THE THEOLOGY OF THE CROSS FOR THE 21ST CENTURY

The Theology of the CROSS *for the 21st Century*

Signposts for a Multicultural Witness

EDITED BY ALBERTO L. GARCÍA
AND A. R. VICTOR RAJ

CONCORDIA PUBLISHING HOUSE · SAINT LOUIS

Copyright © 2002 Concordia Publishing House
3558 S. Jefferson Avenue, St. Louis, MO 63118-3968
Manufactured in the United States of America

Library of Congress Cataloging-in-Publication Data

The theology of the cross for the 21st century : signposts for a multicultural witness / edited by Alberto L. Garcia and A.R. Victor Raj.
        p. cm.
Includes bibliographical references.
    ISBN 0-570-05288-2
    1. Evangelistic work—Lutheran Church. 2. Jesus Christ—Crucifixion. 3. Christianity and culture. I. Garcia, Alberto L. II. Raj, A. R. Victor.
    BV3793 .T48 2002
    266'.4135—dc21   2002015637

1 2 3 4 5 6 7 8 9 10   11 10 09 08 07 06 05 04 03 02

Contents

Contributors   253

Editors' Preface

The twenty-first century is upon us whether we like it or not. This is true for every person and for every institution in North America. The Christian church is no exception to this reality. At the birth of this new century, we accept that people in North America live in a global village. Advances in telecommunications bring the world daily to our homes as friend and stranger. International commerce and global markets dictate that North Americans are not isolated from any region in the world. However, North Americans live in a global village because North America is a microcosm of the world. During a typical day, North Americans will not only swim in the currents of Western culture, but they will find that other major worldviews are also present in their village. Immigrants from South Asia, East Asia, Africa, and Latin America live here too. In particular Hispanics and Asians increasingly occupy a major role in North American culture. A decade ago Cinco de Mayo was unknown in North America; now it is celebrated at the White House by the president of the United States.

The evidence that we live in a global village can be clearly perceived in our religiously pluralistic communities. North America is no longer a white, Anglo-Saxon, Protestant society. Instead, we find mosques and Muslims, Buddhists, and adherents of the New Age Movement (which is inspired by Hinduism). The Dalai Lama is revered as an important religious leader, an equal to Jesus Christ. The Caribbean African folk religion of *Santería* is increasingly popular among non-Caribbean Americans in key urban centers such as New York, Miami, and Houston. The Roman Catholic Church is becoming increasingly Hispanic, accepting the folk religiosity of the people.

Our pluralistic situation is complicated by another important phenomenon in American culture. Postmodernism is characterized by many attributes. However, whether we consider postmodernism a friend or a foe, it provides the Christian church today with opportunity to witness to the Gospel because of the postmodern culture's radical historical consciousness. Society no longer possesses the modernistic confidence in progress or human achievement; instead, the postmodern community is pessimistic. This pessimism is characterized by a radical social consciousness. Many social analysts are deeply pessimistic in their observations of postmodernism. They find that our culture is driven by little more than self-interest, whether in areas of power, gender, class, or greed. Our pluralistic society also offers conflicting options regarding truth. In this context people deeply long for a meaningful community because one characteristic of our present age is profound pain and suffering. People desire real relationships based on truth. They want to find healing for their pain amid postmodernity's narcissism and pessimism.

The Cold War may be over because of the fall of the Soviet Union. Nevertheless, our world continues to be torn by hatred and war. Our global village seeks meaning and understanding at a time when divisions abound. Our historical wounds run wide and deep. September 11 has awakened new generations of North Americans to the reality of world chaos and division. Palestinian and Hebrew parents cry at the death of their children, a result of generations of hatred and division in the Middle East. Our world seems hopeless. This is our time, the right time, our *kairós*, for Christian witness in the twenty-first century. How may we offer a genuine biblical witness that is sensitive to our global village and to our postmodern times?

"CRUX sola est nostra Theologia" [The cross alone is our theology]. Martin Luther spoke these significant words at a time of crisis during the Reformation.[1] All the authors in this volume share a similar vision. We see the witness of the cross as the central witness of our Christian faith and our theology. Central to this witness are two dialectical or dialogical principles. In light of Luther's theology of the cross, we point to the difference between a "theology of glory" and a "theology of the cross." A "theology of glory" points to the human condition and our tendency to create idols that distort our value as God's creatures. A "theology of the cross" identifies our incarnate and crucified God, Jesus Christ, with our human sin and suffering. The witness of the cross is sensitive to our human context but also points to redemption only through the crucified and risen Christ. The authors also employ the principle of Law and Gospel. The Law points to our human predicament and our "theology of glory" so we might find grace and God's unconditional love in the "theology of the cross."

A key to this global witness to the cross is that we pursue and follow a discipleship of the cross. Our witness to the cross is not based on academic theology. We find in Jesus Christ the living God who comes to us in Word and Sacraments to stand with us in community. God cares for our pain and suffering in this global village. Luther's insight is that catholic evangelical Christians *are theologians of the cross*. He underscored the cost of discipleship in this witness to the cross: "For one becomes a theologian by living, by dying, by being damned and not by mere intellectualizing, reading and speculating."[2] Our proclamation is grounded in a living incarnational witness of our Lord Jesus Christ.

A unique characteristic of this book is that though all the contributors share a common evangelical witness to the cross, they offer their witness in light of a specific world culture. Five of the authors were born and raised outside mainstream North American culture. They share perspectives and understandings sensitive to the cultures of South and East Asia, the Caribbean, Africa, and the African American context. One author has lived and worked among people who adhere to the faith of Islam; another has lived and worked among the people of Eastern Europe. Four of the authors write in light of their Western cultural context concerning issues and themes important for the witness of the Gospel in North America.

The book is divided into three parts. Part 1, "Signposts for Multicultural Witness," discusses important theological signposts related to the theology of the cross that are crucial to the witness of the Gospel in our global village. The three essays lift high the cross to critique our present human situation while also offering a timely and sensitive witness to our multicultural and postmodern world. Part 2, "Global Themes for Witness," opens readers to an important dialogue with the major worldviews of East and South Asia, the Islamic world, Africa, and Eastern Europe. Themes such as harmony in *T'ai-Chi*, the use of the Law in relationship to *dharma* and *karma*, the Jesus of Islam, sacrifice in Africa, and mystical suffering in Russia are explored in light of the incarnate theology of the cross. Readers will discover how the authors affirm important values and perspectives within the specific world cultures without giving up the way of salvation in light of the theology of the cross. Part 3, "North American Themes for Witness," is the most diverse section. Three of the authors explore the specific needs and opportunities for witness presented by postmodernism, the present bioethical revolution, and the New Age Movement. These contemporary North American movements are explored in a pastoral and apologetic manner to offer a witness of the cross within the present situation. The final two authors explore specific cultural themes within the Hispanic and African American cultural experience in the United States. Important themes such as *mestizaje*, popular religiosity, human dignity, and worth amid suffering are explored to offer a faithful witness of the cross in a serious attempt to hear and lift high every voice.

We pray that this book guides readers to key signposts of our faith under the cross as they gather insights from our global village and seek to proclaim that Jesus is Lord of the nations.

Eve of Pentecost
Alberto L. García
A. R. Victor Raj

NOTES

1. *The Commentary on the Psalms* (1519–1521) includes Luther's lectures on the Psalms, which he delivered during one of the most difficult periods in his life. The lectures were delivered as he waited to appear before Charles V at the Diet of Worms. These lectures offer a living witness of the cross by Luther, a disciple of the cross, even during difficult times in his life and in the church. Cf. WA 5:176.32f.

2. WA 5:163.29–30.

Abbreviations

ELCA	Evangelical Lutheran Church of America
GWN	God's Word to the Nations
KJV	King James Version
LCMS	The Lutheran Church—Missouri Synod
LW	Luther, Martin. *Luther's Works.* American Edition. Gen. eds. Jaroslav Pelikan and Helmut T. Lehman. 56 vols. St. Louis: Concordia; Philadelphia: Muhlenberg and Fortress, 1955–1986.
NRSV	New Revised Standard Version
RSV	Revised Standard Version
TDNT	*Theological Dictionary of the New Testament.* Edited by G. Kittel and G. Friedrich. Translatesd by G. W. Bromiley. 10 vols. Grand Rapids, 1964–1976.
WA	Luther, Martin. *D. Martin Luthers Werke. Kritische Gesamtausgabe. Schriften.* 68 vols. Weimar: Herman Böhlaus Nachfolger, 1883–1999.

PART 1

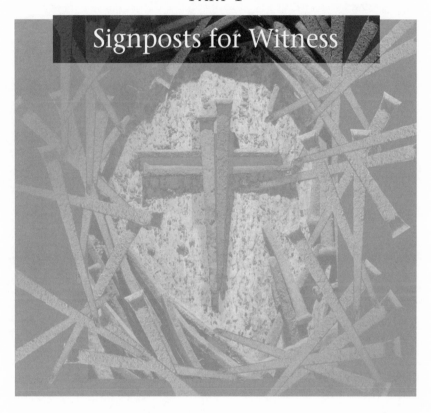

Signposts for Witness

1

Signposts for Global Witness in Luther's Theology of the Cross

ALBERTO L. GARCÍA

> Christ must be apprehended as Man, before he is apprehended as God: and the cross of his humanity must be sought after and known, before we know the glory of his divinity.—Martin Luther, *The Commentary on the Psalms* (1519–1521)[1]

Signposts are like road signs that point the way on a journey. Two important conditions are essential for a road sign to be effective. First, the sign must be clear to follow. Second, the sign must guide us along the right path. Everyone can relate to a time when a particular road was missed because the sign was not clearly marked or was not even posted at the crossroad. We also have been frustrated in our travels because we have been sent on a wild-goose chase with the wrong directions. The last thing that I want to do is to give you confusing signposts to follow for the witness of the cross in the twenty-first century.

My assignment, therefore, requires humility. It is risky at best to lead the reader through important elements in Luther's theology of the cross that will serve as signposts for global witness. As the late Reformation scholar Lewis Spitz Jr. once noted in jest when asked to illustrate Luther's incredible theological output: On the day Luther died, as his left hand was setting into *rigor mortis*, his right hand prepared to write another treatise. Luther's theological output was astronomical and is still being digested by Luther scholars in this century. Therefore, I can only lead you through some signposts in Luther's theology of the cross and hope that they lead us along the way in a more faithful and dynamic global witness.

Our contemporary global village presents another important challenge to our witness. Many cultures coexist in the United States of America. Hispanic and Asian cultures, for example, are growing at a rapid rate on the North American continent. In terms of twenty-first century missions, the world regions that offer the greatest opportunity for global witness are Asia, Africa, and Latin America.[2] These regions express ways of life and ways of thinking, that is, cultures, that are different from the predominant North American or European ways of thinking. At the same time Christian missionary scholars face many challenges created by the Enlightenment and postmodernism. Andrew Walls, a world missions scholar from the University of Aberdeen in Scotland, presents these realities as the most critical challenge for Christian scholars and missionaries.[3] Walls, however, points to a theological sign that makes the missionary enterprise possible in our global village. He finds that there is "a certain vulnerability, a fragility at the heart of Christianity." He calls this fragility, this important signpost to our Christian witness, "the vulnerability of the cross."[4] The theology of the cross points to the reality that there is not one culture that owns the Christian faith. There is no "Christian civilization" or "Christian culture." Sherwood Lingenfelter points also to this important realization.[5] He uses the term "cross-cultural" as a double-edged sword or double entendre. In *Agents of Transformation: A Guide for Effective Cross-Cultural Ministry*, Lingenfelter wants to guide missionaries across cultures so they can live and proclaim the Gospel for the benefit of specific tribes and nations. His vision is directed by a theology of the cross as a criterion for this cross-cultural missionary work. In his own words:

> An agent of transformation is one who brings the good news of the gospel to members of a community and who brokers that message in such a way that those who accept it become disciples of Jesus Christ and learn to live spiritually transformed lives within the context of their community and culture. The outcome of this process should not be the replication of western churches and communities, but rather the establishing of vital communities of faith that exert a positive effect on the wider culture in which they are found.[6]

Lingenfelter's efforts are directed under the Gospel to break our cultural biases and to proclaim within each cultural matrix and beyond the transforming message of Jesus Christ. He is primarily motivated by the incarnational reality of the cross. This is at the center of his skillful cultural anthropological studies. This *modus operandi* permits Lingen-felter to engage other cultural value systems and methods of commu-nication for mission. It also permits him to appropriate other cultural value systems and methods of communication in living the disciple-ship of the Gospel.[7]

You will read in this present book other essays that will point to specific ways the theology of the cross is able to navigate the waters of multiple cultural matrixes for global witness. For example, the essay offered by Professor Wong Yong Ji, "Luther's 'Theology of the Cross' and Eastern Thought," is a vivid example of a constructive missionary vision under the cross for global witness. Under Luther's incarnational theology of the cross, Dr. Ji is able to explore the fundamental Asian dimension of harmony as a key principle to theological discourse and the witness of the Gospel. He moves, therefore, beyond the boundaries of a Western theological discourse and witness, which is primarily lin-ear and directed to explanations and contradictions within a subject and object pattern of thinking.[8]

What are some of the key elements in Luther's theology of the cross that allow us to be Christ's faithful disciples? How does Luther's theology of the cross provide faithful and clear signposts for the Gospel to create vital and indigenous communities of faith? Signposts for faithful and dynamic global witness need the light of the Gospel, as well as an honest look at the terrain that we must travel. I find in Luther's theology of the cross four key signposts for a faithful twenty-first century global witness of Christ's love for the world. These four elements are:

1. Countercultural
2. Incarnational
3. Eschatological
4. Sacramental

THE COUNTERCULTURAL DIMENSION

Lingenfelter reflects on Romans and Galatians to unmask the reality of our human condition.[9] He makes reference in particular to Romans 11:32, where Paul speaks concerning how "God has bound all men over to disobedience." In this particular context Paul is making refer-ence to the human condition of both Jews and Gentiles. Lingenfelter incorporates in his argument the theory of cultural bias in the social sciences. Several social science scholars, such as Thompson, Ellis, and Wildavsky argue that all human beings are constrained by the cultural bias inherent in the particular social environments in which they live and work. Lingenfelter discusses in the first chapters of *Agents of Transformation* how to unmask our social and cultural biases. I agree with this author that the first signpost that we need to promote in our global witness is a self-awareness of our cultural biases and how these cultural biases hinder our witness to other cultures. The dynamics present in Luther's theology of the cross help us toward the same end. This is quite evident in Luther's Heidelberg Disputation of 1518 as he affirms the theologian of the cross in dialectical opposition to the theologian of glory.[10]

Luther clarifies who is a theologian of the cross versus a theologian of glory in thesis 19: "He is not worth calling a theologian who seeks to interpret the invisible things of God on the basis of the things that have been created."[11] Luther's critique in this thesis is not against a system of thought. He is not speaking against the use of reason in theology. His thesis is a critique of our human condition.[12]

When Luther wrote these theses, he had already lectured on the book of Romans. He was intensely aware, because of his study of Paul, of our totally sinful heart and lives before God.[13] Luther's criticism of the theologian of glory goes beyond a critique of Rome's theology of works. It is a critique of our total human reality of sin, and it is a critique against building altars to the gods fashioned after our own image. These altars destroy our lives and our human culture. In this idolatrous vision, we call good those things that we fashion as evil. Also we look at the good and beautiful things that our God has made and call them evil and despise them. It is in this light that Luther offers his critique in thesis 21: "A theologian of the cross calls the thing what it actually is."[14] In this thesis Luther refers specifically to our human condition of pride and our common rejection of God. He is not commenting specifically about human culture. However, every student of culture knows that culture is everything people do and fashion as human beings.[15] God blessed His people at the time of creation to fashion a world, a culture, in light of His creative work (Genesis 1:28). Nevertheless, it is because of human sin and pride that the tower of Babel was constructed. Our human condition distorts the things we make in church and society. This is why we need to apply, in light of the theology of the cross, a countercultural dimension to our witness.

History is quite clear concerning the violence Christians have imposed on others in the name of the Gospel. The Gospel has been used as an excuse to impose another way of life or culture on other people rather than to proclaim the Gospel in their situation. I direct the reader to the seminal work of David J. Bosch, *Transforming Mission: Paradigm Shifts in Theology of Mission*. He illustrates how the Western missiological enterprise has assumed other cultures to be inferior in appropriating the Gospel in an indigenous and powerful manner.[16] As we engage in the witness of Christ in the twenty-first century, we need to be conscious of how our human condition has created cultural idols that get in the way of the proclamation of the Gospel. As we proclaim Christ, we must look at the cross and reflect on how our human condition gets in the way of the witness. This requires, therefore, that we engage in what Walls calls the "vulnerability of the cross." This is the fragile existence that the missionary appropriates as he or she witnesses to Christ cross-culturally. We call what a thing is in the context of our culture and in the context of the culture to which we bring the witness of the cross. Luther speaks to the vulnerability of our witness in his comments on thesis 11: "It is impossible to hope in God unless one has despaired in all creatures and knows that nothing can profit without God."[17] However, how does this vulnerable witness become the power of God to salvation? How, as God's people, may we move away from our sinful offenses that get in the way of the witness so we may unconditionally embrace every tribe and nation in the name of Jesus Christ? The incarnational dimension of the cross leads us to plant another signpost toward our global witness in the twenty-first century.

THE INCARNATIONAL DIMENSION

In his course on faith and ideologies at the University of Chicago, Juan Luis Segundo began one of his lectures by quoting from Luther's explanation of the First Commandment in the Large Catechism: "The faith and trust that the heart make . . . both God and idols."[18] Segundo quoted Luther to show that every person in her or his faith life has a perspective or point of departure in appropriating the object of faith. This is the reality of our human condition. Luther's explanation of the First Commandment speaks against building idols in each of these human situations. Our Christian witness, however, directs us to find those cross-centered values that confront our destructive idolatry and allow us to live God's gifts of grace to the world. This is where we will find the love of God.

I believe that Luther's incarnational theology of the cross directs us in this important task. Luther writes in his Heidelberg Disputation, thesis 20: "But he is worth calling a theologian who understands the visible back side of God through the revelation present in suffering and the cross" ["*Sed qui visibilia et posteriora Dei per passiones et crucem conspecta intelligit*"].[19] The greatest insight of Luther's theology of the cross is that the cross reveals the crucified God for us. We can only know God's stand for us in the incarnate God who died on the cross. God reveals Himself to us through the presence of His incarnate Son, who hung on our behalf on the cross.[20] Jurgen Moltmann has succinctly summarized what is crucial and central to the dynamic of Luther's theology. He defines Luther's theology of the cross as a "radical development of the doctrine of the incarnation with a soteriological intent."[21] While I disagree with Moltmann's parting with Luther's understanding concerning the atonement, I find that Moltmann has grasped quite admirably two constant realities in Luther's vision of the cross. Luther holds together in a powerful manner the reality of Christ's incarnation with the reality of Christ's death for us. It is in God's relationship of the incarnation to Christ's cross that we find the radical nature of God's presence for us.

Luther grasped this reality in a dynamic existential manner during his second lectures on the Psalms (*Operationes in Psalmos*, 1519–1521). I began this essay with an important quote from the *Operationes* that points to Luther's radical perspective of taking seriously Christ's incarnation in relationship to His death: "Christ must be apprehended as Man, before he is apprehended as God: and the cross of his humanity must be sought after and known, before we know the glory of his divinity."[22] Jesus Christ, the incarnate God, lived a genuine life as a human being. He had compassion on the sick, the poor, the dispossessed, and on every sinful human being. We can read in the Gospel narratives how Jesus' life and work was driven by this complete love for people in their distress and human condition. For example, in Matthew, Jesus is overwhelmed with compassion for all the human problems the world faces (9:36–37). This is why He sends His disciples in the following manner: "As you go, preach this message: 'The kingdom of heaven is near.' Heal the sick, raise the dead, cleanse those who have leprosy, drive out demons. Freely you have received, freely give" (Matthew 10:7–8). While initially this task was given by Jesus within the context of the house of Israel, His approach was the same with the Samaritan woman (see John 4). Jesus is concerned to save and heal everyone in the context of their human relationships and specific locals. The lepers and the demon-possessed were especially disconnected from their communities. The Samaritan woman, because of her personal relationships, was disconnected from her family and her community. We may say that these individuals were also at the margins because of their social location. In each context Jesus brings a word of healing with the word of salvation. In his study of the meaning of σῴζω, George Foerster points out that: "In the healings of Jesus, σῴζω never refers to a single member of the body but always to the whole man . . ."[23] This is quite evident in Jesus' healing of Bartimaeus (Mark 10:47–52).

In the Gospels, Jesus is concerned with the whole person. Unfortunately, the proclamation of the Gospel has been reinterpreted through different ideological explanations. In Latin America, for example, during the last three decades the witness of a theology of liberation that speaks to important human needs has often neglected the message of the forgiveness of sins and our cultural realities. At the same time, in our North American witness of the central scriptural teaching of the forgiveness of sin through faith in Christ, we have often neglected the plight of our sisters and brothers in their communities. This is exactly what has occurred in our North American witness to African American, Hispanic, and Asian communities. Often our witness is clothed in a subtle or not so subtle racism that has grown untamed under our false human pretenses of cultural superiority. I believe that the indictment of Dr. Martin Luther King during the civil rights movement is still relevant: "It is appalling that the most segregated hour of Christian America is eleven o'clock on Sunday morning."[24] We have often neglected the implications of God's salvation in light of the situation of the other.

Christ's imperative call to repentance and to believe in the Gospel because of the nearness of the kingdom of God (Mark 1:14) is a holistic call. This call involves healing in all human dimensions. My reading of the Gospels suggests that Jesus Christ healed people not in isolation but by forgiving them and transforming them from outcasts to faithful disciples of the cross within their communities. Also He directed His witness to the specific communities that kept the outcasts at the margins. The witness of the kingdom of God was clearly directed to the integration of the ones at the margins as valuable members of the community. Luke's narrative of the sinful woman who anointed Jesus is a clear example of this witness of σώζω (Luke 7:36–50).

However, we need to be careful in our witness that we do not engage in what Regin Prenter calls "a theology of the cross without the word."[25] A theology of the cross without the Word engages the theologian in an existential following of the cross that may be grounded in personal false idols of power. This theologian lives and proclaims a limited Gospel of redemption in light of his or her *status quo* in life. This theologian refuses to listen to God's judgments upon our idols of power. By not allowing the Gospel to become incarnate in all our human conditions, we become theologians of glory. The theologian of glory is not attentive to all the wounds of God's creatures. Luther's witness of the Word is grounded in Christ. His witness of the cross and incarnation finds in Christology a unifying theme for this witness. Luther's comments in his Heidelberg Disputation thesis 21 confirm this point: "This is clear: He who does not know Christ does not know

God hidden in suffering."[26] The first two Heidelberg theses set the tone for Luther concerning what is central to this Christological vision. Thesis 1 clearly states Luther's intention. He theologizes from the perspective of the Epistle to the Romans to come to an important realization: "The righteousness of God has been manifested without the Law" (Romans 3:21).[27]

To lead to a theology of the Word, Luther directs his first efforts to God's righteousness apart from all human effort. Thesis 2 affirms this. Luther unmasks our unrighteousness grounded on all human works. Prenter summarizes quite admirably what is central to the Heidelberg Disputation:

> The theology of the cross according to which the cross in my own life destroys all my self-righteousness so that I am judged solely in the light of Christ's action on my behalf through which alone I am made righteous before God . . . The faith which justifies is in essence itself a bearing of the cross . . . because it demands that the sinner surrender every claim to self-justification and fly instead for refuge to the cross whereupon Christ suffered on our behalf.[28]

God's righteousness is grounded on Christ's work for us as the incarnate God. In reality this is what is revealed by the "crucified and hidden God."[29] We are called righteous because the person of Jesus Christ hung in our place on the cross. We are called in that light to live Christ's incarnational love in the world.

The key to Luther's theology of the cross is to see the theology of the cross as an active, living act of discipleship. If you read Luther's Heidelberg Disputation carefully, as well as his *Commentary on the Psalms 1519–1521* (the *Operationes in Psalmos*), he does not engage in an abstract theology of the cross. Luther exhorts us in light of Jesus' call to become theologians of the cross. This is never a call to merely interpret and dissect the good news of God's love as distant and detached subjects. The theologian of the cross is called to a living discipleship. In the same way that we cannot separate the theology of the cross from the Word, we cannot separate the Word from the cross. Both dimensions belong together in Luther's perspective. This is also Regin Prenter's perspective. It was also the vision of Dietrich Bonhoeffer in *The Cost of Discipleship* when he spoke against "cheap grace."[30] The cross must move us from proclamation to action. In the words of Christ: "[A]nyone who does not take his cross and follow Me is not worthy of Me. Whoever finds his life will lose it, and whoever loses his life for My sake will find it" (Matthew 10:38–39). How is Jesus' imperative translated into Luther's theology of the cross? In Luther's life as a theologian of the cross, the crucified and incarnate God calls everyone into question, yet in the same breath and at the same time, He calls His disciples to live and impart Christ's unconditional love and grace in every human situation. It is a call to call worthy those who are despised or considered unworthy because of our human pride and idols of power. God's witness to our unrighteousness and to Christ's righteousness becomes a call to a living discipleship.

This witness only occurs when we do not sit and rationalize the theology of the cross but instead become theologians of the cross through whom God's active love shown on the cross "creates the object of his love."[31] See how Luther lives this act of discipleship as he concludes his reflection on his theological disputation at Heidelberg:

> . . . [T]he love of God living in a man loves sinners, evil men, foolish men, weak men, so that the love of God makes them righteous, good, wise and strong. Thus sinners are lovely because they are loved: they are not loved because they are lovely. This is why human love shuns sinners and evil men. As Christ said, "I came not to call the righteous but sinners" [Matthew 9:13]. And that is what the love of the cross means. It is a love born of the cross, which betakes itself not to where it can find something to enjoy, but where it may confer good to the wicked and the needy. For "it is more blessed to give than to receive," says the Apostle [Acts 20:35]. Whence Psalm 41:1: "Blessed is he that considers the poor and the needy." Yet since the mind of man naturally cannot have as an object of its understanding or love something that is nothing (I mean by that the poor and the needy), but can have that which has being and is true and good, therefore, it judges according to the outward appearance. It looks to the person of men and judges by externals.[32]

This love can only be created by the incarnate and crucified God who stood on our behalf. Luther reflects also on how this living reality of the crucified and incarnate Christ becomes our living reality of discipleship. He points to the "sweetest of miracles," a *dulcissimum spectaculum,* that occurs in receiving the incarnate life of Christ in our witness. This is a most "joyous exchange" in the life of the Christian because Christ's righteousness is exchanged for our unrighteousness as He lives with us and through us the life of the cross. Christ becomes our "identical twin" as we bring the incarnate witness of His love to those who are sinful, not loved, and marginalized.[33] In other words, the reality of Christ's alien righteousness implies more than a forensic declarative justification. Certainly it includes this justification in our witness. However, it is also an effective justification through which we seek to empower the poor, the helpless, and the destitute in our incarnational witness to them of Christ's righteousness. Theologians of the cross live this witness, in Luther's words, as "Christophers," namely, as Christ-bearers in the world.[34] This is how Luther signals the life of the theologian of the cross in one of his sermons. We bring Christ to others, and we also carry others in their burden as Christ would have carried and embraced them. Luther reformed the art of doing theology in this vision. His theology of the cross requires becoming a theologian of the cross.

This vision opens a powerful witness for the twenty-first century. Our theology of missions grounded in this reality is open to speak the Gospel in the context and lives of those we address. Our witness is not offered to speculate, to manipulate, or to intellectualize the message of the cross. It is offered as we proclaim and live Christ's call of unconditional love and righteousness in the world. In the words of Luther: "For one becomes a theologian by living, by dying, by being damned: not by mere intellectualizing, reading, and speculating."[35] This life under the cross involves a certain risk and vulnerability because we are forced to hear other voices in their context and need, rather than only listen to our theological cliches or the sounds of our human righteousness. It also may become a risk for us because when we are open to see things in a different manner through the eyes of Christ, we may be called to change our perspective and look at the world in light of our discipleship of the cross. After all this is what happened to Peter and Paul in the book of Acts.

It is important to see how this incarnational witness of the cross is important to our twenty-first century witness of Christ. I would like to show the relevancy of this witness by engaging the reader in a true narrative from my pastoral ministry. This narrative is directed to the witness of the cross in light of our human suffering, which should be the central focus of our witness in our postmodern culture.[36]

In the summer of 1980 I served as director of the Lutheran Immigration and Refugee Service (LIRS) office at Fort Chaffee, Arkansas, during the unexpected influx of more than 125,000 Cuban refugees through the Mariel boat lift to the United States. I went to Fort Chaffee with great joy and expectation to serve fellow Cuban refugees. During the second week at this military camp, something happened that changed my pastoral practice and the way I witness to the Gospel. Early one morning a security officer brought a 13-year-old girl to me for counseling. These were desperate times, and I was the only one available. The previous night, this young lady had attempted suicide. Her bandaged wrists were signs of her desperation. The officers wanted to know why she had wanted to die. I spent two hours with this torn apart, fragile human being. Her immense suffering changed the way I practiced my ministry of reconciliation and healing. This young lady told me how a young man had befriended her at Fort Chaffee. One night he raped her. The next day he tied her in chains and began to sell her as a prostitute. Although this did not represent the majority of the activities at Fort Chaffee, there was a small, strong criminal element operating in the camp. I was outraged. I also remembered how I came to the United States as a 13-year-old, full of fear but protected by my family.

My first reaction was to find this young man and grab him by the neck. I hated my brother. I wanted to kill him. As I listened to this child, a paradigm shift occurred in my pastoral work. She did not call for blood. She did not question God. She wanted to know, however, if her family would still love her because of the terrible perversions perpetrated against her. She wanted to know if the God of love of whom I spoke also loved her. She also wanted to know if I as a representative of that God loved her. She expressed these feelings in confusing terms. At this point I knew it was senseless to explain God's love to her. I also realized it was useless to assume a position of power. She would not be consoled by my assurances that the criminal would be punished. She wanted to feel the presence of God's love standing with her in her powerlessness. I turned to the cross, I embraced her, and I cried with her in the name of God. It is because God was there in her suffering that I was able to articulate Christ's witness to her.

This brings us to the witness of the cross between modern and postmodern times. The November 13, 2000, issue of *Christianity Today* published a roundtable discussion of six postmodern Christians.[37] Many conservative evangelical theologians want to protest such a dialogue. One of the problems in discussing postmodernism is that many theologians have used this term to underscore the relativism and consumerism of our culture. Many postmodernists have included this inner focus in their agenda. However, there are conservative theologians who also speak in light of postmodernism to confront the modernism present in our culture. In their criticism of our culture, they are antimodern theologians with a valuable metanarrative (namely, a compelling universal witness) of the cross for the twenty-first century. In this discussion, Andy Crouch, editor in chief of *Regeneration Quarterly*, brought into perspective what is central to this postmodernist critique of modernism.

> For some, *postmodernism* refers to a renewed attention to "the other," "the marginalized." . . . This attention to the marginalized has led many postmodernists into a profound skepticism toward modernity's assumptions about knowledge, truth, and

reason. These postmoderns question the extent to which modernity's attempts to make truth claims is valid.[38]

We have inherited from the Enlightenment a modernist conceptualization of God in which God is always directing us to a universal idea of doing good and loving others. These general principles have been formulated with no view toward our real human problems or our human condition. This conceptualization of God's presence has been formulated by a false ideal of a progressive humanity. In this modernistic perspective, there is no room for the incarnational theology of the cross that questions our motives and sees behind the masks of our idolatrous actions. In this sense, the postmodern perspectives of some Christian theologians speak to the importance of the cross and the incarnation. In fact, this is what I discovered in this roundtable. Vincent Bacote, visiting professor of theology at Wheaton College, spoke about the necessity of the incarnation in the proclamation of the cross. He observes:

> Relationships are so pivotal to impacting people with the message. In other words, you can't just use Evidence That Demands a Verdict to prove the faith anymore. I think a core aspect of incarnational theology is becoming incarnational. To use the phrase of some people, "You might be the only Bible anyone reads, the only Jesus anyone ever sees." We have to literally take that on and live that out to people which is an applied incarnational theology.[39]

Lutherans do not usually proclaim the Gospel in rationalistic terms that "demand a verdict." However, we have reduced many times the proclamation of the Gospel to general explanations of the Gospel without exercising the incarnational theology of the cross in a life of discipleship. It is here where the most powerful witness of the cross can be given in our postmodern times.

This witness is also the necessary bridge between the Baby Boomer and the next generations in North America. Boomers have tremendous difficulty proclaiming the Gospel to those who follow them because we assume a general attitude of "father knows best" rather than joining with our children in a life of discipleship and love, in, with, and under the cross. Generation Next wants to see Jesus, not have us only talk about Jesus.[40] Generation Next wants to experience the presence of God as He hears their uncertain cry for the future. In the words of Sherri King, one of the participants in the roundtable: ". . . [T]he idea of the embodied Christ is extraordinarily timely and important in all areas of human life. And this gets to the issue of truth.

At the end of the day, truth is not a syllogism. Truth is embodied in the person and flesh of Jesus Christ."[41]

We also find some theologians in our postmodern times using the incarnation and the particularity of the cross to take a stand on behalf of the poor and the oppressed. Yet in some cases this critical stand is a witness to a particular ideology rather than to the Gospel of Jesus of Galilee, who truly stood in the corner of humanity in the name of God. This is the paradox of postmodernism. It is critical of an oppressive ideology, but it needs another ideology to overcome oppression. The history of the world points to this way of life as a tribalism in which the strong always vanquish the weak. Andy Crouch concludes the roundtable discussion in a similar manner to my arguments. The theology of the cross in the Word is needed as a metanarrative not only to see our human fragility through the incarnate eyes of Christ, but also to lead us to a future beyond our human situations of sin. Crouch argues also for the importance of a theology of the cross in truly living incarnationally:

> I want to put in a plug for a Cross-centered postmodern theology. I take on postmodernism criticism quite deeply, and this has driven me to a rereading of the Cross, because the Cross is what guarantees the Christian gospel against the critiques of postmodernism, specifically the one that says that all metanarratives oppress. The gospel is a metanarrative: it is "the greatest story told"; it claims to tell the truth about the world. The problem of most stories is that they tell the truth in a way that benefits someone. But the Cross is a story in which the other is met by the non-other; God becomes the other and endures the full experience of marginalization.[42]

Andy Crouch's perceptive arguments are, in my opinion, at the center of Luther's dynamic incarnational theology of the cross. God speaks to our sin and has compassion on us in light of the death of His Son, Jesus Christ, for us. The cross clearly reveals that God is there to welcome the alien and the outcast as worthy members of the kingdom. Luther's theology of the cross can also be understood in a dynamic and perceptive manner for twenty-first century witness as we reflect on the eschatological and sacramental dimensions of the cross.

THE ESCHATOLOGICAL DIMENSION

In an important work concerning Luther's eschatology, Ulrich Asendorf has accentuated the relationship that exists for Luther between eschatology and justification by faith.[43] Asendorf points out that the eschatological nature of Luther's theology is always made possible by the "clear unity that exists between Christology and justification."[44] The cross is the place where God always challenges our human righteousness with His lasting righteousness.[45] Some contemporary theologians critique Luther's explanation of the doctrine of the atonement because they read in his theology a mere restitution of our humanity to a former holy state (that is, to a *restitutio ad integrum*). The key to Luther's understanding of the atonement is that he finds God decisively loving us for all times in the person of Jesus Christ. It is God coming to our human situation and standing on our behalf.[46] It is beyond our human grasp how God can stand against Himself in the death of the cross to be with us and for us. His death on the cross, therefore, has to do with looking at things from God's perspective, not our own. God on the cross declares us righteous and looks at us in this act forever.

Luther writes about this eschatological reality when commenting on Psalm 2:5 in *Operationes in Psalmos:* "For Christ is our Mount Moriah because God sees no one and acknowledges no one who is not offered up and built up on this place that is on Christ, and in Christ, for the eyes of God are on this place only. And therefore, he is called the Mountain on which God will look forever."[47] Also in his explanation of Psalm 2:5, Luther points out that Christ's Mt. Moriah becomes our Mt. Moriah in our conformity to His cross.[48] On the cross at Golgotha, Luther finds God's final and lasting stand as He looks at our future. Luther's *Lectures on Romans* unfolds the dynamics to this life of faith under the cross. We realize that we remain "sick in fact" (*re*) but "healthy in hope" (*spe*).[49] In this context, faith is always an experience of God's righteousness and grace in light of our end. It is an experience that feeds itself on the hope that our present condition is not terminal.

Although we cannot read the contemporary ontology of the theologians of hope into Luther, his insights concerning faith are dynamic and eschatological. I prefer this outlook for our witness of the cross. In our understanding of salvation, we proceed from the perspective of our life in Jesus Christ *coram Deo* (that is, before God) rather than from a mere restitution of our previous holy state. This is the life of a Christian who lives in the state of being totally sinful and totally justified at the same time before God (*simul justus et peccator*). It is in this stand that we turn away from ourselves to God's promise under the cross. It is in this stand that we are open to walk in Christ's way of discipleship instead of the pretense of our holy state. We are a holy people as we live in faith God's promise of salvation and concern for the whole world.

In Luther's writings, this promise of God's stand with us is guaranteed by Christ's resurrection. As Luther gives witness to the power of the incarnation in relationship to Christ's passion, he always includes the resurrection as an important component of this eschatological witness.[50] Our suffering in light of the eschatological reality assures us that it is not a masochistic suffering. We only live this cruciform existence because Christ compels us to the cross on behalf of the neighbor.[51] This cruciform existence can only be made possible in light of the end. Luther comments in light of Psalm 22:

> When a person lives on the cross and suffering, every moment seems eternal and he becomes impatient. Suffering is not hard if one can see the end to his suffering. A person thinks that it is just a bad time, a bad day, a bad week, but things will improve in a matter of time. However, if he cannot see the end, all suffering becomes intolerable . . . even if it just lasts a quarter of an hour. Christians need to know that their suffering will have an end and will not last forever.[52]

In light of the eschatological reality of the cross, I cannot look at the world with disdain because God's future under the reality of justification by faith is our common future. God calls us His own in His judgment of grace to the end of times because of the crucified Christ. My faith relationship becomes more than a personal relationship with God. It involves my relationship with the whole world. This eschatological dimension can only depend on our grasping of faith as a gift of grace. It is always cognizant of the fragility of our human existence and of our idols of power. This life is lived as we experience daily the reality of our Baptism. It lives under the cross as the old self dies to sin and the new person resurrects in Christ (Romans 6:4) to a new life.[53] This reality becomes compelling as we explore the sacramental dimension of the cross.

THE SACRAMENTAL DIMENSION

As we look at the history of Christian witness in North America in the last century, we will find a proclamation of the cross that is individualistic in tone. Most evangelistic efforts are directed to leading individuals from sin to grace. This is also reflected in the way that Baptism and the Lord's Supper are interpreted. They are seen somehow as individual sacramental acts of grace for a person to receive the forgiveness of sin. I am not questioning that the individual needs to hear the Gospel to be led to faith (Romans 10:17). However, this proclamation of the Gospel is always given as a sacramental witness in the New Testament. This sacramental witness calls for the coming together and the mutual support of all God's people. It also calls the people of God to exercise the vocation of the cross.

In this last section, I want to explore this sacramental dimension as it is present in Luther's vocation of the cross. Francis Pieper, in his "Prolegommena" to his *Christian Dogmatics,* captures the essence of Luther's vocation of the cross in Luther's formula: *"oratio, meditatio, tentatio faciunt theologum"* [One becomes a theologian through "prayer, meditation, and the afflictions of the cross"].[54] *Tentatio* is a trademark in Luther's theology of the cross. It is, in fact, the key to his radical incarnational theology of the cross. I learned through the scholarship of Lewis Spitz that Luther revolutionized Gabriel Biel's formula of *"tentatio, meditatio, lectio."*[55] The vocation of the theologian consisted for Biel in "prayer, meditation, and reading." Luther substituted *tentatio* in the place of *lectio. Tentatio,* or *Anfechtungen,* are those assaults and trials that come to the Christian because of the vocation of the cross. There has to be prayer and meditation on the Word of God in our witness. However, there is no witness to Christ apart from a vocation to the discipleship of the cross. In Luther's *Operationes in Psalmos,* we find what is meant by this vocation of the cross.[56] It is a life in conformity to Christ in the world. The *Anfechtungen* in this context are not to be seen as the assaults or trials coming from God to us. They are the confirmation that our lives are in conformity to the sufferings of God on the cross. This is clearly evident in Luther's sacramental theology. They are, in a real sense, how we live Christ's sacramental presence.

Luther's sacramental vocation of the cross is expressed in a powerful manner in his sermon "The Blessed Sacrament of the Holy and True Body of Christ, and the Brotherhoods" (1519). The subtitle for this sermon in German reads "Fur die Leyen" ["For the Laity"].[57] This subtitle does not appear in the American Edition of Luther's Works. This is an important subtitle because Luther exhorts in particular the laity of the church to live the vocation of the cross in a sacramental manner. How is this possible? Luther finds under the sacrament of the Lord's Supper a common life, a common sharing, and a common witness. The significance of this sacrament is "that Christ and all saints are one spiritual body."[58] The consequences of partaking of the Lord's body and blood are quite clear for Luther. It engages us in the vocation of the cross:

> In this sacrament, therefore, man is given through the priest a sure sign from God himself that he is thus united with Christ and his saints and has all things in common [with them], that Christ's sufferings and life are his own, together with the lives and sufferings of all the saints.[59]

We share this cost of discipleship on behalf of even the little ones of this fellowship.

In this vision Luther is influenced by St. Paul's writing in 1 Corinthians 12:12–24.[60] Luther's vocation of the cross is an exhortation to " fight, work . . ." and "have heartfelt sympathy" with the community of saints in all their needs and injustices done to them. However, if we are congruent with Luther's eschatological and incarnational vision of the cross, we must include in this sacramental vision a concern and a stand with all those who suffer and hunger in the world community. This is the kind of witness that I also find in the words of Jesus in Matthew 25:35–40. We always stand with the "least."

In conclusion, Luther's countercultural witness of the cross allows us to take a real look at ourselves and the world communities in humility before condemning the various world cultures as less adequate than our own in planting the Gospel. The incarnational soteriological witness opens for us ways to appropriate in a relational, powerful manner the message of salvation for our times in light of God's gift of grace rather than our works. The eschatological vision suggests to us that each day we must begin anew in this witness. We must consider how, in our present situations, God comes anew each day in the Gospel with a message of hope in Him for the future. It opens our witness to move beyond the boundaries of our past experiences, prejudices, and human anxieties to include the hopes and dreams of the world communities. Last but not least, the sacramental dimension points to our witness as the witness of the body of Christ as the people of God. It is a witness "en *conjunto,*" that is, a joint effort. We are no longer foreigners and aliens in our witness but members of the same "*familia,*" that is, household, as we join together in Christ as a living body to build together a dwelling in which God lives by His Spirit (Ephesians 2:19–22). This witness is attentive to the sins, fears, and problems of our world community. I pray that this witness makes us faithful disciples of the cross in our global village in this new century.

NOTES

1. Henry Cole, ed. and trans., *Select Works of Martin Luther* (4 vols.; London: T. Bensley, 1924–1926), 3:184. It reads in the original: ". . . *quod prior sit Christus homo, quam deus apprehendus, prior humanitatis eius Crux, quam divinitatis eius gloria petenda*" (WA 5:129.9–10). This citation is from *Operationes in Psalmos.*

2. "The Expansion of Christianity: An Interview with Andrew Walls," *The Christian Century* (2–9 August 2000): 796–800.

3. "Expansion of Christianity," 794.

4. "Expansion of Christianity," 792.

5. Sherwood Lingenfelter, *Agents of Transformation: A Guide for Effective Cross-Cultural Ministry* (Grand Rapids: Baker, 1996).

6. Lingenfelter, *Agents of Transformation,* 9.

7. See also Sherwood Lingenfelter, *Ministering Cross-Culturally: An Incarnational Model for Personal Relationships* (Grand Rapids: Baker, 1986).

This is a helpful anthropological study. However, we must dig deeper into the incarnational nature of the cross to engage in this kind of purposeful awareness.

8. See in this volume the essay by Won Yong Ji, "Luther's 'Theology of the Cross' and Eastern Thought."

9. Lingenfelter, *Agents of Transformation*, 9–10.

10. See LW 31:37–70. See also James Atkinson, ed., *Martin Luther: Early Theological Writtings* (Philadelphia: Westminster, 1962), 274–307.

11. Atkinson, *Martin Luther*, 290.

12. See Alister E. McGrath, *Luther's Theology of the Cross* (New York: Basil Blackwell, 1985), 67–68. McGrath places Luther within the Augustinian tradition. He does not see Luther upholding the *via moderna*, which followed the metaphysical nominalism of William of Ockham and Gregory of Rimini, over against the *via antiqua*, which promoted the metaphysical realism of the Thomist and Scotist schools. Luther's position is more directed to the Augustinian insights concerning the human condition.

13. See Luther's comments on Romans 6:10 and 7:18, LW 25:314, 346.

14. LW 31:53.

15. See Martin E. Marty, "Articles of War, Articles of Peace: Christianity and Culture," in *Christ and Culture in Dialogue* (ed. Angus J. L. Menuge et al; St. Louis: Concordia Academic Press, 1999), 56–77, for an excellent discussion of culture and Christianity.

16. David J. Bosch, *Transforming Mission: Paradigm Shifts in Theology of Mission* (Maryknoll: Orbis, 1991), 291–313. I discuss this reality in more depth in "Christological Reflections on Faith and Culture," in *Christ and Culture in Dialogue*, 72–75. Earl Shorris, *Latinos: A Biography of the People* (New York: W. W. Norton, 1992), offers a good narrative of how the Hispanic culture in North America is considered inferior by the dominant culture and how Latinos have suffered as a consequence of this perspective. See also Peter J. Paris, "The Religious World of African Americans," in *World Religions in America* (ed. Jacob Neusner; Louisville: Westminster John Knox, 1994), 69–77, in relationship to the African American reality. This way of thinking creeps into our missiological methods and church decisions about missions. These are only two examples from our North American rainbow reality that demonstrate why we need the cross as a countercultural principle that speaks to our human condition as we engage in a twenty-first century witness of the Gospel.

17. LW 31:48.

18. Cf. Juan Luis Segundo, *Faith and Ideologies* (trans. John Drury; vol. 1 of *Jesus of Nazareth Yesterday and Today*; Maryknoll: Orbis, 1984), 33. This book is based on Segundo's lectures at the University of Chicago.

19. This is my translation of WA 1:362.1–2, which takes into account Atkinson, *Martin Luther*, 290, and McGrath, *Luther's Theology of the Cross*, 148. The translation by Harold J. Grimm reads: "who comprehends the visible and manifest things of God" (LW 31:52). This

translation does not take into consideration the reality of the crucified God as the point of departure. It is in the offense of the *"posterio-
ria Dei per passiones et crucem"* that God reveals Himself to us.

20. The concept of the hidden God, the *deus absconditus,* in the Heidelberg Disputation is directed to show Christ as the crucified God for
us. Luther follows this same way of thinking in his *Resolutiones*
regarding thesis 28 (cf. WA 1:613.23–28). Luther interprets the hidden God as an "inscrutable God" and in a different manner in *The
Bondage of the Will* (see LW 33:62–63). See also McGrath, *Luther's Theology of the Cross,* 166; and Erich Seeberg, *Motive und Ideen* (vol. 1 of
Luthers Theologie; Stuttgard: W. Kohlhammer, 1937), 144.

21. Jurgen Moltmann, *The Crucified God* (trans. R. A. Wilson and J. Bow-
den; New York: Harper & Row, 1974), 212.

22. See n. 1.

23. G. Foerster, "σῴζω," *TDNT* 7:990. For an excellent sociological study
of how this holistic meaning of salvation has been neglected in Latin
America, see Christian Smith and Joshua Prokopy, eds., *Latin America
Religion in Motion* (New York: Routledge, 1999), 1–42.

24. Martin Luther King Jr., "Stride toward Freedom," in *A Testament of
Hope: The Essential Writings and Speeches of Martin Luther King Jr.* (ed.
James M. Washington; New York: Harper & Row, 1986), 479. See in
particular the recent article by Edward Gilbreath, "The New Capital
of Evangelicalism," *Christianity Today* (21 May 2002): 41. Gilbreath
points out how this problem is significant in Dallas, Texas, the most
important center for evangelical churches.

25. Regin Prenter, *Luther's Theology of the Cross* (Philadelphia: Fortress,
1961), 7.

26. My translation of *"Patet, quia dum ignorat Christum, ignorat Deum
absconditum"* (WA 1:362.23). See also LW 31:53.

27. See WA 1:335.30–32; Atkinson, *Martin Luther,* 281.

28. Prenter, *Luther's Theology of the Cross,* 4.

29. See Luther's *Resolutiones* concerning thesis 58, WA 1:613.23–28.

30. Prenter, *Luther's Theology of the Cross,* 4.

31. Atkinson, *Martin Luther,* 295.

32. WA 1:365.9–25; Atkinson, *Martin Luther,* 295.

33. E. Gordon Rupp, *The Righteousness of God* (New York: Philosophical
Library, 1953), 225. He quotes from Luther's *Operationes in Psalmos of
1519–1521.* Cf. also Luther's treatise: *The Freedom of a Christian,* LW
31:333–77.

34. See Luther's "Sermon at Coburg on Cross and Suffering," LW 51:202.

35. This quote is my translation from Luther's *Operationes in Psalmos of
1519–1521:* *"Vivendo, immo moriendo et damnando fit theologus, non
intelligendo aut speculando"* (WA 5:163.29–30).

36. See, in particular, Stan Van Hooft, "The Meaning of Suffering," *Hast-
ings Center Report* 28.5 (1998): 13–19. He argues perceptively that suffering is the critical point of dialogue with a postmodern culture concerning our human condition.

37. "The Antimoderns," *Christianity Today* (13 November 2000): 75–80.

38. "The Antimoderns," 76.

39. "The Antimoderns," 80.

40. Cf. Kevin Graham Ford, *Jesus for a New Generation: Putting the Gospel in the Language of the Xers* (Downers Grove: InterVarsity, 1995). Chapter 6 of his book, "The Postmodern Generation" (110–32), deals with some of the same dynamics and cultural characteristics to which I make reference in this section.

41. "The Antimoderns," 80.

42. "The Antimoderns," 80.

43. Ulrich Asendorf, *Eschatologie bei Luther* (Göttingen: Vandenhoeck & Rupprecht, 1967), 12–48.

44. Asendorf, *Eschatologie bei Luther,* 12.

45. Asendorf, *Eschatologie bei Luther,* 13.

46. I agree with Gustaf Aulén, *Christus Victor* (New York: Macmillan, 1969), when he says that Luther's understanding of the atonement is not Anselmian in model. It is closer to the New Testament and the church fathers where God comes to stand with us for all times against the tyranny of the Law, the devil, and sin. I find, however, that Aulén fails to underscore the *Christus Victor* motif under an eschatological vision. By connecting the theme of justification by faith to Christology in Luther's theology, it opens for us an eschatological motif to Luther's vision of the atonement that grounds him to a radical consideration of an incarnational theology of the cross.

47. WA 5:58.17–18; Cole, *Select Works,* 3:184.

48. WA 5:128.31–139; Cole, *Select Works,* 3:184.

49. WA 56:270 (*my translation*); cf. LW 25:258. See how Gerhard O. Forde offers a powerful witness of the cross in light of this eschatological dimension by using the dialectics of flesh/spirit in Luther's theology in "The Word That Kills and Makes Alive," in *Marks of the Body of Christ* (ed. Carl E. Braaten and Robert W. Jenson; Grand Rapids: Eerdmans, 1999), 1–12.

50. Cf. Marc Lienhard, *Luther, Witness to Christ* (trans. Edwin H. Robertson; Minneapolis: Augsburg, 1982), 183–84. Lienhard finds this witness in Luther's *postils* and sermons of 1522.

51. Luther compels us to accept this way of discipleship in light of Matthew 10:38. See LW 51:198. Cf. also LW 51:199–202.

52. See Luther's exposition of Psalm 22 in *Auslegung der 25 ersten Psalmen* (1530), WA 31/1:354.8–13, 442.29–32 (*my translation*). Cf. also Luther in LW 30:23.

53. See, in particular, Luther's didactic teaching on the sacramental power and effect of Baptism in his Large Catechism.

54. Francis Pieper, *Christian Dogmatics* (St. Louis: Concordia, 1950), 1:86. See Luther's "Preface to the Wittenberg Edition of Luther's German Writings," LW 34:285–87.

55. Lewis W. Spitz, "Luthers Bedeutung als Gelehrter und Denker fur den

anthropologischen realismus," in *Humanismus und Reformation als Kulturelle Kräfte in der deutschen Geschichte* (ed. Lewis W. Spitz; Berlin: Walter de Gruyter, 1981), 19.

56. Erich Vogelsang, *Der Anfänge von Luthers Christologie nach ersten Psalmvorlensung* (Berlin: Walter de Gruyter, 1929), 11, 32; Rupp, *Righteousness of God*, 226; McGrath, *Luther's Theology of the Cross*, 171–73. Luther looks at the Christian life and his *tentatio* in light of the dimension of *totus iustus* in his sacramental theology. *Tentatio* in Luther's theology is usually interpreted by many as the afflictions the Christian endures because of his *totus peccator* (totally sinful) reality. Because in Luther's Pauline anthropology the Christian lives under grace as a *simul iustus et peccator*, the language of *tentatio* belongs to both conditions. However, we miss Luther's most radical Christian methodological insights if we do not consider *tentatio* in all its sacramental dimensions. *Tentatio* becomes, then, a key element in our witness of the cross.

57. WA 2:739; see LW 35:47–73, especially 47.

58. WA 2:743.6–12; LW 35:50–51.

59. WA 2:744.8–11; LW 35:52.

60. WA 2:744.1–7; LW 35:22.

FOR FURTHER READING

On Luther's theology of the cross:

Aulén, Gustaf. *Christus Victor*. New York: Macmillan, 1969.

Lienhard, Marc. *Luther, Witness to Christ*. Translated by Edwin H. Robertson. Minneapolis: Augsburg, 1982.

McGrath, Alister E. *Luther's Theology of the Cross*. New York: Basil Blackwell, 1985.

Forde, Gerhard O. "The Word That Kills and Makes Alive." In *Marks of the Body of Christ*. Edited by Carl E. Braaten and Robert Jenson. Grand Rapids: Eerdmans, 1999.

Prenter, Regin, *Luther's Theology of the Cross*. Philadelphia: Fortress, 1961.

Rupp, E. Gordon, *The Righteousness of God*. New York: Philosophical Library, 1953.

On cross-cultural witness:

Berkey, Robert F., and Sarah A. Edwards, eds. *Christology in Dialogue*. Cleveland, Ohio: Pilgrim Press, 1993.

Bosch, David J. *Transforming Mission: Paradigm Shifts in Theology of Mission*. Maryknoll: Orbis, 1991.

González, Justo L. *Out of Every Tribe and Nation*. Nashville: Abingdon, 1992.

Kitamori, Kazoh. *Theology of the Pain of God*. Translated by Shinkyo Suppanska. Richmond: John Knox, 1965.

Lazareth, William, and Péri Rasolondraibe. *Lutheran Identity and Mission: Evangelical and Evangelistic?* Minneapolis: Fortress, 1994.

Lingenfelter, Sherwood. *Ministering Cross-Culturally: An Incarnational Model for Personal Relationships.* Grand Rapids: Baker, 1987.

Menuge, Angus J. L., William Cario, Alberto L. Garcia, and Dale E Griffin, eds. *Christ and Culture in Dialogue: Constructive Themes and Practical Applications.* St. Louis: Concordia Academic Press, 1999.

Neusner, Jacob, ed. *World Religions in America.* Rev. and exp. Louisville: Westminster John Knox, 2000.

Sanneh, Lamin. *Religion and the Variety of Culture: A Study in Origin and Practice.* Valley Forge: Trinity Press International, 1996.

2

"Nothing But Christ Crucified"

THE AUTOBIOGRAPHY
OF A CROSS-CULTURAL COMMUNICATOR

ROBERT A. KOLB

"I resolved to know nothing . . . except Christ Jesus and Him crucified," Paul told the Corinthian congregation (1 Corinthians 2:2). Although God had called him first of all to bring the Gospel to the nations (Acts 9:15), the apostle in fact brought the message of Jesus, the Messiah, who "had to suffer and rise from the dead" (Acts 17:3), to Jews and Gentiles alike. Paul announced to the assembly in the synagogue of Pisidian Antioch that the people of Jerusalem and their rulers had not recognized Jesus as Israel's Savior, so they condemned Him. His death brought about what had been written concerning Israel's deliverer. They took Him down from the cross and buried Him, "[b]ut God raised Him from the dead . . . . What God promised our fathers, He has fulfilled for us, their children, by raising up Jesus." Paul was proclaiming the forgiveness of sins available in Jesus Christ (Acts 13:26–41).

THE CONVERSION OF SAUL,
THE MESSAGE OF PAUL

Paul's epistolary reflections on the Christian life ranged over many topics, but at its heart his message focused on the death and resurrec-

37

tion of his Lord. Christ had died for Paul's sins and risen for his restoration to favor in God's sight (Romans 4:25). The apostle had been crucified with Christ, so the life he lived, he lived by faith in God's Son, whose love for Paul had led Him to give Himself into death for this chief of sinners (Galatians 2:20; cf. 1 Timothy 1:15). The cross revealed to the pious rabbi Saul who God really is and what He had done for humankind by sending His Son into human flesh (Galatians 4:4). The cross also revealed to the apostle Paul who he was and what kind of life God had in mind for one sent across all cultural barriers with the message of the crucified rabbi.

The crucified Jesus called Saul as the rising young star in the leading circles of Jerusalem's society made his way to Damascus to continue persecuting the Name—the Name that suddenly and shockingly approached him out of the light that flashed from heaven (Acts 9:5–6). Obviously from a well-placed family, a Roman citizen, shaping a good career for himself within the Jewish establishment—a man well situated and deeply embedded in Palestinian native culture—the upwardly mobile Saul was looking forward to one more success in Damascus. He was "circumcised on the eighth day, of the people of Israel, of the tribe of Benjamin, a Hebrew of Hebrews; in regard to the law, a Pharisee; as for zeal, persecuting the church; as for legalistic righteousness, faultless" (Philippians 3:5–6). Then the one at whose expense he was climbing the ladder of cultural achievement and attainment, the crucified Jesus from Nazareth, confronted him. Saul was completely turned around—converted. His new way of thinking led him to say,

> Whatever was to my profit I now consider loss for the sake of Christ. What is more, I consider everything a loss compared to the surpassing greatness of knowing Christ Jesus my Lord, for whose sake I have lost all things. I consider them rubbish, that I may gain Christ and be found in Him, not having a righteousness of my own . . . but that which is through faith in Christ . . . . I want to know Christ and the power of His resurrection and the fellowship of sharing in His sufferings, becoming like Him in His death, and so, somehow, to attain to the resurrection from the dead. (Philippians 3:7–11)

Paul was "unable to establish any continuity across this divide, and in virtue of his experience hitherto, of both world and self, he is not even able to recognize one. Rather he is created anew and has his identity permanently outside himself, in another, a stranger."[1] The "rule" or "canon" of Paul's life became his resolve to boast of—and cling to—only the cross of Christ, "through which the world has been crucified to me, and I to the world" (Galatians 6:14). Paul found security neither in the mark of his Jewish culture, circumcision, nor its opposite, the uncircumcision of the Gentiles. He had become a new creation in Jesus Christ (Galatians 6:14–16), and that liberated him to enjoy both cultures in which he moved because he lived as a reborn child in a third, the family of God. As a member of the church, Christ's body, Paul was free to enjoy, support, and criticize elements of each culture into which he entered. He recognized each as a gift of God and a field for the exercise of love toward others. That meant he could make proper use of these cultural gifts—his Roman citizenship (Acts 22:25–29; 25:10–12) and the works of pagan writers (Acts 17:28; Titus 1:12), for example. It also meant that Paul could criticize elements of the culture and call for repentance from false cultural values, even if his call might create tension and hostility. At the same time Paul remained thoroughly Jewish, with Jewish concerns and Jewish commitments (compare his lamentation for his own people in Romans 9–11).

Jesus made it clear from the beginning that His call would bring Saul suffering. First, this devoted advocate of all things Jewish would move out of his comfortable cultural cocoon. He would cross the lines that defined and protected him as a follower of the God of Abraham, Isaac, Jacob, and Moses, and he would "carry My name before the Gentiles and their kings," as well as before the children of Israel (Acts 9:15–16). The abandonment of these cultural moorings as the foundation of his worldview represented a great sacrifice—Paul was relinquishing the heart of his old way of life. He learned to live within his own culture and others not on the basis of the strength they offered, but only on the basis of the Lord's word to him, "I am sending you to [your own people and the Gentiles] to open their eyes and turn them from darkness to light, and from the power of Satan to God, so that they may receive forgiveness of sins and a place among those who are sanctified by faith in Me" (Acts 26:17–18).

Initially those words from Jesus meant death for Saul, death to his old faith and his accustomed way of living. The voice of Jesus crucified Saul's religion and his identity as it brought him into a new life. From that point, Saul, renamed Paul, lived in the shadow of the cross, driven by the wind of heaven that blew through Christ's empty tomb to refresh and revive him and—through the words given to him—to bring true life to many others. The cross of Christ determined the way Paul understood life. It also determined his crossing into the hearts of his hearers in every culture with the proclamation of death for sinners and new life for the chosen people of God. Paul's theology of the cross was not only a method for the practice of theology, but above all it was a report of God's method of salvation and creating anew.

THE THEOLOGY OF THE CROSS
REVEALS WHO GOD IS

As outlined in the initial two chapters of his first letter to the Corinthians, Paul's theology of the cross described God's revelation of Himself. The Creator is Lord of all He has made. He set the nations in their places and assigned them their periods in history (Acts 17:26; cf. Job 12:23). He has given all human creatures dominion over the creation He has entrusted to them. A part of this dominion comes in receiving responsibility for the specific gifts of each culture.

Nonetheless, sinners fail to use these gifts of culture and dominion rightly. They use and abuse these gifts without seeing the Creator and Giver behind them. Therefore, in this fallen world God comes into the lives of His people from outside their normal way of thinking and living, no matter the nation to which they belong. Although the intertestamental Jewish culture and the Hellenistic culture of the Roman Empire in which it was lodged have a certain cultural priority because God chose their vocabulary and thought structures to express the heart of His revelation of Himself, no culture is superior to any other. All cultures bear the marks and scars of rebellion against God, and each culture blinds and deafens itself to the voice of its Creator and Lord in a host of ways. God must come from outside every culture to address people with the Word of life. He comes, however, into the midst of the culture, using its language even as He used human flesh as the vehicle of the climax and perfecting of His revelation to us.

As God brings His Word to a culture through us, He has us assume the concerns and the customs of that culture insofar as they do not contradict His will and insofar as they serve as agents of living the life He has called us to live. He wants us to be freed from our own cultural prejudices and narrowness of focus so we can be agents of His Word, not of our own culture. At the same time God embraces us as the cultural beings we are. He accepts us in the brokenness of our cultural misconceptions and illusions, but He wants to correct these misapprehensions about His world and the life He has given us in it. Through the Word of the cross, God crucifies our errors and transforms our understanding of and appreciation for the many gifts He gives in our own and other cultures.

That was Saul's personal experience. When "God, who set me apart from birth and called me by His grace, was pleased to reveal His Son in me," the one who had tried to destroy God's church, Saul consulted no one (Galatians 1:15–16). Jesus had come to him. Jesus breaks into the rhythm and structures of people in societies in every corner of the world—without invitation, without being welcomed—to deliver

God's wisdom and power, God's gift of dying to false gods and being raised to true life in Christ. Paul made that clear to the Corinthians. God is only to be found in His Word made flesh, the one nailed to the cross. *How foolish! How impotent!* all people, whatever their culture, think. Like God's chosen people at Isaiah's time (Isaiah 45:9; cf, Paul's use of this passage in Romans 9:20–24), everyone wants to play the part of the pot who tells the potter how to form the products of his hands. And all must hear God's rejection of their proposal: "The wisdom of the wise will perish, the intelligence of the intelligent will vanish" (Isaiah 29:14; cf. 1 Corinthians 1:19). "God chose the foolish things of the world to shame the wise; God chose the weak things of the world to shame the strong. He chose the lowly things of this world and the despised things—and the things that are not—to nullify the things that are, so that no one may boast before Him" (1 Corinthians 1:27–29). Jesus Christ alone is God's wisdom, righteousness, holiness, redemption, and no one can know Him apart from revelation from God's Holy Spirit (1 Corinthians 1:30; 2:14).

Reflecting Paul's line of thinking in 1 Corinthians 1 and 2, Martin Luther made the distinction between the hidden God and the revealed God a key part of his "theology of the cross."[2] For the reformer, the term "hidden God" designated both the essence of God, which lies beyond the grasp of creatures—particularly when their rebellion has blinded and deafened them—and the pictures of God that fallen human beings construct as they try to identify and domesticate Him. These "hidden gods" of human construction are, indeed, "god made in human image."[3] In every culture people have constructed such gods. Individuals and cultures hang onto the gods of their own construction for dear life because these gods—whether personal or impersonal, whether systems of thought or of ritual or of human accomplishment—provide the glue that holds society together and supplies life and meaning and security for their adherents. Across the lines of protection drawn by these adherents as they seek to defend and preserve their religion—that which commands their devotion and binds their lives together[4]—Jesus advances, attacking the foes who have stolen His people from Him. As the impotent and foolish crucified convict, He comes from outside their way of imagining God, from above their fragile, failing fantasies of false faith. Jesus had come as a kid in a crib, no way for God to make His entrance in any culture. He had taken His throne as a criminal on a cross. He made His exit, people thought, as a corpse in a crypt. And there is no other way to explain who Jesus is in any culture because that is who God really is. The fact is: Jesus did come into our kind of baby crib, into our way of dealing with criminals, into our kind of dying. He is incarnate. He fully shares all that it means to be human and a part of human culture apart from sin. That must be made clear to all people in every time and place.

Nonetheless, Paul's message, Christ's word for His people, is not a proposition that can be tested against any human—cultural—standard. This message and Word is a person who convicts hearts and convinces minds by personal engagement, by speaking impotent and foolish words that draw people into death and then into life because of the person who is speaking. The message—the person of Jesus, the Messiah—must cross cultural boundaries and overcome cultural barriers sufficiently to make the claim clear. But God remains one who comes from outside. He is one whom every human culture has barred from its center because the forces of this world have sought to arrange and manage life without Him. God is the one who wants to renew all cultures through the presence of His own people, in whom He has renewed truly human life by restoring their faith in Him through Jesus Christ. God confounds cultural values constructed in opposition to His will, but through their love for Him, God renews the ability of His people to enjoy and employ the cultural values that conform to His plan for human life.

Jesus taught His disciples "that the Son of Man must suffer many things and be rejected by the elders, chief priests and teachers of the Law, and that He must be killed and after three days rise again" (Mark 8:31). In the mystery of evil that lies far beyond our explanation, God saw a necessity in dealing with evil in this way. God felt compelled to come to terms with the reality of our sin through the cross. The Word of God in human flesh remains a stumbling block for every culture that would like to claim God as one of its own. Jesus was a first-century Jew, and at the right hand of God He remains just that. But He is a first-century Jew who can and wants to talk with anyone. He can and does send His people to walk the dusty roads of every land and to sleep on the stinking streets of every city. Jesus comes from outside our experience and our domain, but He does cross the boundaries into the territory occupied by every ruler and every professor and every merchant of this earth. He Himself bridges the gaps constructed by every individual and society between themselves and their Creator. He makes Himself and His people at home in every culture because they all belong to Him, whether their power structures defy Him more or less ardently, more or less explicitly. Thus Jesus comes to break down the pride-filled idolatry of maleness involved in *machismo* while affirming the good gift of all the assignments He gives to men and boys. He sets aside the need to defend oneself on the basis of gender and breaks through a feminism that ignores His place in calling women and girls to the proper exercise of their femininity. Sometimes God's people see no way to continue to sing the melodies of an idolatrous culture, but sometimes those melodies can be baptized and used for the praise of Jesus Christ. In every culture the forms of beauty to which a people is accustomed can be used to depict and express God's intervention into our world in culturally apt ways. Each society has forms for organization and governance that can be refitted for use in conducting the life of the church.

And the message of the church finds points of contact with thought in every culture. Paul tried to build bridges to hearers in various places to tell of God's death blow to evil by moving onto their turf and by taking seriously their presuppositions and conceptions of reality. He could point out to the people of Lystra that they, too, had observed the testimony of the God who had showed kindness by giving rain and crops and filled their hearts with joy (Acts 14:17). He could try to win the Athenians' attention by appealing to their attempt to worship the unknown god. But when Paul proclaimed the resurrection of the dead, they sneered—though some believed (Acts 17:22–34).

Despite the common foundations on which conversations between Christians and non-Christians can begin, the gap between God and sinners remains and can be overcome only by His Word. Finally, the people of each culture must hear what the Jews of Pisidian Antioch had to hear: After constructing the appropriate bridges to his hearers, the apostle let them know he had come to announce forgiveness of sins in the one taken down from the tree and laid in a tomb. They had to be warned not to repeat the reaction of their ancestors who—Paul paraphrased—were addressed by the prophet Habakkuk, "Look, you scoffers, wonder and perish, for I am going to do something in your days that you would never believe, even if someone told you" (Acts 13:41; cf. Habakkuk 1:5; see also Acts 13:26–41). To the Israelites the Law had been given as a means of evaluating the performance of their daily lives. As such, it was not only a reference work for holy living, but also, always, a sentence of death. What God had promised was to break the power of the Law—the power of condemnation—with the power of His own death and coming to life again. "The power of God is the power of resurrection, a power that creates new life out of death."[5] Death is the inevitable theological consequence of our encounter with the Law. As Rainer Stahl notes, Luther emphasized in his preface to the Old Testament that the Law forces us, drives us, to Christ because it invites a performance that is impossible for sinners to perform. Thus it sets us up to recognize the failure of our own ability to live the kind of life God wanted us to live.[6]

Such a critique can be delivered from outside a culture or from its edge, at least in theory. But to bring God's Word of life to people and to lead them to trust God through that Word, it is necessary to meet people within their own cultures. Paul knew that, and he practiced his mission in accord with that principle. He became a Jew to the Jews and lived under their Law to win them for the Crucified One. He became weak to win the weak; he became all things to all people so he might save some of them for the sake of the Gospel of the God who revealed Himself in the foolishness and impotence of the cross (1 Corinthians 9:20–23). In his own person Paul sought to avoid anything that would offend Jews or Greeks and to please everyone in every way so they might be saved (1 Corinthians 10:32–33). Parallel to Christ's incarnation, Paul's accommodation with those to whom he brought the Gospel resisted whatever in their way of life threatened the Gospel but brought understanding and appreciation to the gifts of God present in their cultures. Nonetheless, in his message Paul was compelled to preach "Christ crucified: a stumbling block to Jews and foolishness to Gentiles" (1 Corinthians 1:23) because this man on the cross is God, is God's power and wisdom. But "no one can say, 'Jesus is Lord' except by the Holy Spirit" (1 Corinthians 12:3).

Paul's was a theology of the cross, of the one who died on the cross, of the God-man, Jesus of Nazareth, the person who came into the world as God's Word and way of dealing with blind, deaf humankind. This Jesus visits every society and brings to the center of every culture the death of false lordship and the renewal and revival of the gifts that God has given each tribe and nation. The cross puts failing ways of life to death and recreates failing human creatures into fellow citizens who can responsibly renew and revive what God has bestowed for the maintenance and enrichment of human life in specific cultural forms. From Calvary, the Creator who became flesh reveals Himself as the one who preserves and protects, guides and accompanies His people as He transforms and renews them. He does so by empowering them to live by dying to every other claim upon them, any plan for life other than His. In His resurrection Jesus appears to them with new claims upon them and the gifts God has given them in their own cultures. He calls them and sends them into His world with new assignments for taking care of their societies and cultures. That is the God who found Saul in the midst of persecuting his own Lord unawares. That is the God who sent Paul with a message of death and life across the cultural boundaries that had defined his life. That is the God who freed Paul through baptismal death for real human life.

THE THEOLOGY OF THE CROSS REVEALS HOW HIS PEOPLE KNOW GOD

This revelation comes—as it came to Paul—in the form of a promise from the cross, from the resurrected corpse of God, to His people. Promises do not have or need proof of any kind. Promises rest upon the trustworthiness of the one who promises.

Paul's Jewish acquaintances wanted signs. His Greek friends wanted a logical argument (1 Corinthians 1:22). Each culture has its favorite ways of exercising mastery over its own brands of truth. All Paul had to offer his hearers was the promise of death to imprisonment in false faiths and resurrection to new life in Christ. He was not eloquent and had no great wisdom. He had approached the Corinthians with his message of the cross as a weak man, fearful, with knees shaking. He did not find his presentation particularly persuasive. It was a demonstration of the power of the Holy Spirit, who takes words that seem foolish and impotent and demonstrates the power of God through them. That is God's plan because He does not want people to think that their new life has come to them through any other means than His own unconditioned giving (1 Corinthians 2:1–5). So it is that God's chosen people could reject the Word when He became flesh, preferring the darkness of their own religious culture, as they had constructed it, over His light. Those who received Christ, on the other hand, received Him as the light of their lives and became the children of God (John 1:9–12). Thus Paul noted that his proclamation was veiled to the perishing, those blinded by the gods of their own cultural constructions of reality and thus unable to see the light of the Gospel of the glory of Christ (2 Corinthians 4:3–4).

Those outside the faith are not foolish from the perspective of the world as it pursues its existence apart from its Creator. To them the proclamation of the cross does not make more sense than the world's wisdom; it does not have better arguments or more brilliant insights or a more reliable orientation for existence, nor is it even always more effective in transforming society. It is just that the world's wisdom exists without God. To come from their culture's point of looking at human life to the side of the Creator of that life means that people in every culture must experience "enlightenment only as an experience of darkness, kindness only as terror, the presence of God as the absence of God, orientation only as confusion, beginning as end, life as death."[7] When the voice from the cross interrupts the life of any person, that person is called to follow the path to the cross and to die.[8]

In the many cultures of the contemporary world, Christians encounter insistence on proofs of various kinds. Some people want logical proofs, according to the logic of their own cultures and ideologies. Others believe that truth comes only through the scientific method, ignoring the leaps of faith necessary to put the presuppositions for investigation and analysis in place. Still others "prove," or test, the worth of ideas or ways of life with emotions and feelings in various formats. Some think they can be certain if the new worldview brings blessings and benefits; others find confirmation that they have chosen the real truth in suffering. Some cling to hopes based on ideas that produce good works, others to those that spring from good feelings, and still others put their faith in their own faith.

Paul directs all believers away from false objects of trust to the one whose love establishes trust in His beloved children. He is the one who died and rose to deliver His love to His people. Paul anticipated the emphasis on trust found in some modern psychological systems when he acknowledged that the crucified Christ elicited from him the faith that made life possible for him (Galatians 2:20). If trust indeed stands at the heart of human life—as both biblical writers and contemporary psychologists claim[9]—then Paul calls all believers out of the web and woof of cultural faiths of all kinds to the cross of Christ.

Living as they do at the foot of the cross, Christians do not engage in much introspection and self-assessment. Repentance is sufficient preparation for assessing the situation in which God has called them to give witness to His Gospel and for appraising the gifts (both personal and cultural) that God has put at their disposal for this witness. On the basis of such an assessment, all believers proceed from that cross back into their culture, to live out daily life with the gifts God has given them through their culture. They use artistic and literary forms from their culture to tell the Gospel, and they practice Christian love in the forms that their culture needs. But because these newborn children of God have been altered at the heart of their existence, their culture will notice the impact of the cross as its way of life reflects itself in the service performed for all in the culture by those whose hearts have been impaled upon the cross. The cross will crucify the elements of the culture that point to false gods; thus it will change much in the new believer's way of life. It also will point this new believer to the true Lord of the culture and thus enrich the use and enjoyment of the culture's gifts.

THE THEOLOGY OF THE CROSS REVEALS WHO GOD'S PEOPLE ARE

The God who reveals Himself in the cross tells His human hearers who they had been while they were still in rebellion against Him and who they have become through His action on the cross. In so doing God lets His people know how He has recreated their lives as His children.

People of every culture share the experiences of the Ephesians. They had been dead in transgression and sin, following the ways of this world and of Satan, who made them deaf to God's Word for them. Paul knew that he shared that state with them; even he had gratified the cravings of the fallen, corrupted human nature, which had earned the wrath of God (Ephesians 2:1–3), who loves His people so much He wants them to enjoy the human life He made for them. False objects of trust take various forms. Many people are polytheistic because no one god fashioned by human imagination can suffice to provide meaning and security for life in a fallen and fractured world. Many today seek that meaning and security in an impersonal spirit that will suck up all the particles of spirit that have been scattered into the material bodies of the created world. Others look only to human devices—material accumulation, party and ideology, exercise of power for its own sake, worldly wisdom imparted through self-help groups—to provide meaning and security.

To each human creature the shadow of the cross comes as an expression of God's deep disgust at our straying from His family and the good life He fashioned for His human creatures. The cross falls across our lives to crush us. At the same time, "the cross of Christ is also the symbol of the gracious acceptance of us by God, the symbol of our leaving behind all of our own human accomplishments, the symbol of justification by faith."[10] God's unconditional love and the richness of His mercy have also found expression in the cross, and they have made His people alive with Christ though they had been dead in their rebellion against His plan for their lives. God has raised His people with Christ so they might live the lives He had prepared them to live (Ephesians 2:4–10)—within their own cultural contexts, using the blessings of cultural forms and expressions from their own way of life but freed from the false gods their cultures had imposed upon them.

Paul wrote explicitly of the transformation the cross had wrought in the lives of the Gentile believers in Ephesus. They had been the uncircumcised, cut off from the people of God, excluded from citizenship in Israel. They were outsiders, separated from the covenants God had made that conveyed hope and His presence to those to whom He had given His promise of life as His people (Ephesians 2:11–12). All cultural gaps are real, and the cultural divide between those who live in God's presence and those who do not is very, very real—even when it cuts a gulf between those who live in the same culture.

The gulf had been crossed, the gully filled, because Christ's blood bonded into one people, God's people, those who had been brought across the bridge constructed by the cross. This crucified God is the peace that has destroyed all barriers, all dividing walls of hostility, in His own flesh. He abolished some of the distinctive cultural marks of the Old Testament people of God to create one new family. That does not mean that He abolished all the distinctive marks of the Old Testament people of God. It does mean that circumcision and dietary laws, Sabbath observances and festival celebrations, required rituals and distinctions between clean and unclean no longer divided Jews in their culture from Gentiles in theirs. Both had been lifted above cultural distinctions that they might find a home in one new family, the body of Christ. Christ reconciled into one body those who had been separated—both from their Creator and Father and from their fellow human creatures. This reconciliation took place because every evil that plagued human life had been put to death through the cross. Christ had made peace for all and given everyone access to the Father through His death. He has drawn those who were foreigners and aliens into God's household, where they are now part of the temple He has constructed (Ephesians 2:13–22).

Paul's message for the Colossians differed little from that for the Ephesians. Alienated from God, His enemies in their minds and in their behavior, the Colossians had been reconciled to God by Christ's corpse. They could now present themselves holy and free from accusation in His sight because the Crucified One in whom God dwelt fully had made peace with His blood, shed on the cross, and thereby rescued them from the lordship of darkness. Christ had brought them, redeemed and forgiven, under His own lordship, the rule of the man on the cross (Colossians 1:21–22, 19–20, 13–14,). He had taken them into His own death through Baptism and brought them into new life through His resurrection, as its effects were conveyed through faith in God's power, as they encountered it in Christ's resurrection (Colossians 2:11–12; cf. Romans 6:3–11). That meant that those who had been dead in their self-willed separation from God had lost their identity as those accused of rebellion by God's Law. The bill of indictment had been soaked in the blood of the cross, and those false faiths and false gods that had held them captive had been taken captive themselves by the Lord, who disarmed them and made a public spectacle of them because He had triumphed over them by the cross (Colossians 2:13–15). This crucified Lord now rules because the result of His obedience to His Father, even to the point of dying on the cross, is that He has returned to equality with God—something He did not hang onto as He humbled Himself and took on the nature of the servant. Christ has been exalted and is Lord. And He also gives His people the same way of looking at life that He has (Philippians 2:5–11).

Having died in Christ through His Word in Baptism, His people no longer need to focus on their own strength and wisdom, whether they had previously thought that came from their own individual accomplishments, or from their nation or race, or from their party or economic system, or from the achievements and attainments of their culture or society or nation. Paul was struck blind and so could only listen to God; he could do no more than call out to the Jesus who was addressing him (Acts 9:3–9). In the same way God focuses the lives of His children upon Himself, even if it means distracting them from relying on other creatures through the infliction of a thorn in the flesh (2 Corinthians 12:7).

That means that the people whom Christ freed from the curse of the Law by hanging on a tree in their place will bring the blessing of being people of God to those of other cultures (Galatians 3:13–14). It also means that because they have died with Christ to the principles that give life and meaning to and through their own cultures, they will be free from the rules and regulations and controls of this world. Because in Baptism they have been raised to new life in Christ (Colossians 2:11–15), they will have a different way of thinking about how to act within their own cultures. Dead, having a life hidden with Christ, they will put to death every kind of disruptive behavior. They will live from a new identity, one renewed in and through their new knowledge of the image of life's Creator. They will reflect what it means to be God's chosen people, whether they are barbarians, Scythians, slaves, or free. Therefore, their lives will be marked by compassion, kindness, humility, gentleness, patience, and all other godly human characteristics. Above all, their lives will rest upon the peace that flows from the crucified Lord (Colossians 2:20–3:15). Because they have been crucified to their old, dead nature, with the passions and desires it used to secure its world, they live in the fruit of the Spirit: love, joy, peace, patience, kindness, goodness, faithfulness, gentleness, and self-control (Galatians 5:22–24). Thus as individuals and as communities of believers, they invade their own cultures and societies with God's love and goodness.

Their death to the ultimate claims of their culture and its gods separates them from their fellow citizens in their own societies. The one who came to bring a sword not only unites His own people, but divides others (Matthew 10:34–39). Paul recognized that he brought the fragrance of Christ to those whom God was saving, but those outside Christ's people sniffed in him the stench of death (2 Corinthians 2:15–16). At the same time these fundamental human characteristics embrace the good aspects of the culture to which God calls individual

Christians and their congregations. These characteristics enable God's people to let the gifts of their culture come to full blossom.

THE THEOLOGY OF THE CROSS REVEALS HOW GOD'S PEOPLE LIVE

Within the context of the blessings and challenges of culture, God fashions anew His own family. His people serve Him by serving their neighbors amid a fallen and failing world in which all life is marked by the cross, as well as by God's many blessings. Sinners who have died to their identity as children of the lie come to life as people prepared to follow Christ into sacrifice and death as they bring His Word of new life to others. That means they die to every earthly security they have formerly needed, including elements of their own culture that they have regarded as fundamental to life and may still regard as beautiful gifts from God. This has implications for all areas of daily life, as Paul noted to the Colossians (2:20–4:6). Indeed, he viewed the life of God's people as the offering of their bodies as living sacrifices (Romans 12:1). He viewed his own life as one that had been crucified with Christ (Galatians 2:20)—sinful identity buried with Christ, new identity resurrected with Him (Romans 6:3–11)—so he might live by faith in the Son of God who died for him and gave Himself for the rebellious persecutor of His church. Paul did not mind suffering for the Gospel (the power of God) because he knew that God had planned from before the beginning of time to destroy death and bring life and immortality to life through the Gospel of the incarnate Savior, Christ Jesus (2 Timothy 1:8–12).

That suffering was only symptomatic of what it had cost Paul, the proud and successful rabbi with the blossoming career in early first-century Judaism, to have his life interrupted, his old way of life put to death, by the appearance of Jesus on the road to Damascus. Peter's death to his old presuppositions regarding cultural necessities in the practice of the faith may have been more dramatic than Paul's (Acts 10:1–11:18), but Paul's dying to the role in God's service for which he had prepared himself was just as decisive and disruptive. It enabled the apostle to put aside all craving for personal gain for the sake of bringing the good news of salvation in Christ to others. For Paul, nothing dared hinder the course of the Gospel (1 Corinthians 9:12; 2 Corinthians 6:3–10; 11:16–33). He was prepared to relinquish every advantage to deliver new life through the cross to others. God's presence expressed itself in his experience as Christ's suffering overflowed into his life and produced endurance and hope and, therefore, comfort (2 Corinthians 1:3–8; cf. Romans 5:3–5). Paul felt compelled by the love of Christ; he was confident his Lord had died for all and thus had rendered all dead to false gods, raised to live not for themselves but for the crucified Lord, who had died for them and come back from the dead (2 Corinthians 5:14–15). Christ's death has reconciled them to their Father, and they are, therefore, new people in Christ (2 Corinthians 5:17–21). They live as part of this new community under the Word of God and experience life by hearing it and repeating it (Ephesians 4:1–16).

Paul was convinced that the God whose own power and wisdom took form in what appears impotent and foolish to fallen human eyes was expressing His power also in Paul's weakness. The Lord had let him know that His grace was sufficient for the apostle and that His power was being perfected in Paul's weakness (2 Corinthians 12:9). His life exhibited God's power in the same way that Christ had when He was crucified in weakness (2 Corinthians 13:4). Paul's own fragility and failings—he called himself a jar of clay—highlighted God's all-surpassing power (2 Corinthians 4:7; cf. 1 Corinthians 2:3–5). Fragility and failings he had aplenty, but Paul believed that "we who are alive are always being given over to death for Jesus' sake, so that His life may be revealed in our mortal body" (2 Corinthians 4:11). That life came indeed to people of every culture, but it pointed beyond every earthly culture to life with God that never ends (2 Corinthians 5:1–10).

To deliver this life, believers place their schedules and their travels into the hands of God. He determines where and when they do what they have to do. Although Christian witness on occasion takes place in hit-and-run situations, when the Lord opens a brief opportunity to confess His name and His Son's cross, the mission of God most often sends Christians into witnessing situations to stay. They do not live in the big house on the hill and occasionally come down into the dirty, dusty streets of town. They are ready to share the weakness and the failure of the people to whom they come.

The people of God go without fear into their own neighborhoods to confront the idolatries and disobediences of their own societies, realizing that God chooses the weak and foolish for accomplishing His purposes (1 Corinthians 1:26–31). Christian love demands that we struggle and strive for temporal justice and welfare for our neighbors. But the cross reminds us that progress in social justice and economic well being is always fleeting in a world of sin. We share the suffering and the oppression of our neighbors, and we hope and work for the improvement of their situation. But it is precisely in our readiness and our willingness to live in the shadows of life and to suffer its blows that the world experiences change for the better. Our focus on the cross does not let us lose sight of these temporal disadvantages and disasters that take away the taste of goodness from our neighbors within the church and outside it. But we know that the only true freedom and the only lasting improvement comes by clinging to the cross both in the midst of suffering and in its absence. By holding onto the cross, we are given the courage to recognize our own interests and to become free in relationship to them, even to become ready to ignore them, so we can bring true freedom and welfare to those around us. "Only in the shadow of the cross, even when we hardly notice it, do we become free to live a life of solidarity with those around us," which ensures their future.[11] Bearing the burdens of the weak, the fearful, and the exploited, we patiently lift them up again and again, sometimes with their help and sometimes without it. We help them catch a vision of life in Christ, and we assist them in learning how to practice the habit of living under the cross. With understanding and forbearance, we persevere in repeating God's love to them as we serve as the Holy Spirit's weapons in His struggle to bring them beyond their fears and the habits of selfishness and injustice that they practice and of which they are victims.

God so loved the world that He sent His Son into human flesh, into the midst of human culture, onto the cross, and out of the grave. Jesus breathed a breath of re-creation upon His disciples and said to them and all that follow in their train, "As My Father hath sent Me, even so send I you" (John 20:21 KJV). He sends His people into their own cultures and across cultural boundaries. Like Paul, we can never separate ourselves from the cultures into which we were born and those in which we live because they are gifts of God that He has woven into the fabric of human life. They remain gifts for His people. These gifts dare not become prisons that prevent believers from reaching into other people's lives with the cross that bestows salvation and life. The gifts of cultural blessings dare never become objects of trust and worship. God has given His people these gifts for their joy and for their service to others. Amid these gifts, God's children are determined to know nothing but Christ crucified.

NOTES

1. Oswald Bayer, "The Word of the Cross," *Lutheran Quarterly* IX.1 (1995): 47.
2. See the superb study of Luther's theology of the cross by Gerhard O. Forde, *On Being a Theologian of the Cross: Reflections on Luther's Heidelberg Disputation, 1518* (Grand Rapids: Eerdmans, 1997).
3. See Martin Luther's "Heidelberg Disputation," LW 31:39–70, especially the theological theses 1–28. Cf. Ludwig Feuerbach's use of this concept against the Christian faith in *The Essence of Christianity*, (trans. George Eliot; New York: Harper, 1957), 118.

4. The popular etymology that connects the English word *religion* with the Latin *religare*, "to bind together," has been rejected; the word comes from the Latin *religere*, "to regard with awe." Nonetheless, *religion* indeed does function as that which binds together all aspects of life.

5. Rainer Stahl, "Kirche unter dem Kreuz, Konsequenzen für ihre Gestalt und ihr Wirken in der Welt," *Zeitwende* 68 (1997): 77.

6. Stahl, "Kirche unter dem Kreuz," 78.

7. Jorg Baur, "Weisheit und Kreuz," *Neue Zeitschrift für die systematische Theologie* 22 (1980): 40.

8. Dietrich Bonhoeffer, *The Cost of Discipleship* (New York: Macmillan, 1959), 79. It is important to note that in this passage Bonhoeffer is speaking of baptismal faith.

9. Cf., for example, Erik Erikson, *Childhood and Society* (New York: Norton, 1952); and Erik Erikson, *The Life Cycle Completed* (New York: Norton, 1982).

10. Stahl, "Kirche unter dem Kreuz," 79.

11. Stahl, "Kirche unter dem Kreuz," 81–82.

3

A Missiology of the Cross

ROBERT SCUDIERI

Drawn to the cross, which you have blessed
With healing gifts for souls distressed,
To find in you my life, my rest,
Christ Crucified, I come.

Then all that you would have me do
Shall such glad service be for you
That angels wish to do it too.
Christ Crucified, I come.[1]

INTRODUCTION

Mission is something that Christians do because they live under the cross. If there were no great commission (Matthew 28:18–20), would there still be a Christian mission? You might respond, "Yes, because there would still be Luke 24, where Jesus said, "[R]epentance and forgiveness of sins will be preached in [My] name to all nations, beginning at Jerusalem. You are witnesses of these things" (Luke 24:47–48). And there is Mark 16:15 (GWN): "Then Jesus said to them, 'Go everywhere in the world, and tell everyone the Good News. Whoever believes and is baptized will be saved, but whoever does not believe will be condemned.' "

But suppose none of these passages existed, not to mention any of the dozens of Scripture texts that show God's love for all nations and His desire that the world hear the Gospel through His church—what then? Would there still be a mission for the Christian church?

From one point of view, no. There are Christians and Christian churches that understand Christian mission as the result of a command—an order—as in "these are our marching orders." In this regard, God's commands are at the center of mission. But let me suggest another way to look at mission. We might call it an "evangelical missiology"—that is, mission is a result of being a Christian. Mission is something that Christians do because they live under the cross. These Christians would understand Acts 1:8 (GWN)—"You will be my witnesses to testify about Me in Jerusalem, throughout Judea and Samaria, and to the ends of the earth"—not as a command, but as a promise.

In my opinion, too much mission thinking surrounds "technique." Frankly, technique is an essential element of missiology, but at the beginning let us be grounded in a theological understanding of the cause of mission. The "how" flows from this. As Lutherans, let's talk about mission under the cross. Luther called the theology he advocated "*theologia crucis*," the "theology of the cross." Later in life he called it the "theology of the Gospel."[2] The term was made well known in the Heidelberg Disputation of 1518. When he posted the Ninety-five Theses in 1517, Luther had called for a disputation, a discussion, of the theses. The discussion never took place. Instead, Luther was attacked as a heretic. Pope Leo X wanted to silence Luther, and he asked the general of the Augustinians, Gabriel della Volta, to do this. Volta turned the task over to Johann von Staupitz, the vicar general of the German Augustinians.

It was the practice of the Augustinians in Germany to meet every three years on the third Sunday after Easter. In 1518 the meeting was in April at Heidelberg. Staupitz asked Luther to share his views on theology—to introduce the Augustinians to the new evangelical theology. Luther wrote 28 theological and 12 philosophical theses for the debate. The most important of these, and the one that forms the basis for this essay, is theses 24, "Yet that wisdom is not of itself evil, nor is the law to be evaded; but without the theology of the cross man misuses the best in the worst manner."[3]

For a while now I have been considering what kind of missiology would clearly reflect Luther's theology of the cross. In my opinion, a "missiology of the cross" would look at Christian mission from two vantage points:

1. It would perceive that all mission flows *from* the cross.
2. It would perceive that all mission flows *to* the cross.

Others more knowledgeable than I have written about the Gospel as the starting point for mission. Certainly Georg Vicedom's *Missio Dei* is evidence of this perspective.[4] However, I know of no missiology that puts the cross at the center of mission. In what follows I am suggesting that the cross is both the starting and ending point for mission, even as Jesus in Hebrews 12:2 is called, as *God's Word to the Nations* translates it, "the source and goal" of our faith." If in the few pages that follow you come to value the cross as more important for the mission of the church, thank God. If not, maybe someone else will be moved to take up this goal!

ALL CHRISTIAN MISSION FLOWS *FROM* THE CROSS

The created world can tell us only so much about the nature of the Creator. Television news shows barrage us with scenes of destructive hurricanes, tidal waves that wipe out buildings and carry away people, and drought that dries up lives. A popular action movie was made about the terror tornadoes cause in human society. These terrifying acts of nature cause us to ask, "What kind of God would allow these things?"

Luther talks about this knowledge of God as the *"deus revelatus"*— the revealed God.[5] But it is the *"deus absconditus,"* revealed by Jesus, most explicitly revealed by Jesus on the cross, that shows us the true heart of God. In nature God shows His power, glory, and might. On the cross God is revealed as compassionate, loving, forgiving sin by taking the consequences for our sin on Himself. The cross gives us the reason for mission. It shows us the lengths to which God was willing to go to bring broken humanity back to Himself. The cross shows that God is love.

True Christian mission occurs not because of human desire for success or accomplishment. We reject some mission approaches because they make growth in numbers the "bottom line" for mission work and ignore or downplay the top line. The "top line" is disciples formed into faithful, sacrificial, loving Christians. Growth of the church in numbers is not necessarily evidence of God's blessing. "I will boast all the more gladly about my weaknesses . . . when I am weak, then I am strong," Paul says (2 Corinthians 12:9, 10). Conversely, smallness and meanness are not always evidence of faithfulness!

In Colossians 1:19–20, Paul says that God was pleased to bring peace through the blood of Christ. And in 1 Timothy 2:4, Paul states that it is God's desire that all be saved and come to the knowledge of the truth. New churches and the growth of existing churches are each the result of God's grace, His undeserved love. People become disciples of Jesus, hearts are converted, as Article V of the Augsburg Confession says, "when and where [God] pleases."[6] But God does not act alone in this.

We are not antinomians. As the Reformation gained strength in Germany, variations of evangelical teaching began to occur. John Agricola, a former student of Luther, began to teach that it was not correct to urge Christians to do good works. Luther fought this idea. Good works are not necessary for salvation, but they will be done and will be taught as a natural expression of God's love for all.

There are radical elements today that resist teaching Christians how to do the work of outreach. They teach that it is not important or necessary to bring the Gospel outside of the church building and into the world. They say it is enough to care for those whom God sends. Some of them teach that the work of mission outreach ended when the apostles died.[7] They are as wrong as Agricola. Luther explains, "I wish to have the words 'without work' understood in the following manner: Not that the righteous person does nothing, but that his works do not make him righteous, rather that his righteousness creates works. For grace and faith are infused without our works. After they have been imparted the works follow."[8] It is not good works that are bad, it is trusting in good works for salvation. Growing churches are not wrong, but trusting in that growth as a means of earning God's favor or even as a means of salvation is wrong. We should teach churches how to do a better job of reaching out to make faith-filled, sacrificial, loving disciples. But we will also declare that growth or lack of growth in a church will not affect our salvation.

Christian mission does not just happen. God has chosen to work through means—through human beings. Because of this we send Christian leaders to schools to learn how to teach and how to preach and how to lead a worship service; how to start new churches; and how to use the limited resources available to a church to share the Gospel with the most people. Although the power behind liturgy, preaching, and teaching is God's Holy Spirit, we become more effective through study and practice. And because we are broken human beings, we need instruction in mission outreach, but always we live in the forgiveness of sins, trusting God to use our feeble efforts to accomplish what He wants done when He wants it done.

In the present context of a non-Christian United States, we must teach Christians how to be missionaries. In 1992 the LCMS declared North America to be a "world mission field." What does this mean? How is a missionary different from a pastor or a professor or a chaplain? How can we encourage the growth of mission churches—congregations that will see their primary work as reaching out to those without Christ, sacrificial congregations that put the needs of the unchurched neighbor ahead of their own? There is an old saying that seminary professors used to share with their students, "Pray as if everything depended on God; work as if everything depended on you." As in the crucifixion, the results belong to God. The cross gives us the reason for mission. Jesus' cross shows us that the growth of the church is in God's heart and in God's hands. Furthermore, the cross gives us the message for the mission.

Luther was readied for reformation after he heard the message of the Gospel. It is well known that Luther taught that the righteousness God demanded was provided for us by Jesus' life, death, and resurrection. No human could fulfill the demands of God's Law. To paraphrase Paul in Romans 3:21ff., God's way of putting people right with Himself has been revealed, and it has nothing to do with the Law. The Law and the prophets give their witness to it, but God puts people right through faith in Jesus Christ. And in Ephesians 2:8–9, Paul says, "For it is by grace you have been saved, through faith—and this not of yourselves, it is the gift of God—not by works, so that no one can boast." This is the message we have, and our mission is to share this message with those who do not know it so they can become and grow as disciples of Jesus.

The cross gives us the message for the mission. In the Heidelburg Disputation, thesis 20, Luther says, "He deserves to be called a theologian, however, who comprehends the visible and manifest things of God seen through suffering and the cross."[9] The cross gives us the reason, the message, and the urgency for mission. The Gospel writer Mark quotes Jesus, "Whoever does not believe will be condemned" (Mark 16:16); and Jesus says, "Those who don't believe are already condemned" (John 3:18 RSV). Without Christ's death, there is no sacrifice for our sins, there is no salvation, no forgiveness, and no life eternal. "The Gospel . . . is the power of God *for salvation*" (Romans 1:16 [RSV], *my emphasis*). Its purpose is to save.

Yet the church in North America has had an increasingly difficult time getting that message out to its neighbors. According to Dr. George Hunter, church attendance in Canada is one half of what it was 40 years ago; in Australia, one half of what it was 25 years ago. In the United States 50 to 60 million people do not even claim to be Christian. Another 50 million are nominal members of churches.[10] The recent past president of the LCMS, Dr. A. L. Barry (1992–2001), strongly emphasized the reality that the United States is the third largest mission field in the world.

The cross is the source for mission—not human will or efforts. Dona Hoffman made this point eloquently in a poem entitled "Witness":

I sat in the pew and listened
    to the silent anguish of my brothers
Being denounced for their failure to evangelize.
The sloped shoulder, the withdrawal,
    the burdened hearts were mute beggary:
Show us Jesus Christ and we will gladly share him.
We cannot share Whom we do not know.
And after the damning
    we were ushered out to our busywork
Of choir rehearsals and bowling leagues and sewing circles.[11]

Ultimately, all mission flows not from a command but from a love—and not from our love but from God's love. All mission flows from Jesus' cross.

ALL CHRISTIAN MISSION FLOWS *TO* THE CROSS

The cross was the goal of Jesus' mission. Jesus says, "God so loved the world that He gave His one and only Son" (John 3:16). Again in 1 John 3:16 (GWN), "We understand what love is when we realize that Christ gave His life for us." Jesus came into the world to die on a cross. Jesus' death is necessary for us to be forgiven. His death pays the price for our failures, mistakes, and outright sins. In response to the praise of the crowd at Palm Sunday's triumphal city entrance, Jesus reacts to the presence of Gentiles in the crowd by saying, "Unless a kernel of wheat falls to the ground and dies, it remains only a single seed. But if it dies, it produces many seeds" (John 12:24). In the middle of a triumphal procession, Jesus announces His death. Jesus came into the world to die so countless more would live!

Jesus entered the world to go to the cross, and the mission He sends us on takes its characteristics from Him. Christian mission is not easy, it is not always glorious, and there are no magic bullets. Instead, there is sacrifice, hard work, suffering, and faith in God. This was Jesus' way. In the words of our Lord: "Those who love their lives will destroy them, and those who hate their lives in this world will guard them for everlasting life" (John 12:25 GWN). This is the way to the cross.

Africans have a lot to teach us in this regard. When large numbers of African immigrants began settling on Staten Island, New York, St. John's Lutheran Church asked the LCMS for help to reach them. The LCMS appealed to the Lutheran Church of Ghana, asking that church body to send a missionary. Rev. Isaac Gympadu came to the United

States and started five new African immigrant churches within three years. Rev. Gympadu left his family in Ghana and did not see them for three years. He and his family were willing to sacrifice for the sake of the Gospel. Not many North Americans would or could make that kind of a commitment.

As the cross was the goal of Jesus' mission, bringing others to the cross is a part of what it means for Christians to be faithful. C. F. W. Walther, first president of the LCMS (and the preeminent nineteenth-century Lutheran theologian), said in an address to the first convention of the Iowa District: "The church is the mother of us all (Galatians 4:26). Just as surely as we are now members of the church, so surely we should also be fruitful mothers . . ."[12] We might ask what Walther meant by "fruitful." Surely there are many ways of interpreting this. But Walther tells us: "If we are not fruitful mothers, i.e., if we do not produce spiritual children, or fail to do those things whereby such children are produced, then we are not obeying our calling, and then God will not say to us, 'You pious servant' but He will say to us 'you unfaithful servant.' God grant we never hear those words."[13]

Of course we live in the forgiveness of sins, even our sins of failing to evangelize! Luther, commenting on Galatians 3:26–27, says,

Faith is an unswerving gaze that looks on Christ alone. . . . So if you want to be comforted when your conscience plagues you or when you are in dire distress, then you must do nothing but grasp Christ in faith and say, "I believe in Jesus Christ, God's Son, who suffered, was crucified, and died for me. In his wounds and death, I see my sin. In his resurrection, I see the victory over sin, death, and the devil."[14]

The goal of the church is to bring people to Jesus' cross. This is the church's calling, its mission. We emphasize this mission when we use the adjective "apostolic" to refer to the church. T. W. Manson wrote, "It is a pity that the word 'apostolic' has had its meaning narrowed in the course of centuries—so that instead of declaring primarily the commitment to a great missionary task it registers a claim on the part of the Eastern and Roman Catholic communions to be the lawful successors of the apostles."[15] Echoes of this missionary meaning of "apostolic" are found when we call St. Gall the "apostle" to Switzerland, Willibrod the "apostle" to Holland, and Boniface the "apostle" to Germany.

The church is to go into the whole world with the saving Gospel. This Gospel, as it comes in Word and Sacraments, brings people to the cross of Christ, where they find healing, forgiveness, and life. To say the church is apostolic is to declare that it is missionary—that it has been sent, with the authority of Jesus, to bear the Gospel to a dying world. This is not something the church decides it should do, it is a mission that has been given to it. It is in this light that we consider the Great Commission: Matthew 28:16–20. Is this a command or a promise?

Jesus and His disciples are together outside Bethany. He is about to leave them, and they sense this departure is for good. Matthew observes in verse 17, "They worshiped Him; but some doubted." How can this be? Jesus has been with them for more than 40 days. What can they be doubting? The Greek word translated in this text as *doubt* is *distadzo*. Literally it means trying to stand in two places at the same time. The only other time it is used is in Matthew 14 when Jesus comes to the disciples at night, walking on water. At first the disciples are terrified, then one of them shouts, "It's the Lord!" Peter yells to Jesus, "If it is You, Lord, call me out with You." Jesus calls Peter out of the boat, and Peter actually walks on the water for a few steps. Then Matthew records that Peter "saw the wind." He took his eyes off Jesus, which is when he began to sink. Peter's attention shifted from Jesus to himself: "Look at me. I am walking on water! Uh oh!" Then Jesus pulled Peter back up and said, "Why did you *distadzo*?"

Peter wasn't doubting Jesus, he was doubting himself, which was true of the apostles in Matthew 18. They knew Jesus was about to leave, and they were thinking, "What are we going to do without Him? How will we get along?" Their *distadzo* was for themselves. That is when Jesus says, "As you go, make disciples—but remember, I will be with you to the end of the age." The focus is on the presence of Jesus with His church as it carries out the mission. The Great Commission is not a command, it is a promise. It is the promise of God to be with His church as it goes out to do His work of bringing His love to all people.

As Jesus came into the world to go to the cross, so His church goes into the world, with His Word and Sacraments to bring those separated from God to the healing cross of Christ. But the church does not go alone or on its own authority or power. Jesus goes with us. Furthermore, when people are brought to the cross, the cross shapes them, making them more like Jesus. The cross shows us the commitment required for mission, what it is necessary to suffer, and what God was willing to suffer and how committed He was to the mission. Why would God come into the world and allow Himself to be killed on a cross? John explains this: "God is love. Those who live in God's love live in God, and God lives in them" (1 John 4:16 GWN). "We understand what love is when we realize that Christ gave His life for us" (1 John 3:16 GWN). The theology of the cross is a constant reminder that though the war has been won—Christ is alive, interceding for us before the throne of God, victorious over death, the devil, and sin—the conflict continues. And there are daily casualties.

New Mount Olive Lutheran Church was started in Detroit in the mid-1980s. The Rev. Venice Douglas, an African American LCMS pastor, was the mission developer. Pastor Douglas started the church in the way new African American and Hispanic missions typically begin: without large subsidies but with the guidance of a visionary leader and the help of dedicated members from other local congregations. What little money is contributed from local churches is used for outreach, thus the new developer is most often bi-vocational, working at another job for income until the church grows large enough to support itself—which usually takes eight to ten years. Pastor Douglas drove a cab, sold vitamins, and did odd jobs until the church began a child development center that produced enough income to allow him to be a full-time pastor. Such a situation creates a tension between the joy and hope that fills missionaries and the knowledge that outreach requires hard work, disappointment, sacrifice, tears, and pain.

What do disciples look like? They are hard pressed, worn out, confronted by new challenges every day. They look like their Lord; they look like sacrificial love. Sacrificial love is the hallmark of Jesus and of Christians. Jesus says, "By this all will know that you are My disciples, if you use the old hymnal." No. "If you grow your church very large." No. "By this all men will know that you are My disciples, if you love one another" (John 13:35). Yes!

Paul is no different. The apostle says, "He who loves his fellow-man has fulfilled the law" (Romans 13:8). And John adds, "We love because [God] first loved us" (1 John 4:19). Paul the apostle agrees. Every Christian knows Paul's important insight in 1 Corinthians 13: "If I speak in the tongues of men and of angels, but have not love, I am a . . . clanging cymbal. . . . And now these three remain: faith, hope and love. But the greatest of these is love." Paul tells us what love looks like (vv. 4–7): "Love is patient, love is kind. It does not envy, it does not boast, it is not proud. It is not rude, it is not self-seeking, it is not easily angered, it keeps no record of wrongs. Love does not delight in evil but rejoices with the truth. It always protects, always trusts, always hopes, always perseveres." The cross shapes those brought to it—it recreates us into loving people and churches, and it forms us into sacrificial people and churches.

In Matthew 10:38–39, Jesus instructs His first missionaries. He has called the Twelve together to give them the authority to do their mission—authority to drive out evil spirits and to heal diseases (Matthew 10:1). These first are not sent to those outside the church—they are not sent to the Gentiles but only to the people of Israel. The first to have the opportunity to know the great news are the people to whom Christ was promised. It turns out they have the right of first rejection.

Jesus prophesied that the missionaries will be flogged in synagogues and will be brought before governors and kings as prisoners. Family members will betray them. This is the mission on which they are sent. They will, because of who they are, be sacrificial. It is in their nature because it is in the nature of Jesus. And Jesus is clear about this. In Matthew 10:38, He says, "Anyone who does not take up his cross and follow Me is not worthy of Me."

Before Constantine ascended to the throne as ruler of the Holy Roman Empire, before the church became "established" as a part of the culture and the government, mission work was more risky, more sacrificial. But it disregarded the cost. There was little bureaucracy involved in mission work, after all, churches were not allowed to own property or to worship in public. Itinerant preachers spread the Word of God, and they supported themselves—much like the apostle Paul. This same model existed in the United States Lutheran church prior to World War II. In every city someone can point out the "mother church": the congregation that started congregations.

After World War II most LCMS mission work in North America was carried out by synodical districts. We like to say that districts act on behalf of congregations, but too many times they act instead of congregations. By the 1970s, it became clear that districts could not and should not do mission work apart from congregations, but old habits die hard. It was not until the 1980s that districts seriously began to work in partnership with congregations to begin new missions. As one example, the Rev. Dr. Paul Heinicke, at that time the mission executive of the Michigan District, asked the district in convention to reduce giving to Synod by 4 percent and redirect this amount to fund district mission work. Dr. Heinicke told the convention that if it did not make the change, there would be no funding for new mission starts in Michigan. The convention voted against the proposal.

What was Dr. Heinicke to do? He knew one thing he was not going to do: He was not going to stop planting new missions. Instead, he traveled to every circuit and challenged them to establish local mission committees that would provide local support for all new missions in addition to nominal support from the district. Michigan District circuits and churches responded enthusiastically. A wave of new missions began, more than could have been started under the old strategy of district subsidy.

Today almost every LCMS judicatory realizes that it is best to begin new missions in partnership with local churches. The work has become more sacrificial, grounded in the love that comes from the cross. And it is more faith oriented. In the late 1980s some new churches were started with child development centers. The ministry to children, the opportunity to reach the adult family members, and the income such a center could provide to support the new mission made this a useful strategy. But finding funding to start the first church with a child care center was not easy. Ascension Lutheran Church, Atlanta, Georgia (a congregation that worshiped 130), recognized the opportunity to begin a new church with a child development center in Alpharetta, about 20 miles north of Atlanta. The congregation, as a part of its thirty-fifth anniversary celebration, raised more than $400,000 to begin this mission. The new church, Shepherd of Christ, worshiped for six years in the great room of the child care center. Income from child care helped pay the mortgage, then they built a large sanctuary. Today Shepherd of Christ has more than160 children in its child care program and more than 500 attend worship each Sunday. None of this would have happened were it not for the sacrifice of the faithful people of Ascension.

New churches are both the base and the goal of mission work. It is in churches that the Gospel is preached and the sacraments are administered. It is in the church that God does His work of transforming lives. Mt. Holy Cross Lutheran Church, Vail, Colorado, takes its name from a mountain. Mt. Holy Cross received its name because of the image of a cross that appears when the snow collects on the mountain. The snow is shaped by gullies and valleys into an image of the cross. Longfellow wrote a poem about this mountain, but he never saw the mountain or the cross; someone told him about it.

If the cross is the center of mission work, then the overflow of joy at being saved by grace, through faith cannot be contained by one person or by a church building. This joy must spill over, will spill over, into the lives of people everywhere. People will tell other people—starting in Jerusalem but moving to Judea, Samaria, and to the ends of the earth. This is the essence of mission work. Mission flows from the cross, then back to the cross. Christian mission is under the cross, as Paul Speratus wrote:

> Faith clings to Jesus' cross alone
> And rests in him unceasing;
> And by its fruits true faith is known,
> With love and hope increasing.
> For faith alone can justify;
> Works serve our neighbor and supply
> The proof that faith is living.[16]

NOTES

1. *Lutheran Worship*, 356.1, 4.
2. Heino O. Kadai, "Luther's Theology of the Cross," *Concordia Theological Quarterly* 63.3 (July 1999): 169.
3. LW 31:55.
4. Georg Vicedom, *The Mission of God* (St. Louis: Concordia, 1965).
5. E. Lueker, "Deus absconditus; Deus revelatus," *Lutheran Cyclopedia* (ed. Erwin L. Lueker; St. Louis: Concordia, 1975), 233.
6. Theodore G. Tappert, ed. *The Book of Concord* (Philadelphia: Fortress, 1959), 31.
7. Tappert, *Book of Concord,* 40.
8. LW 31:55–56.
9. LW 31:52.
10. George Hunter, presentation to Gospel and Our Culture Network, Chicago, Illinois, February 1992.
11. Quoted in Paul G. Bretscher, *The Holy Infection: The Mission of the Church in Parish and Community* (St. Louis: Concordia, 1969), 112.
12. C. F. W. Walther, address to the first Iowa District Convention, unpublished translation by the Rev. Bruce Cameron.
13. C. F. W. Walther, address to the first Iowa District Convention, unpublished translation by the Rev. Bruce Cameron.
14. *Through Faith Alone: 365 Devotional Readings from Martin Luther* (St. Louis: Concordia, 1999), reading for January 18.
15. T. W. Manson, *The Church's Ministry* (Philadelphia: Westminster, 1948), 35.
16. *Lutheran Worship*, 355.5.

FOR FURTHER READING

Kittelson, James. *Luther the Reformer*. Minneapolis: Augsburg, 1986.

McGrath, Alister. *Luther's Theology of the Cross*. New York: Basil Blackwell, 1985.

Scudieri, Robert J. *The Apostolic Church: One, Holy, Catholic and Missionary*. Fort Wayne, Ind.: Lutheran Society for Missiology, 1997.

Vicedom, Georg. *The Mission of God*. St. Louis: Concordia, 1965.

PART 2

Global Themes for Witness

4

Luther's "Theology of the Cross" and Eastern Thought

WON YONG JI

INTRODUCING THE SUBJECT:
ITS *TERMINUS A QUO* AND *AD QUEM*

The pregnant observation of Rudyard Kipling (1865–1936) many years ago, "Oh, East is East, and West is West, and never the twain shall meet," frequently stimulates my thinking and arouses my curiosity. Is there not indeed some way the two can meet and at least appreciate and respect each other without sacrificing each other's identity and uniqueness?

This essay—with an unconventional content from such a curiosity and with a desire to pursue a new paradigm for Luther study in the East Asian context (a context that now is on American shores and growing)—notes an intriguing similarity between Luther's paradoxical way of thinking and the classical *T'ai-Chi* cosmology. The latter's wisdom and Luther's thought are key in resolving some complex postmodern issues and promoting harmony. "Harmony" is an important concern in East and West for internal coherence and balance between faith and culture without unnecessary discord. This insight may also help to reduce the polarization that causes much tension, confusion, and strife in society and among adherents of various religions.

First, harmony calls the attention of Luther students and scholars to a possible *Anknüpfungspunkt,* or contact point, between Luther's thought, which is often summarized in the *theologia crucis,* and the *T'ai-Chi* matrix, which is used not in the pop-culture jargon but in the classical sense in East Asia. This connection can be a mutual reference point and a point of cultural adaptability of Luther's thought in East Asia.

Second, harmony reminds us that there may be a significant similarity in these thought schemes. Such a similarity may exist in the way of thinking about and the attitude toward reality and the "center." This similarity may offer mutually edifying experiences and spark discussion.

Third, harmony promotes through such deliberation the necessary connections that will ultimately increase peace among the people instead of distrust and misunderstanding. Harmony will not merely help East and West to come closer, it also will help each to appreciate the other. Harmony also helps highlight fundamental differences and sheds light on what is unique and essential to each. Furthermore, while non-Christian traditions and cultures have been, to this point, largely a hypothetical concern, at least for many Europeans and Americans, they are now a practical reality almost everywhere, chiefly as a result of the general decline of Christianity in the West and the rise of religious pluralism. Indeed, pluralism comes to us with enormous problems, as well as unlimited challenges and promise.

The idea to use the *T'ai-Chi* matrix to examine Luther's thought grew out of a simple practical question concerning whether Luther has something meaningful and helpful to say to the East Asian mind. Can one make an analogy between Luther's thought and some Eastern thoughts? Such an excursion, we realize, may offer some benefits, as well as invite some necessary caution. Nevertheless, it can be a worthwhile venture.

CONTRAST AND HARMONY

Let's examine a common perspective of contact that appears to be recognizable in both Luther's paradoxical way of thinking and in the *T'ai-Chi* principle: Each reveals a totality of the universe with two distinct, but not opposite and separable, elements. These elements are the most basic components, namely, the Yin/Yang Axis. The *T'ai-Chi* principle, representing "the Center," contains "balance" between these two contrasting elements.

There seems to be a considerable similarity between Luther's way of handling "truth" and some Eastern methods of perceiving "the Great Ultimate." Specifically, Luther's "paradox" paradigm and the Eastern *T'ai-Chi* matrix appear to have great affinity: They are relational and "both/and" oriented.

In the practical level of life, there are pressing needs for a positive encounter between East and West (and North and South). One may rightly ask: How can we live together, peacefully and harmoniously, in the East and West with others who are perceived to be disagreeable and even unattractive? Can religion in general help this situation? In particular, can Martin Luther and his globally significant "Great Discovery" assist us? What aspect of Luther's thought can be highlighted to approach this issue? How can we make Luther's thought more relevant for the twenty-first century? In the shifting winds of postmodern cultural trends—in which the virtual cyberworld, individual identity, and ego are blurred—everything becomes passive, cynical, insecure, relative, and negative for the contemporary postmodern person. Luther's thought deals with the sharply contrasting tensions between faith and life, sin and grace, the known and the unknown, the church and the world, etc. In approaching these tensions and their relation to each other, we encounter real paradoxes. We can also find a relational aspect that does not necessarily oppose the other. From this point of view, Luther seems to be more Eastern than Western in his thinking.

THEOLOGIA CRUCIS AND THE PRINCIPLE OF HARMONY

Luther's *theologia crucis* (WA 5:176.32f.; 5:179.31; 5:163.28–29 [*Operationes in Psalmos*, 1519–1521][1] and many other references in his writings) and an Eastern way of reasoning, such as the *T'ai-Chi* matrix, for example, may shed light on how to ease the mutual tension and misunderstanding concerning many unresolved sensitive subjects, such as issues related to the Christian faith and indigenous beliefs in non-Christian lands, Christian mission and modern cultures, the theology of religions, etc. For certain, Luther is not merely another great figure in the history of the West nor merely the "guru" of the Lutherans. His great discovery has often been summarized in his "theology of the cross," reflecting the true meaning of divine grace and the outpouring of God's love for humanity through Jesus Christ, which can be apprehended only through faith. In the process of explicating this meaningful truth, Luther has left us some helpful insights, such as the idea of *simul iustus et peccator* (being righteous and sinner at the same time); the concept of being a free person *and* a complete servant (1 Corinthians 9:19; Romans 13:8; Galatians 4:4; Philippians 2:6–7); God as the hidden *and* the revealed (cf. *De Servo Arbitrio*);[2] the insights on two kingdoms; and the view of human bondage (sin) *and* freedom through divine grace in the same breath. In summary, immutable Law and full Gospel in one divine revelation are certainly intriguing.[3] We can comprehend such contrasting theological notions only in the experience of their opposites. Both notions are positively correlated and held truly in tension. From this perspective, Luther and the East are neither fully identifiable nor incompatible.

THE *T'AI-CHI* COSMOLOGY

T'ai-Chi is an anthropologically oriented East Asian cosmology with a unique approach to reality. It is based upon "Yin-Yang" philosophy, which teaches that balance and harmony are maintained in all the perpetual changes that occur in the universe. Its origin may be traced to the Chu Dynasty in China (1027 B.C.–256 B.C.). That is when the cosmological literary work *I-Ching* (the *Book of Change*) was written.[4] *T'ai-Chi* is the unity and harmony of Yin-Yang, which are opposed yet united in the *T'ai-Chi*. Although existentially opposite in character, they are essentially united and inseparable, that is, the division of the undivided. Yin-Yang are different not in substance and entity, but in dynamic of change. They are relational symbols, in complementary relationship and harmony, not a conflicting but a complementary dualism. The application of Yin-Yang thought in religious Taoism and in the development of the most refined Confucian philosophy is known as Neo-Confucianism, which was completed by Chu Hsi (A.D. 1130–1200), the *Li* School of the "Unchanging Principle."

The "Eastern Latin" (my coined expression) word to the left reads in Chinese *T'ai-Chi*, in Japanese *Tai-Kyoku*, and in Korean *Tae-Guik*, with virtually the same meaning in all three languages and cultures. The literal meaning of *T'ai-Chi:* "the greater [than] the extreme," which equals the Center, the Middle, that is, the Balance or Harmony. *T'ai-Chi* is often used today to refer to a physical exercise and martial arts.

The *T'ai-Chi*, an ancient symbol, vividly illustrates a paradigm of diversity and harmony in the universe. One is urged to consider, for example, the harmonious relationship between Yin and Yang, the negative and positive forces of the "ridgepole" of the universe, the breaths of heaven and earth. In the *I-Ching* they are named as the two *Ch'i*. *T'ai-Chi* may mean infinity, creativity, absolute, harmony, etc. Yin and Yang are the two basic elements that express the dual aspects of the cosmos in a complementary way, not opposing each other. These dualistic elements in *T'ai-Chi* show that while there is a constant movement within the sphere of infinity, producing a constant creative tension, there are always balance and harmony. Within infinity (*T'ai-Chi*), with diversity, there still prevail unity and harmony. (Choo Yum-Ke, during the Song Era, proclaimed *T'ai-Chi*, *o-hy_ng*, and *yin/yang* in his book: *Tai Geuk Do-Sul*.) Frequently a contrast is also made: *T'ai-Chi* as the *one* through which the *Tao* manifests itself, then differentiates into two forces, *Yin* and *Yang*. The Koreans, for example, have adopted *T'ai-Chi* in their national flag.

What the *T'ai-Chi* principle maintains is not a Manichean dualism of opposing forces such as good and evil, but it indicates the contrasting qualities that belong to or describe the same reality, two indispensable components in one true Reality. *T'ai-Chi* requires both components and a maintenance of a perfect balance of the two elements. *Yin* and *Yang* are equally necessary sides of the same reality—a complementary nature of the two aspects, the paradoxical poles, appearing to be in contradiction but in reality in harmony and in balance, not as a conflicting dualism of "either/or" but as a complementary symbiotic relationship of "both/and." Indeed, *Yin* and *Yang* do not contradict each other but require each other. One can see a contrast between the following two pictures:

In the West   In the East

We encourage interested persons to engage in further research into the *T'ai-Chi* cosmology—with its relational symbol, the harmony of opposites (Yin/Yang)—from the classical age in the Orient to modern understandings, but to do so without being misled into wrong conclusions, as has happened to some contemporary occultic groups. Unfortunately, the legitimate meaning of and concern for harmony and balance in life are being infiltrated and captivated by some of the eccentric and quasi-pagan religious sects. We sometimes see the Yin-Yang symbol used for religious and commercial logos or trademarks. Thus the symbol and meaning of *T'ai-Chi* is frequently misused just as the symbol of the cross is at times misused. We are also aware that the concept of harmony existed among some primal folk religions, for example, those in Korea and other parts of the world. *T'ai-Chi* cosmology reminds us of the speculation of Teilhard de Chardin. One may also consult the profitable volume *The Unity of Nature and History in Pannenberg's Theology*, by Cornelius A. Buller (Lanham, MD: Littfield Adams, 1996).

In summary, the concept of harmony in *T'ai-Chi*, which is based upon the Yin/Yang principle of contrast and balance, may provide a road map for our somewhat polarized generation, visible in family and society, as well as among individuals and nations. Harmony appears to be a crucial need for the twenty-first century. We may give serious attention to this proposition without sacrificing or compromising our faith in Jesus Christ and the concerns of Martin Luther.

BOTH/AND WAY OF THINKING

The "both/and" way of thinking is best represented by the concept of complementary dualism, which is in contrast to the "either/or" way of thinking that excludes "middle." Both/and is an inclusive manner of thinking that presents the "whole" because it actually embraces the either/or category. The inclusion of opposites is found in the symbol of the ultimate reality, *T'ai Chi*. For example, light is relative to darkness because light is light because of darkness. They are always in relation to each other.

What is the practical implication of what has been said so far about the theology of Luther and the *T'ai-Chi* principle? In Luther's thoughts there are the distinct elements of "negative" and "positive," particularly from the viewpoint of being "sinner" and "righteous." That is, there is negative in sin, positive in salvation by free grace; negative in being a servant, positive in being a free person; negative in the wrath of God under the Law, positive in the grace of God with the Gospel. God in His majesty is hidden; God in His mercy and love is revealed in the incarnation of Christ. All these aspects are present in Luther's theological thinking based on the Holy Scriptures and may attract the Eastern mind and its way of thinking. This is by no means a syncretistic overview nor an attempt to confuse them. It is rather an attempt to illustrate mutually complementary aspects through which a deeper understanding and mutual appreciation may be possible. There can be flexibility without losing the theological center, open-mindedness without emptying the content, and generosity without displaying bias or favoritism. After all, was not Luther himself a relational thinker who expressed antithetical contrasts related to each other, for example, invisible and visible, spiritual and carnal, hidden and manifest, divine and human, *coram Deo* and *coram hominibus*, etc.? (Consider also the dualism in Luther's first lectures on the Psalms[5] and other similar references in his writings.) Furthermore, wasn't Luther a both/and thinker rather than an either/or thinker? The idea of both/and seems to be the paradigm of Luther and Lutherans in the subsequent generations. (Consider C. F. W. Walther's so-called "Middle View" on the doctrine of ministry and his succinct analysis of Law and Gospel.)[6]

One may make an analogy between the relationship-oriented *T'ai-Chi* matrix and the orthodox Christian understanding of the paradigm of the relationship among the three persons of the Holy Trinity (Exodus 3:14; John 1:1f.) and, furthermore, in the *communicatio idiomatum* that is ascribable to the hypostatic union and ultimately related to the Holy Trinity. There are, in fact, networks of relationships in Christian teaching that are expressed in its traditional creedal statements. At any rate, we ought not to perceive these in additive terms ("+," for example, $1 + 1 + 1 = 3$) but in a relational manner (namely, in "x," that is, $1 \times 1 \times 1 = 1$ or $1 \times 1 = 1$. Compare: $9 + 9 = 18$; $9 \times 9 = 81$). *T'ai-Chi*, for example, is Yin x Yang. So is the Holy Trinity. Is not Luther's understanding of Law and Gospel in that sense? Lack of balance causes a negative correlation.

A complex problem that remains unresolved is the understanding of the ineffable Christian term "I AM" or "I AM WHO I AM" (Exodus 3:14) and the Eastern counterpart terms: *T'ien* (Heaven), *T'ien-ju* (= Master of Heaven), *Tao* (equivalent of *logos* in the Greek tradition), *Kamisama* (God in Japanese), *Hananim* (God in Korean), etc. The word *Tao* is frequently used in various connections in the Bible of East Asian languages. For example, John 1:1 reads in Chinese: "In the Great Beginning was the *Tao*." As we know, in the early twentieth century, there was an animated debate concerning the name of God in China, as well as considerable discussion in other parts of East Asia on the same topic. Furthermore, what should be the real meaning of "harmony"? Does it mean the restoration of the relation between God and humanity, reconciliation of humanity to God through the cross and resurrection of Jesus Christ, or a "humanistic" horizontal adjustment of relationships? All these suggest further reflection and investigation. At any rate, the concepts and terms are vitally important for our generation because of the increasing traffic of religions and religious concepts, notions, and practices that are multiplied everywhere through the advanced global network of electronic communication media and rapid transportation. One may conceive of "dialogue" between concepts and ideas, for example, *logos* and *Tao* (*Dao*), *God* and *Tien*, Spirit and *Ch'i* (*Ki*), etc.

Luther's way of presenting his insights in paradoxical contrast has global relevance. His way may meet some significant allies in the East. Behind Luther's thinking, is there not an intention of harmony and balance? Could not this insight possibly be the "one thing more," the needed wisdom, that the East and West ought to take seriously? Jesus spoke in paradox. So biblical teaching is expressed frequently in paradoxical language.

The search for "harmony" in nature, in family, in society, in the world, and even in religions appears to be the indispensable necessity for mutual survival. Otherwise the world appears to be on the brink of destruction. Can the welter of religions offer some positive direction? As they are today, the prospect does not inspire optimism. Religions in general seem to create more tension and cause more strife. A creative rethinking is needed, not my truth-claim at the expense of others but my witness among them as my unique contribution. We should find points of contact rather than contention. No either/or dichotomy can clear the road for mutual coexistence.

TOWARD A COEXISTENCE PARADIGM OF HARMONY

Since the Reformation, the theological tradition of Lutheranism has been mindful of the proper distinction, not separation, between contrasting aspects, such as Law *and* Gospel, the righteous *and* the sinner, etc. Upon reflection, behind such a tenet, is there not the concern and interest for proper balance? More by coincidence than by design, it seems, there is an intriguing similarity between this unique way of Luther's thinking and the content of the East Asian *T'ai-Chi* paradigm. In this paradoxical approach to reality was, for Luther, the divinely revealed truth; in the East, this paradoxical approach reveals the *T'ai-Chi* cosmology. At any rate, in the wisdom of "harmony" there appears to be a common key that unfolds and resolves some of the complex postmodern issues for both East and West, including tension, conflict, and misunderstandings. Harmony might have been an important concept in sixteenth-century Europe, as well as in the ancient East, and it seems to remain as important and as elusive today in the West and in the East as we search for internal coherence and harmony without discord in all human endeavors, including theory and practice, theology and witness (mission). In a practical sense we need more discussion and less argument.

By no means is this a naïve attempt to Asianize Luther's thought or to Lutheranize the concept of *T'ai-Chi*. Instead, my intent is to take a close look at the distinct aspects of Luther's Reformation thought, known as *theologia crucis* in its early period, in which the cross of Christ is the focal point of God's revelation and the foundation and center of Christian theology. Indeed, the cross is an authentic symbol of total degradation and ultimate victory in resurrection. Here the cross becomes the key to the whole of theology. From this perception of theology proceeds the implied consequence, such as the concepts of *iustus/peccator*, sin/grace, Law/Gospel, etc. Under the umbrella of *theologia crucis* is the authentic presence of all the components and implications of the three *solas* of the historical epoch of the Reformation. On the other side we observe in this essay the pregnant classical Eastern pattern of thinking: the *T'ai-Chi* matrix and its cosmology of contrasting but harmonious elements. These contrasting aspects from the East and the West, through meaningful analogy, may enable each side to contribute mutually to the remedy for the polarized way of thinking that causes considerable confusion and strife.

This recognition of the similarity between Luther's way of perceiving reality and the *T'ai-Chi* paradigm may provide to the West and to the East a new form and ideal for the future with reciprocal spiritual enrichment and peaceful coexistence. Somehow we must learn the art of how to understand each other in this shrinking and crowded "global village."

LUTHER STUDY IN EAST ASIA

Martin Luther is not totally new nor strange in East Asia.[7] In the past several centuries, his name was mentioned whenever the Western world was introduced in history books and also through limited travels to Europe, especially Germany. Luther and the Reformation usually occupy a significant portion in textbooks, chiefly the sociopolitical-religious "reformatory" movement against the papacy and medieval systems and worldviews. For this writer, the personal experience of encountering Martin Luther at an early age led him in later years to the Lutheran faith and to become a lifelong student of Luther.

In the most recent century, Luther's writings have occupied a challenging, though still limited, place in academic circles. Not including all the references to Luther and his contributions in history classes, many books, essays, articles, and scholarly monographs have been written about him by Lutheran and non-Lutheran scholars. Although not an exhaustive list, some outstanding Japanese examples include:

- Shigehiko Sato: *Luther's Basic Thoughts on Romans*, 1933 (in Japanese). Cf. *Concordia Journal* (October 1997): 379.

- Chitose Kishi: *Luther's Commentary on Hebrews* (in Japanese). Also served as editor for *Luther Past and Present*, 1983, a collection of essays from various authors in observation of the 500th anniversary of Luther's birthday (in Japanese).

- Shigeru Watanabe: *German Reformation—Thought and History*, 1968 (in Japanese). Also other writings in Japanese.

- Isao Kuramazu: *Luther and Karl Barth*, 1988 (in Japanese).

- Yoshikazu Tokuzen has contibured many scholarly articles on Luther in Japanese and in German.

Furthermore, a number of Luther's writings have been translated into Japanese, for example, two volumes on Romans (Matzuo, 1959–1960) and "Freedom of a Christian" (M. Fujita, Iwanami Bunko). Many years ago, a work on Luther's anthropology appeared. The ambitious undertaking of the Japanese Edition of Luther's Works, which began in 1963, is extraordinary. So far, 14 volumes have been published, and more translations are underway by competent scholars in the original languages. This project by the Japan Society of Luther Research (Yoshikazu Tokuzen, director) in a non-Christian land is a noteworthy venture. For a comprehensive list of books and articles on the study of Luther in Japan, see Y. Tokuzen's article on "Luther" in vol. 15 of *Reformation, Senshu* (Tokyo: Kyobunkan).

In Korea, too, Luther's Reformation and his work were dealt with by historians and theologians of various backgrounds. Naturally their assessment of Luther was somewhat limited. Most of the world history books give note to the Reformation and to some portion of Luther's writings. Understandably, more serious attention has been given to Luther since the advent of LCMS mission work in Korea in 1958. Again in addition to essays and articles on Luther's Reformation by Lutheran and non-Lutheran scholars, a number of books have appeared, such as *The Life of Martin Luther* (1960); *Luther's Thought: Theology and Education* (1961); *Luther and the Reformation* (1965), etc. The publication of the Korean Edition of Luther's Works (in 12 volumes), the Korean translation of *The Book of Concord* (1988), and the Korean translation of C. F. W. Walther's *Law and Gospel* (1993) are significant additions in a predominantly Roman Catholic and Reformed land that also has a long history of traditional Confucianism, Taoism, and Buddhism. Furthermore, the Luther Study Institute of Luther Theological College/Seminary in Korea is attempting to promote Luther study.

Now a new dimension is being added to Luther study in East Asia, namely, the great subcontinent of China. On Luther and his Reformation, some similar aspects are observable in China as in Japan and Korea. In fact, the influence of the West and Christianity in China has a long history. Consequently, the Reformation was widely known, especially in academic circles. More than a century ago, Youwei Kang was known as the "Confucian Martin Luther." Numerous scholars, frequently non-Christians, dealt with Luther and his Reformation in their academic work in universities. Meanwhile, a few volumes of Luther's writings have appeared (1968, 1992). More recently, a plan for a more extensive Chinese Edition of Luther's Works, possibly in 15 volumes, is underway.

The 1998 visit of Professor Yutian Lei of Guangzhou Normal University in the People's Republic of China to Concordia Seminary, St.

Louis, Missouri, was an important landmark, this writer believes. It will be an historical event when the plan materializes for a joint international project between the Luther/Reformation scholars in the People's Republic of China and Luther scholars outside the People's Republic. The LCMS Board for Mission Services and Concordia Seminary are assuming the supportive and coordinative leadership for this timely venture for the twenty-first century. On November 7, 1998, Professor Lei wrote in a personal letter to this writer: "According to your suggestion, we have now been preparing for forming a Luther Study Center under the leadership of the Comparative Culture Institute of Gaungzhou Normal University [PRC]." In a later correspondence (24 March 1999), Professor Lei mentioned: "According to the suggestions of some Luther scholars in China it is better for this Luther Study Center to be a national one."

Luther study in East Asia seems to be realistic and encouraging. Like the historical Luther Renaissance in the West more than a century ago, a similar, though modest, resurgence in interest in Luther, including a serious study of his theology, may become a vivid historic reality in the intellectually sophisticated East Asian lands. To assist and to promote such a trend in East Asia, Luther study seems to be a sublime task for the coming generations and a privilege and honor for those who are involved in the unique mission for the Lord.

Luther's thought, epitomized in his *theologia crucis,* may provide some unique insights and wisdom and serve as an unmistakeable signpost for twenty-first century witness to the people in East Asia and elsewhere!

NOTES

1. WA 5. An English translation of the *Operationes in Psalmos* is available in Henry Cole, trans. and ed., *Select Works of Martin Luther* (4 vols; London: T. Bensley, 1924–1926).

2. LW 33.

3. *"Enarratio Psalmi LI,"* WA 40/1; *Selections from the Psalms,* LW 12; and *Lectures on Galatians* (1535) and (1519), LW 26–27. See especially WA 40/1:327.31ff. (1532); 352.33ff.; LW 12:311f., 328 (Psalm 51); LW 26:117 (Galatians 2:14), 342 (Galatians 3:23); SL 9:802 (Galatians 3:23–24). Cf. LW 27:54 (Galatians 5:14) on faith and works.

4. Cf. *I Ching* (trans. Alfred Huang; London: Inner Traditions International, 1998) for a contemporary translation of this important work.

5. *Dictata super Psalterium* (1513–1516), WA 3:498, 164, 144, 583, 574; 4:11, 222, 250. Cf. LW 10 and LW 11.

6. Cf. C. F. W. Walther's *Church and Ministry* (trans. J. T. Mueller; St. Louis: Concordia, 1987); and C. F. W. Walther, *Law and Gospel* (trans. Herbert J. A. Bouman; St. Louis: Concordia, 1981).

7. Cf. "Luther in East Asia," *Concordia Journal* 20.1 (January 1994]): 33–38.

FOR FURTHER READING

Brief list of reference works on Eastern thought

On topics related to this paper (excluding Luther and his works), volumes could be written and have been written. Besides the *I-Ching* and its many translations, there are numerous scholarly works, some of which deserve mention. Jung Young Lee has done considerable work in English for Western readers. His works include: *Embracing Change: Post-modern Interpretations of the I-Ching from a Christian Perspective* (Scranton: University of Scranton Press, 1994); *The Trinity in Asian Perspective* (Nashville: Abingdon, 1996); *The I-Ching and Modern Man* (Secaucus, N. J.: University Books, 1975); *The Theology of Change* (Maryknoll: Orbis, 1979); and other publications (all in English). There are also many Korean works (as well as those in Chinese and Japanese) on *T'ai-Chi* and related thoughts that have either direct or indirect connection with the *T'ai-Chi*, including:

"*Tae-Kuk (T'ai-Chi),*" *The Standard Dictionary of Confucianism* (Seoul: Bak-Young Sa, 1990), 1612–19. *T'ai-Chi* as the First Cause of the Origin of All. "The word *T'ai-Chi* is originated from *I-Ching*. In *yuk* (*I*) is *T'ai-Chi.*"

Tae-Kuk Do *and Chinese Medical Theory*: Ju-Yuk *and Chinese Medicine*, by Yang Yuk. Trans. into Korean. 1995. See pages 135–53.

Understanding of Ju-Yuk *Philosophy*, Byung Suk Chung, 1995.

Ju-Yuk (I Ching) Kang Hae, Suk Chin Kim, 1993.

Ki Chul-Hak San-Jo, Yong Ok Kim, 1992. See pages 25–133.

Ki-featured articles in the journal *Ministry and Theology* (in Korean) (November 1995): 45–111.

The Concept 'Ch'i' in East Asia, by Prof. Hyun Sup Um. 1996.

It can be especially meaningful for researchers on *Tai-Chi* to do an analogical study of its concept with the *Li* (reason) and *Ch'i* (spirit) debate in the subsequent generations of Neo-Confucianism in East Asia.

For English readers, the following works can be recommended related to Neo-Confucianism: *The Four-Seven Debate* (ed. Michael C. Kalton; Albany: State University of New York Press, 1994); Edward Y. Chung, *The Korean Neo-Confucianism of Yi T'oegye and Yi Yulgok*

(Albany: State University of New York Press, 1995). For a reappraisal of the *Four-Seven Thesis* and its practical implications for self-cultivation, confer *sa-dan*: *in, ui, ye, chi*; *chil-ki*: desire, hate, love, fear, grief, anger, joy (cf. *Doctrine of Mean*, chapter 1).

Some reference works on Luther's *theologia crucis*

In addition to those already mentioned in this essay, there are many primary sources (such as Luther's writings) and secondary materials (written by Luther scholars) on this subject. The following deserve mention: Luther's writings on the Heidelberg Disputation (1518), especially theses 18–21; *Commentary on the Magnificat* (1521); *Lectures on Hebrews* (1517–1518) (Cf. WA 57:29, 20; also WA 5:176.32f., 179.31, and 163.28f.); *Bondage of the Will* (1525); *Lectures on Genesis* (1545), etc. For the secondary sources (studies), one may list the classic by Walther von Loewenich, *Luther's Theology of the Cross* (trans. Herbert J. A. Bouman; Minneapolis: Augsburg, 1976), as well as the works of Heinrich Bornkamm, E. Gordon Rupp, Philip Watson, E. G. Schwiebert, U. Saarnivaara, and many more. Noticeable is the essay by Heino O. Kaidai on Luther's "theology of the cross" that was written in commemoration of the 450th anniversary of the Reformation in 1967 and recently reprinted by *Concordia Theological Quarterly* (July 1999).

The above is by no means a comprehensive list of references.

5

The Witness of the Cross and the Islamic Crescent

C. GEORGE FRY

ISLAM: AN URGENT MATTER

More tha 30 years ago, I published my most famous and my most controversial article. It appeared in *Christianity Today*. The title? "Christianity's Greatest Challenge."[1] The essay argued that Islam was the church's major difficulty and its major opportunity. I penned the article in less than 20 minutes, the result of a sense of spiritual urgency that had been generated by a summer spent studying the secularization of Turkish politics in Anatolia.[2] My time in Turkey was pleasant, my hosts were generous, the hospitality left nothing to be desired, and my studies were fruitful—generating several scholarly works, a book, and two new university classes.[3] That is not my point. After living for an extended period in a Muslim nation—albeit a secularized one—I was impressed, even in 1969, with the resurgence of Islam that was underway. Conversations with students and scholars, imams and edi-

---

Editors' Note: This essay was written before the tragic events of September 11, 2001. We believe that Dr. Fry's insights are more urgent today. We need to understand the people of Islam not as followers of a monolithic religion. It is also imperative that we listen to their hopes and aspirations in our incarnational witness to the cross.

tors, cab drivers and docents convinced me that, spiritually, Islam is *the* greatest challenge Christendom will confront. From that impression came the essay that evoked such response.

In part, the response was positive. The Fellowship of Faith reprinted the article from *Christianity Today*—and it has been circulated by the hundreds of thousands here and everywhere. Long after I am dead and gone, that one pamphlet will be my memorial, of that I am certain.[4]

In part, the response was negative. Readers wrote to *Christianity Today* insisting that I was spiritually blind, insensitive to reality, oblivious to the obvious. Two other challenges were suggested by those writers: Communism and secularism. Surely, they contended, these vastly eclipsed Islam as a challenge to the church.

One of the advantages of living long is to be able to see your adversaries shamed. After three decades, my assessment stands, but theirs fell.[5] As to Communism, well, we can say that Marxism has been relegated to the dustbin of history because it was a challenge to the church for only 70 years (1917 to 1987). The Berlin Wall tumbled; the Cold War ended not with a bang but with a whimper; the Soviet Union dissolved, quietly, like ice under a spring sun; and everywhere from St. Petersburg to Vladivostok, from the Arctic Circle to the Central Asian steppes, Marxism is now lamented by many as one of the most tragic socioeconomic experiments ever tried by humans. Prayers are said by Orthodox priests in the Kremlin, mullas call the faithful to prayer near the Cosmodrome, and except for Cuba—and a few corners of the American college system—Marxism is now considered about as relevant, or as interesting, as Pythagoreanism. As to secularism? Well, that was a fad of the 1960s, long since forgotten as the United States and the entire world moved into a New Age. The Canadian historian Richard Nienkirchen said that "the Third Great Awakening has begun, and it is being led by the pagans, not the Christians."[6] It is hardly secularism or a "world come of age" that dominates thinking from Seattle to Sydney, from Denver to Dresden. What has been called "the Third Wave" is sweeping our society, with an emphasis on the spiritual.[7] We are being reminded, as never before, that we do not live by bread alone, but we have profound religious appetites that will be met—and nongodless systems, either Marxism or secularism, can't meet these appetites. One movement, poised to benefit from that resurgence of spirit, is Islam.

There are, I think, five longstanding reasons why Islam is an urgent matter for the Christian community.

1. Islam is the only major world religion to rise since the birth of Christianity. There have been minor ones, such as Christian Sci-

ence and Mormonism, and a few serious contenders, such as Sikhism and Bahai. So far the appeal of these has been marginal. But Islam is completely different. Born 622 years after Christ, it has major appeal to millions of humans. Instantly and consistently successful, Islam contends that it is God's final word to our species before the Great Judgment. That means Islam has a precedence in time that makes it appear to be a substitute or supplement or replacement to Christianity.[8]

2. Islam is the only major world religion to claim to reform Christianity. Of course within the Christian community we have had many "reformations," from that of Pope Gregory the Great to Martin Luther, from St. Bernard of Clairvaux to William Booth and the Salvation Army, from St. Francis to the Social Gospel. All these have come from within our tradition, and each has accepted to great measure the fundamental assumptions of our religion. Islam is a reform from without—and it has rejected to a fundamental degree the central teachings of our faith. Theirs is a profound claim: Christians corrupted the Scriptures, instituted idols, substituted man-made for God-given Law—and that the real reformation of the church was not in Germany in 1517 but in Arabia in 610 and was led not by the monk Martin Luther but by the merchant Muhammad.[9]

3. Islam is the only other major world religion to use many of the same Scriptures, symbols, thoughts, and sentiments that prevail in Christianity but to employ them with a different conclusion. Although Hindus venerate Jesus, and some, such as Mohandas Gandhi, honored Him, it is only Islam that names Isa as a major prophet, second only to Muhammad. The prophet Isa was born of a virgin, was mighty in word and deed, wrote a book named the Gospel (or *Injul*), now lost, was spared death on the cross because of a substitutionary crucifixion by another, perhaps Judas Iscariot or Simon of Cyrene, and then ascended into heaven, promising that the comforter, namely, the prophet Muhammad, would come. If such revision is not astounding enough, recall that Islam also includes most of "our" prophets—Moses and David, Mary and Solomon, to name but a few. If that is not sufficient overlap with modification, one need only move to the central concept, namely, monotheism. Most other world religions do not deal with the notion of God. Buddhism was begun by a *de facto* atheist. Hinduism centers in a polycentric spiritual world. Confucianism is a passion for moral order in society. Taoism is a search for harmony with the impersonal *Tao*. Shintoism is "the

way of the gods" as it impacts the Japanese. Islam, like Judaism and Christianity, named one God, Allah (or El or Elohim, as in Beth*el* or Emmanu*el*), and states that his revelation to Israel and to Christendom was corrupted only to be restated finally in Islam.[10]

4. Islam is the only major world religion to which Christianity has lost vast provinces. It is a sad thing to travel in large parts of the world and see the ruins of ancient sanctuaries, to stand in landmarks familiar in Scripture and church history and to sense only the ghosts of a vanished church. The Levant—land of the first church, home of Jesus and the disciples, and once site of a vibrant Christian community from the time of James to Jerome—is now Muslim. Egypt—the home of the Alexandrian fathers, where Clement wrote, Origen preached, and Athanasius taught—is now the center of Islam's largest university, Al Azhar in Cairo, and Christians are a shrinking minority along the Nile. North Africa, home of the Latin fathers, Tertullian, Cyprian, Augustine—the spiritual birthplace of Western Christianity—is now virtually devoid of Christians. Anatolia, the home of the seven churches, the three ecumenical creeds, the seven ecumenical councils, numerous Greek Fathers, is Muslim. Of course there was a certain compensation by the Holy Spirit. Western Asia was lost but Western Europe was gained under Charlemagne. North Africa was lost but Northern Europe was added—and the locus of Latin Christianity shifted from the Mediterranean to the Rhine. Anatolia was lost to the Turks in 1453, but the Americas were added, beginning in 1492. Lest we forget, it was out of thanks to God for delivering Spain from the Moors that Ferdinand and Isabella financed Columbus in his ventures across the Atlantic. Compensation? Of course. Painful amputations from the body of Christ? Absolutely! Prior to the discovery of the Americas, the Old World for the European Christians was Western Asia. That was *Outre Meer*, the "land beyond the sea," the "primal home." Even three hundred years of crusading could not end the longing that some day Syria and Turkey, Tunisia and Egypt would once more be restored.[11]

5. Islam is the only major world religion poised for a significant missionary offensive during the third millenium. Other faiths have a "live and let live" philosophy—but Islam, like Christianity, has an imperative to evangelize. Perhaps the Dalai Lama preaches in Central Park, and perhaps the Maharishi gathers a commune in West Virginia, but Islam seeks diligently and ardently the conversion of the West. It is believed that Christianity cleared the

ground of primal paganism, as it did in the Orient and North Africa, but now Europe and North America are ripe for conversion.[12]

There are three major mission fields facing the church in the twenty-first century. One is China, with 1.2 billion people. The Bamboo Curtain is rising, and the church there is growing. Another mission field is India, with 1 billion people and the promise of conversion yet to be fulfilled, though evangelists from St. Thomas to Billy Graham have labored there. Finally, there is Islam, and I repeat, as I said in 1969, it is "Christianity's Greatest Challenge." With perhaps 1 billion people, Islam urgently invites Christian investment of time, prayer, and personnel.

ISLAM: A RECENT MATTER

ISLAM REMAINS CHRISTIANITY'S GREATEST CHALLENGE

I suspect that if we had met in the days of Truman, not Clinton and George W. Bush, our perspective might have been different. The Muslim world in 1945 was a different place from what it is at the dawn of the twenty-first century. Imagine, if you will, seven great changes that have transformed Islam within the last two generations, in the five decades between the end of World War II and the close of the Cold War. These seven events I call collectively "the Islamic Revolution" or the "Third Muslim Renaissance." I see Islam as having had three creative chapters: One was under the Arabs, from 622 until 1258, from the founding of Medina until the fall of Baghdad. This was the Era of Nascence. The second great era occurred under the Turks, the Persians, and the Moghuls, from 1130 until about 1689. It featured centers of political power in Istanbul, Isfahan, and Old Delhi. This era is the Muslim equivalent of the Western Renaissance. The third great era is now, 1945 to the present, the onset of the Muslim Resurgence. Seven traits characterize it.[13]

1. One is demographic, or "population is power." In 1945 Islam perhaps numbered 250,000,000 adherents, a population slightly smaller than that of the United States today. By 2000 there had been a fourfold increase to more than one billion Muslims, or a census approximate to the population of mainland China. This growth in numbers is both biological and missiological. In part it is caused by a high birth rate, the "propagation of the faith" in the primary sense. In part it is caused by a high conversion rate, the evangelization of outsiders as a secondary means of growth. If our world's population is now six billion, then one out of every

six people is Muslim. This means Islam is the second largest religion, second only to Christianity, and that Islam and Christianity are growing at equal rates in the Third World. Within a half century, one of the two will be firmly established as the number one world faith. As the only two aggressively evangelistic religions, they will face off by 2050, seeking the assimilation each of the other.

2. One is geographic, or "location is power." In 1945 Islam seemed "far away" and "remote," like Dorothy in the Land of Oz. It was something in old Bing Crosby-Bob Hope films about *The Road to Morocco*. Muslims inhabited places quite distant from the United States, some six or seven days away by steamer. When Bill Miller went to Iran in 1919 as a missionary, he was out of touch with his family and friends in Virginia for an entire year. He traveled by ship to Europe, then across the Mediterranean, then round Arabia and up the Persian Gulf, then by horse over the great deserts of Iran—the Dasht-i-Lut and Dasht-i-Kavir. One viewed the Muslim world as a belt that encircled the globe slightly above the equator—including North Africa, Western Asia, Egypt, Central Asia, parts of India, and Indonesia. That was the "living core" of Islam that grew from the "heartland of Arabia." Today, however, Islam has expanded beyond that empire, which was defined by the Arabs in 711 and enhanced by the Turks and Mongols by 1452. Islam is growing southward through conversions in Black Africa (Africa south of the Sahara). By 2050 the destiny of Africa will be Muslim or Christian or a confrontation of the two. Islam is expanding northward into Europe by what one scholar called "reverse colonization." Turks in Germany, Algerians in France, Pakistanis in Britain, and Moroccans and Indonesians in the Netherlands are settling so by 2000 Islam is "the silent nation" within the European Union. There are now more Muslims in England than Methodists, and Islam is the second-largest religion in France (outnumbering Protestants), and a third faith in Germany alongside Catholic and Protestant. Occasionally a news item reveals this. Princess Diana died on a date with a Muslim boyfriend in Paris. A major mosque is planned for Rome near the Vatican. Berlin now ranks as one of the largest Turkish cities in Europe. Eastern Islam has grown in the Pacific Rim, with a new sense of Muslim identity in Indonesia, Malaysia, and even China. In the West, Islam has now come to North America with more Muslims in the United States than Episcopalians or Congregationalists (two of the founding faiths), and within the decade there will be more Muslims than Jews. Perhaps there are now six

million Muslims—a result of immigration, our own home-grown Black Muslim movement, and conversions. It is not by chance that the U.S. post office issued a Muslim postage stamp in 2001. This vast "Muslim Diaspora" means that Muslims are in Dearborn as much as in Damascus, in San Francisco as much as in Cairo.

3. One is political, or "politics is power." In 1945 most of the Muslim world was under Christian hegemony. Western powers and the Soviet Union possessed nearly all the lands of Islam. The French were established in North Africa and Syria; the Italians in Libya, Eritrea, and Somalia; the British in East Africa, India, Malaya; the Dutch in Indonesia; and the Soviets in all of Central Asia. Most Muslims were under the tutelage of London and Paris, the Hague and Rome. Those of us who learned geography in those days knew that a few colors could explain most of the earth—red for the British, blue for the French, yellow for the Dutch, and so it went. In the wake of World War II, independence movements swept the Muslim world. Iran, a defacto partition between the Soviets and the United States, asserted itself, first under the Pahlavi Dynasty, then decisively in 1979 under the Ayatollah. The British left every dominion east of Suez—with a bevy of Muslim states, such as Pakistan and Bangladesh, rising out of the ruins of the Raj. French imperium ended, despite a prolonged war in Algeria, so the Arab West, or Magrhib, became free of foreign rule. Italy's empire was forfeited, and that of the Dutch was forsaken. By the 1980s the last imperial power, the Soviet Union, faced its demise, and six new Muslim states emerged in Central Asia. By 2000 there were 44 member states of the Islamic Congress, 21 or 22 of them being Arab.

With independence came assertiveness. *Time* magazine a decade ago spoke of a "Crescent of Crisis" from Morocco to Micronesia. Armed conflict in Bosnia, Kosovo, Lebanon, Afghanistan, Israel/the West Bank, North and South Sudan, Iraq, and Kuwait indicates that "Islamic rage" is a reality to be confronted. One scholar, contending that the collapse of ideology in the Cold War left the world free to return to ancient cultural divides, spoke of the coming Age of Clashing Civilizations—with Islam and the West on a collision course.

4. One is economic, or "money is power." In 1945 one thought of the Muslim portion of the planet as a sort of extended but exotic Dogpatch, a kind of esoteric Appalachia, with "Lil Abner" in a *khafiya* and Daisey May in a *chador*. Turkey was known for valo-

nia nuts, Iraq for dates, Persia for cats and carpets, Egypt for papyri and sarcophagi—and that was about it. Then came oil. As Charles Issawi once quipped, "Where there is oil, there are Muslims." Explorations begun between the two world wars paid off in oil discoveries beyond imagination. Much of the region moved from poverty to plenty, from indigence to affluence. Petrodollars created a modern tale of Cinderella and Cinderfella. By 2000 a major transfer of the world's wealth was underway as the Persian Gulf provided most of Japan's and Western Europe's energy. A Persian Gulf War over Kuwait at the start of the 1990s indicated the significance of that source to the industrialized world. The full impact of this wealth has yet to be imagined. Of course some Muslim states, such as Bangladesh, remain desperately poor, but that ought not eclipse the missionary potential of these billions of petrodollars!

5. One is psychological, or "to will is power." In 1945 it appeared to many that Islam was either dead or dying. The former *Columbus Citizen* predicted on its editorial page in the late 1940s that Islam would soon be as lifeless as the sands of the Sahara. I was so impressed with that "prophecy" that I clipped it and placed it in the family Bible. Meanwhile the *Columbus Citizen* is defunct, but Islam is alive and well. The Muslim world has moved from decadence to renascence, from a former sense of inferiority to the West to one now of moral superiority. Many wonder if it is not the West that is facing a Dark Age or moral collapse, an erosion of identity and vitality. Muslim apologists are arguing that only Islam can save Europe and North America from their impending malaise. That assertiveness was dramatically illustrated in 1979 when the mullas of Iran overthrew in the name of Allah and Shi'ite Islam a dictator supported fully by the CIA and U.S. power and prestige. Astounded Western reporters watched a holy man, of the stripe of Oliver Cromwell, do in Persia what had not been seen in the West since Naseby. Despite predictions that the mullas would fail or falter, the revolution still stands, 21 years later, and is a reminder that Islam has vitality and the ability to release enormous power.

6. One is theological, or "belief is power." Belief rests on faith. When faith can find a rational articulation, then one has two pillars of power—trust and reason. Even the late Samuel M. Zwemer, apostle to Arabia, contended at Princeton Seminary in the 1940s that Islam was theologically bankrupt, that it was devoid of intellectual vitality. Muslims seemed defensive, and secularism appeared

to be the wave of the future for the Muslim world, with Turkey leading the way. The late Mustafa Kemal Pasha Ataturk made "secularism" one of the "Six Arrows" by which he intended to lift Turkey from one culture to another, literally moving a nation of 60 million (now) from Asia to Europe, from Islam to the West. Even as late as the onset of the 1960s, many felt that Ataturk was the "prophet" for Islam's future. Somehow Islam would compress into a generation or two all the changes the West experienced in the Renaissance, the Reformation, the French and American Revolutions, the Industrial Age, and nineteenth-century capitalism. Few expected Islam to instead ignore the ideological changes that transpired in the West and to borrow the technology without the philosophy. Why we are surprised, I'm not sure. Japan did it. China is doing it. The Muslim world is falling in line. One need not accept FDR's "Four Freedoms" to make an atomic bomb, nor need one accept Thomas Jefferson's credo to operate a computer. Technology is proving itself able to be divorced from Western ideology, able to be married to Islamic philosophy, which is what is being attempted in Iran.

7. One is spiritual, or "prayer is power." In 1945 most observers denied any value to conservative or fundamentalist forms of spirituality. Perhaps, with the exception of scholars such as Evelyn Underhill, religion was defined more in rational rather than mystical terms. The debate between religions was regarded as a truth encounter, with the expectation that the "more rational" would commend itself in some kind of dialogue. To the surprise of many, spirituality began to emerge in the 1970s as a powerful current among the new generations in both the West and the East. Even sedate American denominations such as the Lutherans and the Episcopals were upset by the Pentecostal presence, let alone demand for participatory "contemporary worship." That same "wonder where the wonder went" began to sweep the East. Contrary to Harvey Cox and the "Secular City" and Thomas Altizer and the death of God, we are, in fact, living through one of the greatest spiritual revolutions in human history.[14]

Victor Wahhby was a Coptic Presbyterian teaching at the Yale University Medical School. I met him at a missions banquet in Grand Rapids, Michigan. When I asked him to explain the current revival of religion, he did so in medical terms. The old religions, long regarded as being in an arrested state, are being shocked to life by the powerful traumas of the late twentieth century. These are awesome and frightening times. Nuclear proliferation and atomic annihilation are more possible now than in 1945. The promise of the American way of life, promulgated by CNN on a global basis, as the secular fulfillment of paradise on earth will never prove possible for the masses of young people in the Third World. If the American way of life is heaven, they are condemned to hell. The tumbling of ideologies, such as Communism, the demise of nations—as small as Yugoslavia, as large as the USSR—mean that great "faith quakes" are underway. Like electroshock, they bring back to life the dead or dying religions to a new vitality never before imagined. Buddhism, Judaism, Christianity, and Islam are the four most affected. Of the four, Christianity and Islam are the two most poised to speak to the needs of the world.[15] Islam is Christianity's greatest challenge—it is not only an urgent reality, it is a recent one as well.

ISLAM: AN ANCIENT MATTER

Islam is not merely recent, it is ancient. It is not a new but a long-known challenge to the church. Christendom and Islamdom have faced each other for 1,400 years. One could easily say that Islam has been Christianity's most consistent challenge for the loyalty of human hearts. It is only our American insularity (or sense of superiority) that has permitted us to be "shocked" at the resurgence of Islam in what supposedly was "our" century.

Jesus once suggested that a wise scribe takes many treasures from his trove and learns from both the antiquities and the novelties. If we look at a millennia-and-a-half of Christian thinking about Islam, we find that the church's mind has been divided on this subject. As I have time and you possess patience, let me suggest four divergent Christian views of Islam. All accept Islam as a challenge. No two concur on how to capitalize on the opportunity.[16]

1. ISLAM IS A CHRISTIAN HERESY

That was the earliest interpretation of this new religion sweeping out of the Syrian desert into the settled lands of the Mideast. This perspective was proposed by St. John of Damascus (born ca. 700), the last of the great "fathers" of the Eastern Church. His was a theology rooted in the incarnation and expressed liturgically in the veneration of icons. St. John systematized for us the classics of the Greek doctors in his work *The Fountain of Knowledge*. As a student of the first seven centuries and the initial seven councils of the undivided church, St. John knew that all heresies are ultimately Christological. Christ is "the way, the truth, and the life," and "no one comes to the Father but by Him." Any confusion over the nature and ministry of Jesus is a profound heresy. In his work *The Heresy of the Ishmaelites*, St. John saw Islam as Arianism revived with a passion. In Islam are the three components of classical

Unitarianism: (1) The oneness of God is paramount, to the exclusion of variety within the Divine Personality; one has a God who is an undifferentiated unit, rather than a harmony of diversity in unity. (2) To that rigid monotheism add moralism, or the preaching of the Law to the exclusion of mercy with a reliance on works at the expense of the Gospel. (3) The humanity of Jesus is emphasized at the cost of His divinity; one has a master saturated in the supernatural, unique among mortals, sinless, able to work miracles and give wonderful sermons but unable to save. For St. John, Islam was but the latest and most successful manifestation of the heretical notions of Arius—so the movement ought to be seen not as a separate religion but as a deviation within Christianity.[17]

Perhaps St. John has a point. Twelve centuries later and two continents removed, Phillips Brooks once said from Boston that "All Christian heresies tend toward Islam, all Muslim heresies toward Christianity."[18] Surely Socianism and Unitarianism, like ancient Arianism, resemble Islam just as Muslim Sufism has a strange kinship with Pietism and Methodism.

To this analysis one must add a twofold critique: (1) There is the question of intent. Is this what the prophet Muhammad deliberately intended? As one who was not baptized, who never was a member of the church, whose connection with Christianity was, at best, tangential, is it fair to label him a heretic? Can an outsider do what only an insider does? (2) There is the issue of the extent of Muhammad's knowledge of Christianity. In the Qur'an he made blatant errors, identifying Mary, the mother of Jesus, with Miriam, the sister of Moses, or asserting that the Trinity was Jesus, Mary, and God. It takes a certain measure of knowledge to give one credibility as a heretic.

Perhaps St. John has a point but not the entire truth.

2. ISLAM IS A TUTOR TO CHRIST

This was another early analysis. Islam was not to be seen as a falling away from but as a climbing toward Jesus. Muhammad was viewed as a precursor to Christ, with the Qur'an serving the same role for the Arabs as the classics did for the Greeks or the Old Covenant for the Jews. Nicholas of Cusa, (1400–1464), a learned German cardinal and philosopher, who later became bishop of Brixen, took this position. Possessing a versatile mind and able to write with equal ease on law and philosophy, science and religion, Nicholas of Cusa stressed the profound limits of any perspective (see his work *De Docta Ignorantia*). For him, as Plato and Aristotle trained the West and Moses and David educated the Jews, so Muhammad took the Arabs from paganism to monotheism.[19]

There is a point, of course. Muhammad ranks as a major reformer of Arab society. He ended the worship of idols, banished polytheism, spurned superstition, and gave his people, for the first time in their history, pride and purpose and unity. In a variant of this thesis, Paul of Antioch viewed Muhammad as a prophet with "a limited mandate," "the teacher of the Arabs" who was sent by God to bring them from darkness to the dawn.[20] Western critics often have failed to realize the enormous impact of Muhammad on the language and customs of the Arab people.

To this analysis one must add a word of criticism. Two points stand out. One is coherence. As a prophet of monotheism, why did Muhammad not seek information on the other monotheisms of his day? We have no evidence that he sought, read, or studied the Christian Scriptures, let alone contacted those learned in the faith of the church. Any tutor needs to know the master to whom he would take his charge. Another is consequence. Has Islam, in fact, led many to a fuller faith in Jesus, or has it, instead, caused many to stumble and to fall from a profession of faith? I suggest that the silent churches of the East give us an answer, one that is loud and resounding. In practice Islam has led more from Jesus than to Him.

3. ISLAM IS THE SCOURGE OF GOD

Muhammad is not a confuser of Christ, or a tutor to Jesus, but a persecutor of disciples. A variety of Christians, ancient and modern, have held to this thesis. One of them was the late R. C. H. Lenski (d. 1936), at one time professor of New Testament at the Lutheran seminary at Capital University. His skill as an exegete is still honored. For Lenski, Islam ranked alongside the Vikings, the Huns, and the Slavs as one lash used by God in the Dark Ages to punish an apostate church. In part Lenski saw this previewed in the *Apocalypse of St. John* (in such passages as those portraying Christ spewing forth a lukewarm church onto the earth). In part Lenski and other exegetes saw such punishment in the reputation of the Ishmaelites or Arabs in the Old Testament, the slavers who carried Joseph into bondage or the raiders who devastated an apostate Israel in the age of the judges.[21]

This line of thought can go in one of two directions. For some Muhammad becomes the very Antichrist of God. Or at least an Antichrist. Islam is one with "the powers of darkness that spread against the revelation of God in Christ." The movement was born at night, in a cave, during an era still known as the Dark Ages, and the symbol of the religion is a crescent moon, the sign of darkness not light. George W. Peters wrote, "I am inclined . . . (to) see in Islam a 'supra-humanly designed, anti-Christian religious movement to offset and oppose the gospel of our Lord Jesus Christ.' "[22] For others Muhammad is not so much malicious as delusional. One who was insane, a Meccan madman who "heard voices," he is not so much to be decried as "satanic" as to be "pitied" as one who is sick. The appeal of this "crazy man's babblings" can only testify to the naiveté of a large part of the human population.[23]

As to Muhammed's sanity, I can only argue that skeptics have questioned the mental health of nearly all great religious teachers. Even Albert Schweitzer did a *Psychological Study of Jesus,* who was criticized both in New Testament times and during the nineteenth century as being "mad." Muhammad's skill as a warrior, administrator, legislator, and judge, and his genius as a poet and orator argue, in my thinking, against any case for his madness.

As to Islam serving as a scourge, of course no one can deny that. Martin Luther would be the first to see Islam in that light. A famous Reformation hymn places pope and Turk in harness as twin foes of the Gospel, as Luther prays, "Lord, keep us steadfast in Thy word." That God permits persecution none can dispute—and Islam has been so used at times.

Perhaps it is Islam's denial of the cross and resurrection that gives the most credence to this position. As Lutherans, we know that justification is the central doctrine of Scripture, the entire point both of revelation and of the ministration of Jesus. Ludwig Ihmels (1858–1933), a professor at Erlangen and Leipzig, later Bishop of Saxony, said that all Christian truth must be based on the Fourth Article of the Augsburg Confession. St. Paul advised us that any other Gospel, even if preached by an angel, was to be avoided. Or as Ihmels wrote in compelling verse,

I build on this foundation
That Jesus and His blood
Alone are my salvation,
The true, eternal good.
Without Him all that pleases
Is worthless on earth;
The gifts that I owe to Jesus
Alone my love are worth.[24]

Any teaching—Mormon or Muslim—that denies the cross is to some measure profoundly anti-Christian. To say, however, that Muhammad is *the* Antichrist is not only to offend potential converts, but it is to neglect much of the textual material of the New Testament.

4. ISLAM IS A WAY TO GOD

This way to God may be different from the method of Christianity, but it is valid for Muslims. This is the old argument of the mountain: There are many paths to the summit, no one is to be preferred, each must find his or her own line of ascent. Perhaps one exponent of this position was Johann Gottfried Herder (1744–1803), who taught and preached in Riga and Strasbourg before becoming a church official in Weimar. Herder, though a child of the Age of Reason, was one who felt that "different places necessitate different cases." Once he said that just as "different standards apply to children, adolescents, women and men," so it is by different criteria that we evaluate various cultures and creeds.[25] All humans have a religious capacity because humans are "an intermediate development between the brutal and the divine," but that humanity is worked out painfully under the laws of nature and reason. "The all merciful Architect" gives grace to those who try, and in the earthly journey toward perfection, each does as best he can, given his time and place.[26]

Islam makes sense in that light. Abraham had two sons, Isaac and Ishmael. Each inherited part of the ancient legacy. Ishmael, child of Hagar, is, in fact, an heir of Abraham. In these latter days the three great religions—Judaism, Christianity, and Islam—are all Abrahamic. They ought not, said Herder, argue as to which is superior. That is to deny the order of birth. In fact they are like three sons who are given three rings by their father because they each envied the one ring he wore on his hand. Long they quarrelled over who had the true ring when, in fact, no one could tell, and the father refused to reveal it. In fact, each had the true ring—for him. For Herder, the challenge was one of toleration and mutual affirmation. Until the Golden Age dawns, when our species is perfected, we will need to live with diversity— accepting it as evolution's price for progress.

The popularity of this stance in the early twenty-first century is obvious. My reply is phrased in the language of the late Dr. Christy Wilson, longtime missionary to the Middle East, then professor of missions at Gordon Conwell Theological Seminary. While it is true that many trails may lead to the top of the mountain, what we really need is an ascension that will take us from earth to heaven. Only Jesus can provide that.[27]

Another observation is in order. While perceptions of truth may be relative, truth itself remains constant. If I ask, "What time is it?" one will say in Milwaukee that it is noon, while in Columbus the answer would be 1 P.M. or in Denver 11 A.M. or in Singapore it is midnight. That relativity of perception does not repudiate the absolute nature of temporal measurement. Because, by Herder's own admission, "globalization" is the ultimate aim of our species, then "localized views" will have to pass before "universal values," or else through "pluralism" we will construct a tower of Babel, not a New Jerusalem.

ISLAM: AN EMERGENT MINISTRY

"Islam Is Christianity's Supreme Opportunity."[28] That was the title of a tract I co-authored with Raymond Joyce, a colleague from the Fellowship of Faith for Muslims in Toronto. Let me offer three suggestions for the ministry to Muslims that is now emerging.

1. There will be a recognition of the great variety within Islam. This movement is not a monolith, and one style alone will not suffice in our witness.

Years ago when I was teaching the Bible as literature to Muslim women under the auspices of the Presbyterians at Damavand College, Tehran, Iran, I heard the late Margaret Mead give a compelling lecture on great religion at the Iran-American Society. Dr. Mead contended that any major world faith must possess two traits: (1) On the one hand, it must have universality; all the circumstantial elements of life must be surpassed. It must transcend the gender gap and be for women and men. It must cross the racial divide and be for black, white, yellow, brown, and red. It must surmount the economic barrier and be for rich and poor and those in the middle. It must conquer the language issue and be for Mandarin and Norwegian, for Spanish and Korean, making sense in all known tongues. It must overcome the barrier of culture and be for those in the East and the West, the North and the South. It must be bigger than learning and be for the wise and the simple, the learned and the ignorant, and the half-lettered in between. It must be larger than morality, for the good, the bad, and the indifferent. All the peripheral matters of life must be overcome in a compelling unity. A great faith can issue a universal invitation, "Come unto me, all," because it can in fact offer something for everybody. (2) On the other hand, said Dr. Mead, to do this a great faith must be capable of an almost infinite adaptability, the capacity to adjust to a great variety of needs and conditions. Within each world religion will be a multitude of schools, parties, sects, denominations, orders, and factions. Only in such creativity can the great faith minister usefully to the multiplicity of needs encountered.[29] I remain impressed with Dr. Mead's analysis.

I consider Islam one of the seven or eight truly great religions of our world. I do so because it has been able to meet the needs of more than a billion people on all six of the inhabited continents, people who live in contexts as diverse as sub-Saharan Africa and suburban North America. Within the world of Islam there is the modernism of a Sir

Muhammad Iqbal of India and the fundamentalism of an Ibn Saud in Saudi Arabia. There is the mysticism of the Sufis of Arabia and the rationalism of an Avicenna in Persia. There is the secularism of a Mustafa Kemal Pasha Atatürk in Turkey and the deep spiritualism of Mevlana and the whirling dirvishes. There is a national Islam preached by Sukarno in Indonesia and an ecumenical one articulated by Hosein Nasr at Harvard University. There is the radical Islam of the Algerian Revolution, and the conservative Islam of Shaykh Zayid of the United Arab Emirates. There is the intellectual Islam of the graduate seminar and the folk Islam of the bazaar. One scholar estimates that there are at least 1,500 varieties of folk Islam on our planet. I am sure this itemization has not done the topic complete justice. Islam is a house with many rooms, each with different furnishings, each with a totally divergent view.[30] To be at ease in such a place, one needs to be aware of where one is at and how one ought to act in such a place.

2. There will be a recognition of the great variety within the Christian mission to Muslims.[31]

There are a variety of gifts. Some go as teachers, others as healers, others as linguists, some as evangelists. Paul himself spoke of witnessing as being like tilling a field. One plows. One plants. One weeds. One waters. One watches. Finally another harvests. All are needed. One ought not despise the others.

There are a variety of methods. Ray Register, long effective for the Southern Baptists on the West Bank, has urged friendship evangelism. Or to phrase it another way, "They don't care how much you know until they know how much you care." George Braswell, a former colleague who is now at Southeastern Baptist Theological Seminary, has advocated understanding so we end up not with a diatribe of the deaf but with a conversation between listeners. Kenneth Cragg, longtime Anglican bishop among Muslims, would add to friendship and understanding the gift of presence. Can one walk humbly with God in the footsteps of Jesus but do so in a Muslim context and do it with grace and truth? There is also a time for rebuttal of error, granted that, like Paul, we speak the truth in love. This was the gift of the late Samuel M. Zwemer. According to the late Herrick Young, service is yet another avenue, one pioneered by medical and educational missionaries in the Muslim world, to be an incarnation of Christ in a place where He is not fully known.

Among these methods I have yet to mention the contextualization urged by many, that we shed our Western accoutrements of Christianity to let the Gospel, without our accents, speak directly to Muslim peoples. Dialogue, both Roman Catholic and Protestant, has at least clarified issues and moved people to talk rather than sulk. As we contend for the faith, it is necessary to remember that our purpose is not to win an argument but to make a disciple. This is why the witness of the cross occupies the center stage in our outreach to Muslims. It is in this witness that we live the presence and loving service of the crucified and risen Christ. It is in this living witness that we proclaim the unconditional love of Jesus, who died for our sins and rose for our justification. The witness of the cross leads to the making of disciples of our Lord.

The witness to Muslims is like the building of a great medieval cathedral: It will take a long time, involve a large crew, and each member will do a different task. Some are masons, some carpenters, some glassblowers, and some metallurgists. Some are cooks, preparing food for the laborers. Others are tailors, giving them garments for the cold winter's chores. Others are monks, praying for God's blessing. Others are the bishop-architects, overseeing the master plan. All, however, are essential.

The late William McElwee Miller, longtime missionary to Iran, once said to me, "George, the resistance of Islam is not due to the perversity of the fish, but to the paucity of the fishermen."[32] With only 2 percent of the world's mission force deployed in the Muslim world, I can only concur. Perhaps "Christianity's Greatest Challenge" is being reserved for this generation, the children of the new millenium, who will rise up, lifting high the cross, and cause the ancient church to flower—not only by the reformation of the church in the West, but also by the restoration of the church in the East.

NOTES

1. C. George Fry, "Christianity's Greatest Challenge," *Christianity Today* XIV (7 November 1969): 9–12.
2. See C. George Fry, "The Resurgence of Turkish Islam Today," *Vidya* IV (Spring 1970): 64–75; and C. George Fry, "Islam and Social Change in Turkey," in *The Middle East in Transition* (ed. C. George Fry and James R. King; Columbus: Capital University, 1970), 63–73.
3. See C. George Fry and James R. King, *The Middle East: Crossroads of Civilization* (Columbus: Charles E. Merrill, 1973).
4. See C. George Fry, *Christianity's Greatest Challenge* (Toronto: Fellowship of Faith for Muslims, 1969) (several subsequent editions).
5. Perhaps I was not entirely alone in seeing a "resurgence of Islam" in the 1960s. Cf. Alexandre Bennigsen and Chantal Lemercier-Quelquejay, *Islam in the Soviet Union* (with a Foreword by Geoffrey E. Wheeler; London: Pall Mall, 1967,); and James Kritzeck and William H. Lewis, eds., *Islam in Africa* (New York: Van Nostrand-Reinhold, 1969).
6. Richard Nienkirchen, "The Third Great Awakening" in a speech at Winebrenner Theological Seminary, Findlay, Ohio, 4 April 2000.

7. There is a vast literature on "the Third Wave." See, for example, Wade Clark Roof, *Spiritual Marketplace: Baby Boomers and the Remaking of American Religion* (Princeton: Princeton University Press, 1999); or Leonard Sweet, *Faithquakes* (Nashville: Abingdon, 1994). For an evangelical response, see Robert Webber, *Ancient-Future Faith: Rethinking Evangelicalism for a Postmodern World* (Grand Rapids: Baker, 1999). Samuel P. Huntington believes that the dichotomy of the Cold War world is being replaced at the dawn of the new millenium with *The Clash of Civilizations and the Remaking of World Order* (New York: Simon & Shuster, 1996). For Huntington, Islam is one of the seven or eight major world-cultural systems capable of challenging the traditional dominance of the West.

8. See C. George Fry and James R. King, *Islam: A Survey of the Muslim Faith* (Grand Rapids: Baker, 1980).

9. See C. George Fry, *Islam: An Evangelical Perspective* (Fort Wayne, Ind.: Concordia Theological Seminary Press, 1976).

10. See Geoffrey Parrinder, *Jesus in the Quran* (Oxford: Oneworld, 1996).

11. Perhaps this "loss" evokes an "anger" not felt toward most other faith traditions. How else could one explain this remark made by Alexander, papal nuncio in 1521, referring to "the frightful state of barbarism and desolation which the superstitious Mohammed has brought upon Asia"? Quoted by W. M. Blackburn, *History of the Christian Church from Its Origin to the Present Time* (Cincinnati: Hitchcock and Walden, 1879), 393.

12. Christians struggle to arrive at a correct response, ranging from dialogue to diatribe. Bishop Kenneth Cragg, longtime Cairo resident, has urged both conversation and shared prayer. See his *Common Prayer: A Muslim-Christian Spiritual Anthology* (Oxford: Oneworld Publications, 1999). Cragg also has written *Muhammad and the Christian: A Question of Response* (London: Darton, Longman & Todd, 1984). More negative appraisals can be found, ranging from a description of Muhammad roasting in hell (in Dante's *Divine Comedy*) to classical Lutheranism's characterization of him as "an anti-Christ."

13. There are many classic studies of Muslim history. Outstanding among them is Marshall G. S. Hodgson, *The Venture of Islam: Conscience and History in a World Civilization* (Chicago: University of Chicago Press, 1974). Two popular appraisals of the "resurgence of Islam" by a noted journalist are V. S. Naipaul, *Among the Believers: An Islamic Journey* (New York: Random House, 1981); and V. S. Naipaul, *Beyond Belief: Islamic Excursions among the Converted Peoples* (New York: Random House, 1998).

14. Some Western writers have done masterful work in trying to understand Muslim piety and its appeal. See, for example, Constance E. Padwick, *Muslim Devotions: A Study of Prayer-Manuals in Common Use* (Oxford: Oneworld, 1996). Of course the Qur'an itself is a powerful spiritual text. See H. V. Weitbrecht Stanton, *The Teaching of the Qur'an, with an Account of Its Growth and a Subject Index* (London: SPCK, 1919). The most famous form of Muslim spirituality remains Sufism, and the premier study of it remains A. J. Arberry, *Sufism: An Account of the Mystics of Islam* (New York: Harper Torchbooks, 1970).

15. A conversation with Dr. Victor Wahhby at the Reformed Bible College, Grand Rapids, Michigan, 10 April 1974.

16. I am indebted to a masterful survey of "Christian Assessments of Islam" in Lewis R. Scudder III, *The Arabian Mission's Story: In Search of Abraham's Other Son* (Grand Rapids: Eerdmans, 1998), 33–42.

17. See Daniel J. Sahas, *John of Damascus on Islam: The "Heresy of the Ishmaelites"* (Leiden: E. J. Brill, 1972).

18. In an unpublished lecture by Francis P. Weisenburger, Department of History, The Ohio State University, Columbus, Ohio, 12 February 1964.

19. In addition to Lewis Scudder's analysis (see n. 16), see also Clayton Ellsworth, "Nicholas of Cusa," *The Encyclopedia of Religion* (ed. Vergilius Ferm; Secaucus, N. J.: Philosophical Library, 1945), 534; and "Nicholas Cusanus," in *Dictionary of Philosophy and Religion: Eastern and Western Thought* (ed. William L. Reese; Atlantic Highlands: Humanities Press, 1989), 389–90.

20. See Paul Khoury, *Paul d'Antioch, Évêque Melkite de Sidon* (Beirut: Imprimierie Catholique, 1964).

21. Conversation with Gerhard Lenski, Capital University, Columbus, Ohio, 12 February 1966.

22. See Don McCurry, ed., *The Gospel and Islam: A 1978 Compendium* (Monrovia, Calif.: Missions Advanced Research and Communication Center, 1979), 401.

23. Perhaps one of the fairest biographies of Muhammad in English is that of W. Montgomery Watt, *Muhammad: Prophet and Statesman* (Oxford: Oxford University Press, 1962).

24. See O. W. Heick and J. L. Neve, *History of Protestant Thought* (vol. 2 of *A History of Christian Thought*; Philadelphia: Muhlenberg, 1946), 165, 166.

25. See Thomas Mautner, "Herder," *The Penguin Dictionary of Biography* (New York: Penguin Books, 1999), 246–47.

26. See "Johann Gottfried Herder," in *Biographical Encyclopedia of Philosophy*, by Henry Thomas (Garden City: Doubleday, 1965), 119.

27. Personal comment to the author, Damavand College, Tehran, Iran, 10 September 1973.

28. Raymond Joyce, "Christianity's Supreme Opportunity" (Toronto: Fellowship of Faith for Muslims, 1979).

29. Margaret Mead, "The Great Religions," The Iran-America Society, Tehran, Iran, 12 March 1974.

30. For some of the varieties within this faith, see Fazlur Rahman, *Islam* (Garden City: Doubleday, 1968); C. George Fry, *Iran and Japan: Two Models of Modernization* (Fort Wayne, Ind.: Concordia Theological Seminary Press, 1983); and C. George Fry, "Islam in Asia" in *Great Asian Religions*, by C. George Fry et al (Grand Rapids: Baker, 1984), 163–92. One of the favorite Muslim modernists remains Mustafa Kemal Pasha Atatürk (see Andrew Mango, *Ataturk: The Biography of the Father of Modern Turkey* [Woodstock, N. Y.: Overlook Press, 2000]).

31. For a variety of approaches, see Larry G. Lenning, *Blessing in Mosque and Mission* (Pasadena: William Carey Library, 1980); Phil Parshall, *New Paths in Muslim Evangelism: Evangelical Approaches to Contextualization* (Grand Rapids: Baker, 1980); and C. George Fry, *Raymond Lull, Apostle to the Muslims* (Fort Wayne, Ind.: Concordia Theological Seminary Press, 1983).

32. Personal conversation with William McElwee Miller, Capital University, Columbus, Ohio, 3 March 1975.

FOR FURTHER READING

Cragg, Kenneth. *Muhammad and the Christian: A Question of Response.* London: Darton, Longman & Todd, 1984.

Fry, C. George et. al. *Great Asian Religions.* Grand Rapids: Baker, 1984.

Fry, C. George, and James R. King. *Islam: A Survey of the Muslim Faith.* Grand Rapids: Baker, 1980.

Huntington, Samuel P. *The Clash of Civilizations and the Remaking of World Order.* New York: Simon & Shuster, 1996.

Miller, Roland. *Muslim Friends: Their Faith and Feeling.* St. Louis: Concordia, 1997.

Naipaul, V. S. *Beyond Belief: Islamic Excursions among the Converted Peoples.* New York: Random House, 1998.

Parrinder, Geoffrey. *Jesus in the Quran.* Oxford: Oneworld, 1996.

Parshall, Phil. *New Paths in Muslim Evangelism: Evangelical Approaches to Contextualization.* Grand Rapids: Baker, 1980.

Scudder III, Lewis R. *The Arabian Mission's Story: In Search of Abraham's Other Son.* Grand Rapids: Eerdmans, 1998.

Stanton, H. V. Weitbrecht. *The Teaching of the Qur'an, with an Account of Its Growth and a Subject Index.* London: SPCK, 1919.

Watt, W. Montgomery. *Muhammad: Prophet and Statesman.* Oxford: Oxford University Press, 1961.

6

The Theology of the Cross
and Hindu Spirituality

A. R. VICTOR RAJ

Comparing apples and oranges is perhaps not the best image to con-trast the meaning and application of the cross in Christianity with other major world religions.[1] Oranges and apples are of the same genus of fruit. Both are edible, and both are of nutritional value for the human body. The cross, however, has in stock a distinctively Christian definition to it that, no doubt, is not present in other world religions. Hence, a comparison of the cross and cross-related concepts in world religions is practically out of order. The image of a vertical pole and a beam fastened horizontally to it, for almost two thousand years now, has held a unique association with one person in history. Thus the cross in most cultures and among most peoples the world over sym-bolizes Jesus Christ and His life and work and everything people do who bear His name.

Arguably the cross has also become a figure of speech in ordinary language. Banking heavily on its Christian content, the cross, amid a myriad other definitions, communicates a message of suffering, trial, trouble, and tribulation. Not surprisingly, suffering is an ordeal that causes people to turn toward spiritual and religious matters. In most world religions suffering is a means to an end, though different reli-gions understand and interpret the meaning and implications of suffering differently. For example, Siddhartha Gautama, the Buddha, after strenuous experimentation, introspection, and meditation, came to the conclusion that, after all, life is suffering. In fact the Buddha ranked suffering, or sorrow, as the first of his four noble truths. He surmised that the cause for suffering in the world is nothing but desire, craving, or thirst, which according to him was the second noble truth. The Buddha became convinced that desire can be brought to its cessation, and with that suffering brought to an end. To achieve this goal, as the fourth noble truth, the Buddha proposed a comprehensive eightfold path, suggesting the proper application of wisdom, ethical conduct, and meditation.

Undoubtedly, a comparative study of various religions that represent completely different worldviews is challenging and engaging. Equally challenging is any attempt at exploring a common premise in one religion and contrasting it with another religion in which the theme is relatively absent. The student who embarks on such a task doubtless is bound to enter this arena with his or her own agenda. Such is the task of this writer, who maintains that the "theology of the cross" as it is understood in the Christian religion is outside the sphere of the Hindu view of life. Even so, interacting the theology of the cross with Hinduism, particularly with that religion's preponderant teaching of karma and dharma, is a useful exercise for the purpose of witnessing the Crucified One among people of the Hindu persuasion. We venture this fully aware that we are not comparing apples and oranges!

UNDERSTANDING RELIGIONS

There are numerous ways of understanding religions. Studious individuals broach this vast subject from a philosophical, psychological, theological, or sociological point of view. This kind of analysis is highly beneficial from an academic slant. Religion, as it is played out in real life, nevertheless, has a personal and spiritual dimension. Religion is both soul-searching and soul-soothing for individuals. An aggregate of individuals gives shape to communities and societies. Both the personal and the social dimension of a religion must, therefore, be borne in mind as we explore its foundational principles and how the followers apply these principles to their own lives. To be sure, there are many in our world who perceive religion as nothing more than a means to run an orderly earthly course, a stimulus for discovering meaning and purpose in life and for building relationships. W. Richard Comstock has offered a comprehensive contemporary Western definition of religion as the sense of the sacred; as ultimate concern, as loyalty to the Good, the love of man, allegiance to the Gods. It has been said that it is what we do in our solitude; but also what we do to maintain our society; that it is about limit- situations; but also about everyday life. It has been called resignation, but also hope; release from this world, but also a way of living in this world more effectively. Some claim it is an encounter with the Wholly Other; others say it is the crucial meeting with one's own Self.[2]

Definitions reflect the presuppositions upon which they are put together. N. K. Devaraja, another student of religion from a predominantly Hindu background, defines religion in 25 words or less. According to him, religion "aims at bringing peace and tranquility to the soul of man, and to foster good will and amity among individuals and groups."[3]

Almost everything Comstock ventured in his summary statement of religion, Devaraja also included in his straightforward, much less sophisticated, definition, though the latter preceded the former by 10 years. The driving force in both definitions of religion is the quest for peace and tranquility within a person and within a community. Those who resort to resignation and release from this world do so because they think that they are lost in this world and the world has really turned against them. As a last resort they turn against the world, and their souls remain restless. Suffice it to say, they are themselves lost. A well-rested "soul" enables a person to live in this world effectively, fostering goodwill and amity among peoples and communities. If religion aims at bringing peace and tranquility, then these delights need to be brought from elsewhere to here where they are not. Peace and tranquility are relational concepts. Both necessitate an encounter with others or with the Wholly Other; better yet, they constitute the encounter with others *and* with the Wholly Other.

Rooted in the foundational principle of a God who created the cosmos and everything in it, Christianity sees God and human beings in relational terms. God is distinct from His created order, including humanity. Against that backdrop a Christian may be quick to respond that Devaraja's desire for peace and goodwill have already come true for all people the world over in the person of Jesus Christ, heralded by the angelic declaration of these heavenly blessings at Christ's birth. Nevertheless, against such hasty comebacks, E. P. Sanders cautions that we should not be comparing religions where comparisons are not possible. To further elucidate this counsel, Sanders notes, "a religion will function even if the end is not salvation from perdition."[4] Those who compare religions must, therefore, be able to speak as insiders on all religions they are comparing because an adherent of a religion knows best the proper context of that religion and how that religion functions. Strongly discouraging piecemeal comparisons, Sanders maintains that "what is clearly desirable is to compare an entire religion, parts and all, with an entire religion, parts and all."[5]

A wholesale comparison of Hinduism and Christianity to the extent required by the above observation is beyond the scope of this study. For the purpose at hand, a comparison of a dominant theme or related themes in both religions must suffice. From a Christian viewpoint the theology of the cross is not an abstract entity but an everyday life-oriented theme. In that sense the theology of the cross "might be better thought of as the *spirituality of the cross*. It has to do with Christ's work, His presence, and how we draw closer to Him. The theology of the cross also deals with the difficulties and hardships that Christians must live through in an utterly realistic and honest way."[6]

UNDERSTANDING HINDU SPIRITUALITY

"Hinduism" is the designation visitors to India coined to identify for convenience a complex phenomenon of faith and culture that encompasses the Indian subcontinent.[7] In fact, the word *Hindu* is of Persian and Islamic origin, a nomenclature that assumed its Indianness through usage, first by visitors, then gradually by the natives themselves. The original word that signifies Hinduism is *Sanathana Dharma*, translated the "Eternal Way of Life and Thought." Hinduism operates on its own phenomenology: It can at the same time be polytheistic and monotheistic, monistic and dualistic, pluralistic and pantheistic. As a devout follower of Hinduism has put it, "Hindus believe that this universe is the God, creator and creation, unlimited by time and space, and beyond all attributes. [In spirituality] one perceives the unity of God in all living beings and Nature, and has respect for all creation as it is."[8]

As a religion, therefore, Hinduism remains unparalleled to anything in the average Westerner's faith and practice. There are no known ways of knowing the unknown mysteries of this religion of the transformation of consciousness. We are quickly drawn to resort to the cliché "it takes one to know one" to enter the religious world of Hinduism.[9] Yet Hinduism has within itself a composite of almost everything most world religions have within their own independent traditions. Accordingly, Devaraja dubbed Hinduism "a welter of beliefs" because it

> includes practically every type of religious dogma and opinion
> that may be met within the numerous religious traditions of

106

the world; likewise, on the practical side it has tolerated, if not encouraged, practically every form of propitiation and worship of God and gods, and almost every style of meditation and spiritual discipline, from fetish-worship to *yoga* or mystic contemplation, that might have prevailed in any age of man's history, and in any part of this planet.[10]

To be sure, over the past two hundred years, religions from the East have invaded the soul of the West in an unprecedented way. Scientific research, technological advancement, and the capacity to travel and to disseminate information at a faster pace enabled the traditionally Christian West to look unduly critically at Christianity while at the same time embracing Eastern spiritualities uncritically and often in a frantic and frenzied mode. This is a quaint paradox. Her own children subjected the Christian theological enterprise, the foster mother of Western intellectual tradition, to deconstruction. The centrality of God and scriptural authority were brought to trial in the courtroom of rationalism and found wanting. Faith succumbed to reason, assurance to doubt, history to myth, and absolutes to relativism. The religion that has always stood on a well-balanced view of life, here as well as hereafter, the material and the spiritual, became lopsided out of all proportion, stressing either the earthly or the heavenly, most often one at the expense of the other.

Conversely, no other religion has either levied or permitted such grandiose criticism from within its own household against its own moorings and tapestry despite modernization. Instead, other religions have become apologetic about their prescientific, traditional positions and unequivocally claimed their authenticity and specific relevance for the postmodern age. The Hindu religion, for example, has no specific dogma to promulgate, except its own generalist view that all religions are the same, which paves the way for pluralism and universalism. Such juiciness remains within Hinduism until it comes face-to-face with a different religion that has its own exclusive claims. The basic creed of Islam—there is no God but God, and Muhammad is his prophet—on the lips of every Muslim who has submitted his or her will to Allah theoretically has left no room for either inclusivism or inclusive language. The public is little aware of a "textual criticism," if any, of the Qur'anic text, and a member of the Islamic community, including the new convert, covets the skill to recite at least portions of the Qur'an in the Arabic original. The Christian religion, conversely, has inherited its own "scandal" as at the same time it proclaims one God of all and what He has done once for all in one person, Jesus Christ.

Historically, few other religions have either taken the initiative or exhausted their energies by entering into a dialogue with another religion as much as Christianity has. Christian contributions in this area, however, are too numerous to narrate. As a by-product of such interaction, at the popular level, whether through literature, movies, mass media, commercials, or motivational seminars, snippets of Eastern spiritualities have found their niche in the West's daily errands. The mysterious world of advertising lures the consumer into buying a product by making scant but pithy references to yoga, nirvana, and reincarnation, to name but a few of the core beliefs of Eastern religions. What is still an unassailable hallmark of a particular religion in the East enters the West with a presumed innocence and neutered spirituality, as if it had nothing to do with anything religious.

American transcendentalists such as Thoreau and Emerson have, by their own admission, drawn heavily from the *Bhagavad Gita* no small amount of the wisdom that shaped their literary artistry. Twentieth-century Indian revivalists such as Mahatma Gandhi, Pandit Nehru, and Radhakrishnan have, for a reference, given as much importance to the Christian Bible as to scriptures of their native tradition, Hinduism. If Gandhi trusted the *Bhagavad Gita* as his "eternal mother," hardly a day of his life went by without drawing some light from Jesus and the New Testament. What was once a privilege of a select few has now become a syncretistic warehouse for anyone, including those who might consider themselves grown out of religion and spirituality.

THE CROSS: POPULAR MEANING

The cross continues to be the most common and most unmistakable identity marker of Christianity throughout the world. As do other symbols, the cross also suffers from use and misuse. The cross is another metaphor for suffering. At times it has become the insignia of ideologies and movements that are diametrically opposed to what the Crucified One, Jesus Christ, stood for and taught. Peoples and societies impress the cross on jewelry and their wardrobe and use it as a signifier for a level crossing, emergency vehicles, rescue missions, and medical aid. Despite *The Exorcist*, in the world of religions the cross signals Christ, Christians, and Christianity. Few, except a majority of Muslims, doubt if Jesus of Nazareth was fastened to the cross and died on Good Friday. Almost everyone sees in the cross of Jesus Christ the quintessence of self-sacrifice, shedding of innocent blood, and love for others par excellence. They also see gruesome humiliation, the smothering of justice, and an outright denunciation of the poor and the oppressed by the establishment.

What they fail to see, regrettably, is the uniqueness of the cross of Christ and the purpose it has accomplished in God's plan of salvation for all. On the cross, God's righteous indignation directed against human sin was poured out on His own Son as expiation. Human sin and guilt were washed away completely in the cleansing blood with no stones unturned; and as the "blessed exchange," purely on God's initiative, divine righteousness was traded for human sinfulness. Those who believe this and trust in it for Christ's sake are no longer dead but alive, no longer slaves but free, never just earth- and time-bound but forging ahead into heaven and timelessness. The Christian cross bleeds, but it also comforts. It signifies death, but it also brings hope. It brings the present life to its end, but at once it embarks on a new life. The cross renders sin powerless and takes away the sting of death. It contemplates little for itself and stretches out for others. At the foot of the cross a Christian looks within and sees the emptiness and looks above and sees God's love lavished in its fullness. The cross enables Christians to look away from themselves. The cross of Christ puts the suffering of the Christian in perspective. It has the appearance of defeat, but it is the sure sign of victory. Thus Christians lift high this cross for a witness to the world, properly interpreting life here and promising a full life hereafter. If it appears to be a dialectic, then "it is in the affirmation that Christ Jesus was crucified and raised from the dead that the dialectical pattern characteristic of so much [Christian] discourse is grounded . . . its significance was hidden from the world; it is a secret (*mysterion*) revealed to the Christians alone."[11]

From a Christian vantage point, it is normative to view the theology of the cross relationally. The theology of the cross speaks directly to a worldview that perceives the present order of existence in relation to things to come, dealing with today's suffering in joyful anticipation of the ultimate realization of the things of heaven, fully aware that the cross of Christ is the climax of all suffering. Religions that radically depart from the idea of the existence of individual human souls, especially postmortem, also interpret suffering differently. For them, suffering is a means to an end. Actions have consequences. The time on earth, therefore, is opportunity for payback for wrongdoings in previous lives.

Eastern religions operate with a different dialectic and, hence, find the Christian view of the cross inconceivable in their matrix. We have noted the Buddha's conclusion that the one-word summary of life on earth is suffering. The absence of a stable self (in Sanskrit *anatman*) is a foundational doctrine for Buddhism. Suffering (*duhkha*) begins the moment humans begin to think *of* and *for* themselves. Those who stop worrying about and for themselves will never worry at all. After all, there is no real self (*atman*) to worry for and about. What is mistakenly taken for the self, the Buddha claimed, is the aggregate of matter, sensations, perceptions, karmic constituents, and consciousness. The self appears to be when matter (physical) and the other four aggregates (psychological) coexist as a psychophysical entity. Existences ceases when they separate.[12] If the language of the cross is relational, from the Buddhist point of view there is practically no one to whom one can relate, except looking within and subjecting the self to vigorous self-discipline.

A THEOLOGY OF THE CROSS IN HINDUISM?

Belief in God as a person and in a personal encounter of all people with Him are essential for presenting the cross in the middle of that encounter for the purposes of restoring and building a previously broken relationship. It appears that Buddhism, at least the way we have featured it here, does not allow that kind of meeting of the divine and the human at any point. Hinduism also, in its purest form, presents a similar difficulty. In philosophical Hinduism, God is not a person but an "IT" without attributes. God is the Cosmic Soul. IT remains all by itself. IT does not relate but absorbs. When individual souls have run their earthly course well, they merge and become one with the Cosmic Soul, thus losing identity as individuals. Fusion with the ultimate, not fellowship, is the final destiny of the human soul in Hinduism. The following lengthy quotation from Vivekananda, the giant who challenged the West to change its mistaken view of Hinduism, proves this point. According to Vivekananda the very talk about a personal God is a Western idea. All one needs to do to see God is to look within. Vivekananda said,

> Western civilization has sought a personal God and despaired at the loss of belief in such. The Hindoo, too, has sought. But God cannot be known to the external senses. The Infinite, the Absolute, cannot be grasped. Yet although it eludes us, we may not infer its non-existence. It exists. What is it that cannot be seen by the outward eye? The eye itself. It may behold all other things, but itself it cannot mirror. This, then, is the solution. If God may not be found by the outer senses, turn your eye inward and find, in yourself, the soul of all souls. Man himself is the All. I cannot know the fundamental reality. There is no duality. This is the solution of all questions of metaphysics and ethics. Western civilization has in vain endeavored to find a reason for altruism. Here it is. I am my brother, and his pain is mine. I cannot injure him without injuring myself, or do ill to

other things without bringing that ill upon my own soul. When I have realized that I myself am the Absolute, for me there is no more death nor life nor pain nor pleasure, nor caste nor sex. How can that which is absolute die or be born? The pages of nature are turned before us like the pages of a book, and we think that we ourselves are turning, while in reality we remain ever the same.[13]

Vivekananda exhorted his audience to rise to their full moral stature, "to be lions, not sheep." With that kind of clarion call for an altered self-awareness, few would look away and beyond themselves for help from without. Everything is self-contained. One makes it or breaks it! It is all in the way one thinks. If there is a god, that god needs to be found within, and he would help only those who help themselves. Those who do not help themselves get no help at all. There is no talk about sin in this kind of language, at least the way the biblical revelation warrants it. What is termed *sin* is simply ignorance and weakness caused by the hypnosis of *maya,* an inadequate reflection of what is really real.

According to Vivekananda there can be no creation nor any personal God who brings the world into existence *ex nihilo*. Rather, the world is "evolved" from God, as a spider spins its web out of its own body. The talk about God creating anything is incompatible with God's immutability. If the *atman,* or soul, is created, it must also be perishable, which is impossible. The Hindu interpretation of the individual soul (*atman*) emanating from the world soul (*paramatman*) is irreconcilable with the Christian doctrine of creation. A doctrine of redemption also is moot because the individual soul receives little help from without for its deliverance.[14]

The Hindu explanation of salvation connotes ideas that are completely different from its Christian counterpart. Once the sinful state of humanity is acknowledged, and consequently the incapacitated state of humans to save themselves from sin and all of its consequences, then the incarnation of God in Christ and the unfolding of God's plan of salvation in Jesus Christ also receives full acceptance. Then, and only then, does a person begin to see in the cross of Jesus Christ God's own justice and grace coming together, as well as the relevance of the same cross in daily living. In Hinduism, salvation is ultimate release from the cycle of birth and rebirth caused by karma, which operates on a cause-and-effect sequence:

Results of action are like a spiritual substance that entrap the self in the body. But since liberation from the temporary abode of the body is the goal, and it is only by transcending selfishness that one can achieve the ultimate destiny, persons who are bound to their bodies through their actions will experience another incarnation, with another chance to life in touch with the ultimate reality.[15]

THE THEOLOGY OF THE CROSS: A CHRISTIAN VIEW

In both Buddhism and Hinduism suffering visits humans with a vengance. In the Hindu view of life, suffering has close connection with the law of karma.[16] Whether curse or blessing, rebirth into the cycle of life or release from the cycle of rebirth, karma plays a decisive role in the Hindu interpretation of human existence. Of the various themes the cross signifies in the Christian religion, the image of suffering perhaps takes center stage in the phrase "theology of the cross." To keep this idea in focus, we view Christian suffering as suffering *under* the cross of Christ. That the wicked and the ungodly suffer, and suffer terribly, is a foregone conclusion in all religions. But the suffering of the good and righteous has remained an unsolved mystery in all religions, and each religion in its own way has struggled to unravel that secret.

The Christian religion builds on the premise that the cross of Christ is the end of all suffering. Biblical writers have addressed the question of suffering, especially the suffering of God's faithful people, to God Himself. God's answer to this most intriguing question is "faith." The prophets of Old Testament times exhorted God's people to remember from history how God has been leading His people through rough and tumble, at the same time alerting them to look to the future for the total demise of suffering. That future, however, culminated in the cross of Christ, as the New Testament offers a clear witness. Christians, therefore, view suffering in this world holistically, always looking to the cross of Christ for direction.

Christians make no claim to immunity to suffering, nor do they dismiss lightly the effervescence of suffering. Instead, as Martin Luther exhorts in the explanation of the Third Petition in the Large Catechism, they

> surely expect to have the devil with all his angels and the world as our enemies and must expect that they will inflict every possible misfortune and grief upon us. For where God's Word is preached, accepted, or believed, and bears fruit, there the holy and precious cross will also not be far behind. And let no one think that we will have peace; rather, we must sacrifice all we have on earth—possessions, honor, house and farm, spouse and children, body and life. Now, this grieves our flesh and the old creature, for it means that we must remain steadfast, suffer

patiently whatever befalls us, and let go whatever is taken from us.[17]

The Lutheran Confessions speak of sufferings as having a purging effect in the lives of believers. Christians are not spared any suffering that others endure. Nevertheless, those who trust in God through the cross of Christ understand their sufferings "not as a punishment but an exercise and preparation for renewal."[18] The dialectic of Christian living works in such a way that the cross on which it is anchored prompts also the comfort that flows from the same cross. The cross signifies death and at the same time life after death, a physical reality of the resurrection patterned after Christ, who rose again from the dead as the firstfruits (1 Corinthians 15:22). Living under the cross in the present order of existence is literally walking through the valley of the shadow of death, fearing no evil because the Good Shepherd's rod and staff comfort the believer (Psalm 23:4).

Sufferings in the life of a Christian, therefore, are not threats but healthful aids toward a person's spiritual formation. As the apostle Paul exhorted the Christians in Rome, Christians juxtapose suffering and hope and thus rejoice in their suffering because "we know that suffering produces perseverance; perseverance, character; and character, hope. And hope does not disappoint us . . ." (Romans 5:3–5a). Suffering has a purging effect in human life as it brings about discipline and coherence in daily living. It provides the arsenal to quash the advances of the world, sin, and flesh, the ever-so-real enemies of the people of God. Luther shares these comforting words as he sees such provision in Christ's promise of the Holy Spirit:

> Christ has given us his Holy Spirit; he makes us spiritual and subdues the flesh, and assures that we are still God's children, however hard sin may be raging within us, so long as we follow the Spirit and resist sin to slay it. Since, however, nothing else is so good for the mortifying of the flesh as the cross and suffering, he comforts us in suffering with the support of the Spirit of love, and of the whole creation, namely, that the Spirit sighs within us and the creation longs with us that we may be rid of the flesh and of sin.[19]

The theology of the cross takes Christian living, with its attendant sufferings, to the cross of Jesus Christ. In this context Luther's directive to the Holy Spirit's association with the theology of the cross is worthy of emphasis. The Spirit is our defense against anything that intends our harm, including the horrible condition of falling away from faith in Jesus Christ. God has given us the Holy Spirit as the down payment, the deposit, the guarantee of the things to come (2 Corinthians 5:5). Just as much as the Spirit offers hope for the future, so also that same Spirit enables us to deal with the present sufferings in anticipation of the glorious future. Again, in Luther's words, by our sufferings

> we become sure of two things: first, that the great glory of Christ's kingdom is surely ours, and will come hereafter; and, second, that it is nevertheless preceded by crosses, shame, misery, contempt, and all kinds of suffering for *the sake of Christ*. The purpose is that we shall not grow discouraged through impatience or unbelief, or despair of that future glory, which is to be so great that even the angels desire to see it.[20]

The life and ministry of the apostle Paul is a case in point. Paul exemplifies how this theology plays out in real life as one who was himself at one time an enemy of the cross but now turned into its advocate. The cross became Paul's life and mission. He would resolve to know nothing but the "cross of Christ" (1 Corinthians 2:2), and on his body he was wearing the marks (*stigmata*) of Jesus Christ (Galatians 6:17), the signifiers of a life lived out in its fullness under the cross. For Paul, living under the cross is living by faith in Jesus, with whom Paul had been crucified (Galatians 2:20). Christ, therefore, is exalted in Paul's body both in life and death because for him to live is Christ and to die is gain (Philippians 1:20–21). Paul encourages his fellow followers of the Crucified One to imitate him (Paul) as he is, with his companions, playing out a life of sufferings in life's theater as a living testimony to the world (2 Corinthians 4:9–17). Living the Christian life is living under the cross of Christ so the life after the cross also may be revealed to the world.

Thus the theology of the cross puts the suffering of a Christian in perspective. It undercuts the elusive myth of putting a person's stock in human miseries as the way to gain high dividends for a self-sought and self-claimed perpetual nihilistic "fulfillment" (*Nirvana*). Instead, it interprets life in this world as it is, brought to divine justice as the consequence of human sin yet keeping those who trust in the Suffering Servant in the confidence that, as the world ends, so will the sufferings in it also. The suffering of a Christian does not overpower him or her, but it builds perseverance and hope. The theology of the cross interprets life as it really is and promises how it can only be better because of the Crucified One and what He has already done. The theology of the cross, therefore,

> implies a peculiar way that Jesus relates to us. Coming to faith ... involves being broken by the Law, coming to grips with our moral failure. Legalistic religions, in which one saves oneself by

one's own efforts, are very specifically *theologies of glory,* optimistically assuming success and glorifying the powers of the successful, virtuous person. But when we realize just how lost we are, then we cling to the cross, trusting Christ to do for us what we cannot do for ourselves. This is saving faith, the *theology of the cross.*[21]

THE THEOLOGY OF THE CROSS AS WITNESS

Hinduism and Christianity do not share the same understanding of either sin or death. The two religions differ not only in these fundamentals, but also in other bare essentials, such as the one God who created everything and the curse that came upon God's creation because of human disobedience. Our generation is evermore conscious of the constant change in the definitions of words and concepts. Words in any language have limitations. Furthermore, words assume their meaning contextually. This struggle is evidenced in the Christian endeavor to translate Scripture into all languages while frequently updating the already existing translations. Even if the same word is used in two religions, it may signify different meanings in each. As we approach the theme of the theology of the cross as a means for witnessing the Gospel among those who identify with the Hindu way, we should expect to come to terms with such challenges repeatedly.

This does not mean that such issues emerge only when the Christian faith meets other faiths. Even in a historically Christian culture we are bound to switch our mental images when a company tries to sell a cologne by maximizing on a biblical axiom such as "you are the light of my salvation," or when a consumer finds "the taste of heaven" as she consumes a brand-name ice cream, or when a Christian publisher sends "Jesus at bat" to make a salespitch to children for their products. If in the first two instances the secular tries to bag on the sacred, religion tries to benefit from the society's general attitude in the third. All three expressions are literally "up in the air" when they are faced with religions that do not define heaven or salvation in the manner Christianity does, as well as cultures that are complete strangers to the game of baseball.

In Hinduism, salvation is the ultimate release from the cycle of birth and rebirth caused by karma, which operates on a cause-and-effect sequence. Both life and life after death in Hinduism are determined and governed by the law of karma. While Christianity speaks of salvation (soteriology) as God's gift to humankind, Hinduism has proposed what Mircea Eliade has termed "soteriological techniques" for humans to follow on their own. These techniques are deemed enablers that help to emancipate the human soul from the world of suffering. All is suffering; all is pain in Hinduism. "The body is pain, because it is the place of pain; the senses, objects, perceptions are suffering, because they lead to suffering; pleasure itself is suffering, because it is followed by suffering."[22] One specific way to swim against the tide of such obvious pessimism is to work deliberately against the karmic forces.

Karma means "work, action; destiny (ineluctable consequence of acts performed in a previous existence); product, effect, etc." says Eliade.[23] Karma operates on the simple logic that a person's thoughts, words, and actions determine his or her future mode of existence just as the present life resulted from the karma of the previous ones. Each is responsible to himself or herself for personal actions. There is no external judge, no one evoking a threat of judgment or exhorting repentance. Karma literally molds the next life. The soul reaps what it sows, and it cannot grow out of the cast it has built for itself.

Karma begets its natural progeny, reincarnation. Returning to life after death, albeit in a lower form, provides another opportunity for the soul to extinguish the karmic residue, the perennial danger of not succeeding in that endeavor notwithstanding. The results of karma

> are like a spiritual substance that entrap the self in the body. But since liberation from the temporary abode of the body is the goal, and it is only by transcending selfishness that one can achieve the ultimate destiny, persons who are bound to their bodies through their actions will experience another incarnation, with another chance to life in touch with the ultimate reality.[24]

If a rose by any other name is a rose, then, by analogy, we might surmise that the natural knowledge of the Law is at work in a unique way in the Hindu law of karma. Karmic forces crush the human soul to the extent that the soul fails to acknowledge its impotence to seek the path to freedom or to receive the gift of freedom from outside of itself. The karmic residue has entrapped the self in the body, in the darkness of sin, and turned off the exit sign. This is prime time for the light of the Gospel, which radiates from the face of Jesus Christ, to work its transforming power in the individual. Transforming the mind and enabling the soul to receive God's mercy and grace would then occur as God initiates such activity. God's grace, once received, delivers the human soul from the powers of darkness, opens the door for the soul's final resting place, and takes away the tingle of "reincarnation."

A Christian understanding of the theology of the cross hinges on a relationship, though broken by human sin, between God and human beings. God on His own took the initiative to mend that relationship through the redemptive sacrifice of His Son, Jesus Christ. The language of sacrifice, and its redemptive significance, is familiar within the Vedantic tradition of Hinduism.[25] Prayer and sacrifice have been the two significant constituents of Vedic religion. These sacrifices were expressions of worship and devotion to gods with the desire to establish an intimate fellowship with the deities while at the same time pleading for mercy on those who have done injustice. Those who offered such sacrifices "sought to establish intimate communion between themselves and the gods, and hoped to induce the [gods] through prayer and worship to come to their aid against their enemies and to make them happy by granting them health, wealth and progeny. Sometimes they are also found praying for fame and immortality."[26]

Thus, though philosophical Hinduism presupposes fusion with the cosmic soul as the spiritual ideal for the individual soul, in practical living, Hinduism does operate on a divine-human relational dimension, hardly ever underestimating the depravity of the human race. Cries of desperation arise from the Hindu heart, and the desire to commune with the deity takes center stage in every act of worship. Hindus also live with restless hearts until they rest in God, now working hard at trying to undo past karma, now crying out in distress toward a deity that they are not sure is not visiting the iniquities of the fathers upon generation after generation. Here is where the cross of Christ fits in simultaneously as the incarnation of human sin and divine grace, alienation and reconciliation, and the finality of death and the ushering in of the resurrection life.

Despite the mystical element in Hinduism and the conviction that the identity of the individual soul is "lost" in the world soul, for those who are on the road to that depth of understanding of the self, Hinduism suggests a catalog of virtues by which to live. Cardinal and ethical virtues such as humility, self-control, love, and compassion for others, Hindus believe, flow spontaneously from such beings without being cultivated artificially or imposed by external authorities. The *Bhagavad Gita,* for example, encourages the devoted to learn to perform actions without egotistical concern for their fruits by living out one's own share of dharma purely because it *is* one's dharma.[27]

Dharma is moral law. It sets the standards for a deeply satisfying life and strongly encourages humans to live simply and with modesty, setting aside pleasure and success in personal life for the sake of the wellness of community and society. It also stipulates specific duties for individuals, depending on their particular station in life. Dharma also is the order of the universe, and whenever the world is in disarray, the deity incarnates to reinstate that order. On a practical and personal level, dharma encourages people to surrender to God's will and accomplish it willingly.

Granted, in our capsule description of both karma and dharma, there are several aspects of these two concepts in Hinduism with which Christian theology is in constant conflict and even total disagreement. Hinduism does not clearly identify the source or the cause of either karma or dharma. But as a working hypothesis, both karma and dharma, as the natural law written in human hearts, provide a premise for Christians to witness the Gospel of Jesus Christ among those who are persuaded by the Hindu way of life. If karma pricks the Hindu conscience of not having done enough (or of never being able to do enough) to obey the laws of a transcendent God, it is preparing the same heart also to heed the accusing and condemning function of the Law of God the Lawgiver. If dharma makes a Hindu duty-bound to work for harmony and bring about goodwill among people, in the Christian order of daily living these ideals are played out as the natural outcome of the redeemed people of God, claiming no merit for anyone but reflecting the transformation that occurs in lives because of God's redeeming work in Christ. In either case Hindu spirituality would be drawn to the foot of the cross so it might take the eyes away from itself and afix them to the Crucified One.

Hinduism maintains that being born human is just one step away from attaining ultimate liberation. In fact it is the *sine qua non* for entering into immortality. Existence as human beings is deemed extremely rare and the most difficult to achieve. By rightly using the mortal body, one can attain immortality. Having been born as a human being, no one should lose the chance for eternal life. If in Hinduism the origin of the much coveted status of becoming a human remains a mystery, Christianity unravels that mystery by acknowledging the simple biblical revelation: Humanity is God's design for the one He created as custodian and steward of His entire creation.

Each religion has its own story to tell as it interprets suffering in the world and seeks to alleviate it. Modern science is capable of explaining physical pain in psychological terms. It is said of the philosopher and mathematician Bertrand Russell who, while sitting in a dentist's chair, was asked, "Where does it hurt?" Russell responded, "In my mind, of course!"[28] The cross of Christ, however, does not explain suffering away; instead, it puts sufferng in perspective. Suffering is as real as the cross of Christ. The cross brings comfort, and the Crucified One speaks His word of promise, "My yoke is easy, My burden light!"

NOTES

1. The word *religion* is used in this essay in its basic and most common usage. What is not secular, though not always sacred, is religious. Some have called religion a "way of life" or a "worldview." Most Christians hesitate to call Christianity a religion because Jesus Christ never founded a religion. In the New Testament *religion* can mean superstition (Acts 17:22). In its early years Christianity was known as "the Way," as, for example, the apostle Paul calls himself "a follower of the Way" (Acts 24:14).

2. W. Richard Comstock, "Toward Open Definitions of Religion," *Journal of American Academy of Religion* LII.3 (September 1986): 499.

3. N. K. Devaraja, *Hinduism and the Modern Age* (Bombay: Current Book House, 1975), ix.

4. E. P. Sanders, *Paul and Palestinian Judaism: A Comparison of Patterns of Religion* (Minneapolis: Fortress, 1977), 18.

5. Sanders, *Paul and Palestinian Judaism*, 16.

6. Gene Edward Veith, *The Spirituality of the Cross* (St. Louis: Concordia, 1999), 56 (*my emphasis*).

7. The name *India* also has a similar history. India gained independence from British occupation in 1947. Since then, and particularly in the last two decades, most of the native names of states and cities have been reinstated. Hence, Bombay is known as Mumbai and Madras as Chennai.

8. Stuart Rose, "Is the Term 'Spirituality' a Word that Everyone Uses, But Nobody Knows What Anyone Means by It?" *Journal of Contemporary Religion* 16.2 (2001): 203.

9. Thus it makes sense that until the modern era, particularly until Christianity began its grand-scale missionary movement, Hinduism remained a religion for India and Indians. In its prolonged history, Hinduism was never meant to be a missionary religion. A person didn't have to be catechized to practice this way of life. It almost came naturally to anyone who lived in India, hence fascination with Hinduism grows within those who encounter this worldview spiritually.

10. Devaraja, *Hinduism and the Modern Age*, 1.

11. Wayne A. Meeks, *The First Urban Christians: The Social World of the Apostle Paul* (New Haven: Yale University Press, 1983), 180.

12. For further explanation of this sophisticated doctrine with illustrations, see Richard S. Cohen, "Shakyamuni: Buddhism's Founder in Ten Acts," in *The Rivers of Paradise* (ed. David Noel Freedman and Michael J. McClymond; Grand Rapids: Eerdmans, 2001), 121–232.

13. *Swami Vivekananda in the West* (July 1899–March 1900) V, 184–86.

14. R. H. S. Boyd, *Indian Christian Theology* (Madras: Christian Literature Society, 1967), 60–61.

15. John Renard, *Responses to 101 Questions on Hinduism* (New York: Paulist Press, 1999), 44.

16. We will discuss this briefly in the following section.

17. Robert Kolb and Timothy J. Wengert, eds., *The Book of Concord* (Min-

neapolis: Fortress, 2000), 448:65–66.

18. Kolb and Wengert, *Book of Concord,* 214:151.

19. LW 25:37.

20. LW 35:266 (*my emphasis*).

21. Veith, *Spirituality of the Cross,* 60 (*Veith's emphasis*).

22. Mircea Eliade, *Yoga: Immortality and Freedom* (2d ed.; Princeton: Princeton University Press, 1969), 11. Eliade quotes Anirudha, commenting on *Samkhya Sutras,* II:1.

23. Eliade, *Yoga,* 12.

24. Renard, *Responses,* 44.

25. The Vedas are a collection of ancient hymns and ritual poems dating between 1500 B.C. to 900 B.C. They are arranged particularly for the purposes of liturgy, prayer, and sacrifice.

26. Devaraja, *Hinduism and the Modern Age,* 7.

27. *The Bhagavad Gita,* literally "The Song of the Blessed Lord," is perhaps the most popular piece of all Hindu literature. It has been translated and widely used in college classrooms and as reading material. It is part of a magnum opus of Hinduism called *Mahabharata,* which was composed over a period of 800 years, from 400 B.C. to A.D. 400. The *Gita* projects the image of dharma, "duty," over relationships. For a recent English translation, see Stephen Mitchell, *Bhagavad Gita: A New Translation* (New York: Harmony Books, 2000).

28. T. Patrick Burke, *The Major Religions* (Cambridge, Mass.: Blackwell, 1996), 63.

FOR FURTHER READING

Dhavamony, Mariasusai. *Classical Hinduism.* Rome: Università Georgiana Editrice, 1982.

Gopinatha Rao, T. A. *Elements of Hindu Iconography.* 2 vols. New York: Paragon Book Reprint Corporation, 1968.

Klostermaier, Klaus K. *Liberation, Salvation, Self-Realization: A Comparative Study of Hindu, Buddhist and Christian Ideas.* Madras: University of Madras, 1973.

Raj, A. R. Victor. *The Hindu Connection: Roots of the New Age.* St. Louis: Concordia, 1995.

Richardson, Peter Tufts. *Four Spiritualities: Expression of Self, Expressions of Spirit.* Palo Alto: Davis & Black, 1996.

Sivaraman, Krishna, ed. *Hindu Spirituality.* Vol. 1. New York: Crossroad, 1989.

Sundararajan, K. R., and Bithika Mukeruji. *Hindu Spirituality.* Vol. 2. New York: Crossroad, 1997.

Urquhart, W. S. *Pantheism and the Value of Life in Indian Philosophy.* New Delhi: Ajay Book Service, 1982.

7

The Theology of the Cross in the African Context

ESHETU ABATE

INTRODUCTION

Africa has always been related to the cross ever since the Suffering Servant, our Lord Jesus Christ, found Himself heading to Golgotha, carrying the cross. Simon, the father of Alexander and Rufus, who helped our Lord carry the cross, was from Cyrene, an important Libyan city in North Africa.[1] After the resurrection, the Ethiopian eunuch was among the first to hear the message of the cross from Philip the Evangelist as the two traveled to Gaza. The eunuch was reading the text of the Suffering Servant from Isaiah 53. Still today Africa is close to the cross of Christ in many respects. The focus of this essay is to show the multidimensional relevance of Christ's cross within the African experience and reality.

HISTORICAL BACKGROUND: THE CROSS AS A WAY OF CAPITAL PUNISHMENT

The Roman Empire most likely inherited the cross as an instrument of capital punishment from the Carthaginians.[2] This cruel instrument of punishment was used in the empire particularly against rebellious foreigners, violent criminals, robbers, and slaves.[3] It was a horrible punishment. Death on the cross was slow. Besides the hunger, scourging, and the ill treatment endured by the victim, he also had to carry the horizontal bar of the cross to the place of the crucifixion. There, after lying on the ground, the hands of the criminal were nailed or tied with a rope to the bar. After that the criminal was hung on the vertical bar that had been erected on the site of the crucifixion. The crucified person then had to suffer from the heat and cold, the bites of insects and birds, as well as complete exhaustion. One of the victim's great problems was the inability to breathe as the weight of his body pulled him down. After this prolonged, excruciating suffering, the criminal died. Sometimes the victim's bones were broken so he would not be able to support his body, which would hasten his inability to breathe, thus hastening death. Seneca, the Roman writer, observes the following concerning the awfulness of death on the cross:

> Can anyone be found who would prefer wasting away in pain
> dying limb by limb, or letting out his life drop by drop, rather
> than expiring once for all? Can any man be found willing to be
> fastened to the accursed tree, long sickly, already deformed,
> swelling with ugly weals on shoulders and chest, and drawing
> the breath of life amid long-drawn-out agony? He would have
> many excuses for dying even before mounting the cross.[4]

As to the shape of the cross, two kinds are suggested. The one looks like the English letter T while the other variety looks like the plus sign (+). Because of the inscription over the head, many think the kind of cross upon which our Lord was crucified might have had the shape of the plus sign.[5]

What is important theologically is not to master the details of death on the cross, however beneficial they may be as historical description. The important thing is to know that the cross is the greatest suffering a person may experience. Why did the innocent Son of God die on the cross? What does Jesus' suffering and death mean within our African experience? We must consider our Lord's death in light of the African personal, social, political, and economic life. These are some of the areas we will address.

THE AFRICAN AND THE SHEDDING OF BLOOD

The author of the book of Hebrews opens for us a door to find God in light of Christ's cross:

> Therefore, brothers, since we have confidence to enter the Most
> Holy Place by the blood of Jesus, by a new and living way

opened for us through the curtain, that is, his body, and since we have a great priest over the house of God, let us draw near to God with a sincere heart in full assurance of faith, having our hearts sprinkled to cleanse us from a guilty conscience and having our bodies washed with pure water. (Hebrews 10:19–22)

Africans, like most people in the world, are highly religious. In fact, their worldview and daily existence are permeated by their religious convictions and practices. Whether they farm, trade, or select a bride for their children, their daily living is full of religious meaning. Besides religious practices connected with daily vocations, Africans want to reach the divine and please Him. For that purpose they may sometimes use intermediaries such as rainmakers, ritual elders, diviners, medicine men, etc. These intermediaries prescribe to them certain things to be performed. One of the most prominent prescribed rituals is sacrifice.

The practice and concept of shedding blood for religious purpose is not new for Africans. The sacrifice, especially of animals, has been widely used. The animal sacrificed could be a chicken, a lamb, a goat, or an ox. Sometimes a specific color is prescribed. Why do Africans in general like to sacrifice? It is because of their respect for the divine. It is to be on good terms with the powers that have authority in their daily lives. Their aim is to be obedient so they may be successful in life and also may be saved from the different misfortunes that may occur.[6] Concerning sacrifice by Africans, John S. Mbiti writes:

In African societies, life is closely associated with blood. When blood is shed in making a sacrifice, it means that human or animal life is being given back to God who is in fact the ultimate source of all life. Therefore the purpose of such a sacrifice must be a very serious one. Such sacrifices may be made when the lives of many people are in danger. The life of one person or animal, or of a few of either, is destroyed in the belief that this will save the life of many people. Thus, the destruction of one becomes the protection of many.[7]

The death of an animal and the shedding of its blood speak loud to the religious aspirations of the African Continent. Otherwise nobody would go to the pain of finding an animal that will cost him money and take time to raise. There is an inherent sensitivity in the African to the need for some kind of substitutionary sacrifice to approach and please the divine.

From this point of view, the death of Christ on the cross as the substitution for the sinner is a welcome message for the African people. It is not something new or strange to the African culture, but it makes perfect what has been imperfect. In the African rituals of animal sacrifice, we can find some congruence with the Jewish practice of sacrifice. Just as the Jewish sacrifices prepared them for the ultimate and perfect sacrifice effected on the cross, the African religious culture of sacrifice prepared the mind and hearts of the people for the perfect sacrifice on the cross. Therefore, a believing African can identify himself or herself without any problem with the words of St. Peter: "For you know that it was not with perishable things such as silver or gold that you were redeemed from the empty way of life handed down to you from your forefathers, but with precious blood of Christ, a lamb without blemish or defect" (1 Peter 1:18–19)

As the result of Christ's death on the cross, the African people have found the way of salvation. It is through the cross of Christ that the African has received the privilege to approach God in a clear conscience without any remorse or guilt. The cross of Christ has opened for the African the way to heaven. All Africans who believe in the Lord Jesus Christ know that the way to heaven is wide open for them because of the cross of Christ, regardless of their external circumstances. In His suffering on the cross, Christ brought freedom and relief for the African conscience and mind.

THE CROSS OF CHRIST AS THE WAY OF VICTORY

For Africans there is no dichotomy between the world of the spirits and the physical world.[8] The two worlds are interdependent and, so to speak, operate together. The nature spirits and different kinds of powers operate in their farm, health, birth, cattle, seasons, etc. Africans call upon the respective spirit to have the right relationship and favor. For example, the Wollaytta in Southern Ethiopia considered the first week of the new moon holy. They did not cultivate the fields on the Wednesdays of the first week of the new moon.[9] During this appointed holy day, they also approached the rainmakers and diviners so the gods would provide the necessary rain and health to tend the fields. Now, however, the Wollaytta have found Christ, the most powerful one. Many Africans now believe that Christ crucified and risen is greater than any power or spirit that has had authority over them. Therefore, through their faith in Christ, they are free from the fear of spirits, powers, and principalities.

The confrontation of principalities and powers has been a real phenomenon in the African churches. Whenever the African churches advanced with the message of Christ crucified, this confrontation of principalities and powers has occurred. Sometimes the evil spirits give

124

way to the Spirit of Christ; at other times those who are opposed to the message of the cross resort to violent means.

THE CROSS AS SUFFERING AND PERSECUTION BECAUSE OF ONE'S FAITH

Some may think suffering and persecution because of one's confession of Christ is a relic of past history. However, in the experience of most African Christians it has been a vivid and recent experience. It will be wrong to assume that persecution will stop even in the future as long as there are different and opposing powers behind what the apostle Paul calls "the flesh" and "the Spirit." Of course the persecution may take different forms, from verbal attack to open violence, depending on the situation.

Believing individuals have been martyred for the faith and confession of the Lord Jesus Christ as Savior. The Ugandan martyrs and the female Ethiopian martyrs are good examples. Some have been tortured and imprisoned for years for their confession. A lot has yet to be written about the African confession of Christ and the suffering endured by believers on account of this living witness to the cross.[10]

THE SOCIOPOLITICAL DIMENSION OF THE CROSS

The sociopolitical application of Christ's cross looks beyond what is normally known as the substitutionary death of Christ for our sins. It sees the opposition against human suffering, social injustice, and oppression and the subsequent price one may pay by opposing such systems as constituting the cross. Peter Kanyandago of Uganda writes "The suffering of Jesus is not just a result of a free decision to deliver himself for our sins, but is a result of his stand against and opposition to religious and civil authorities who perpetuate the suffering of others."[11] While explaining his understanding of the cross and suffering, Kanyandago clarifies further the place and function of suffering under the cross.

> Firstly, suffering does not come from God and is an inhuman experience that cannot be justified in any way without taking into account how it comes about. Secondly, a Christian's response, like that of Christ must be to fight against it. Any type of theology, spirituality or devotion that integrates and exalts suffering must be rejected. Thirdly, in the process of fighting against what causes suffering one is bound to meet with opposition which can lead to suffering. This is the type of

suffering that the cross represents and it can be accepted because it liberates others and leads to life.[12]

This idea of the cross, which has the backing of many African theologians and intellectuals, is similar to that of Professor Jon Sobrino of El Salvador. Professor Sobrino is against a purely academic theology, which fails to take an appropriate action in the practical life of people. He also is against the traditional mournful "mystique" of the cross, which is too passive and individualistic. For the cross to be relevant, it has to relate to the modern world and its social injustice. According to Sobrino, "God is to be found on the crosses of the oppressed."[13]

We have to appreciate the above views because they direct us to a holistic meaning and application of the cross of Christ. If we rightly understand and apply the cross of Christ, it is where differences are overcome and all become one. The best model and witness to the effects of the cross of Christ on human communities is the celebration of the Eucharist. It is during this gathering for the partaking of Holy Communion where the body and blood of our Lord Jesus Christ is shared. The apostle Paul clearly admonishes that there should not be divisions because of social and economic standards among those who receive the Eucharist. The poor who do not have any possessions are equal to the rich when they come to the table of the Lord. In fact, the agape meal that they share together after Holy Communion should be equally distributed, regardless of social status (1 Corinthians 11:20–22, 33). The apostles repeatedly reiterate the equality of the people of God in the eucharistic celebration, in worship, and in daily living. This was indeed the practice of the early church (Acts 2:44–45). St. Luke reports in the Acts of the Apostles how: "All the believers were one in heart and mind. No one claimed that any of his possessions was his own, but they shared everything they had" (Acts 4:32). The apostles' teaching was that from where there is much blessing and abundance, it should be shared where there is a need so all shall be even or equal.

From the witness of the apostles, we can understand that the cross of Christ is the place where barriers of all kinds are erased as we share in the Eucharist. The ethnic, economic, sexual, social, racial, and any other kind of barrier must disappear at the Lord's Table. This is the kind of community that our Lord Jesus Christ wanted to create through His death on the cross. This community, diverse yet united through the cross of Christ, can bring change in the society in which we live. Too often, however, the church, which is the community of the cross of Christ, has itself become a poor model instead of the light and the salt of the earth (Matthew 5:13).

Instead of "lifting high the cross" so the world may see it, the church has kept it within its premises. Only those who are permitted to go inside the church's walls have the opportunity to hear the Gospel's message. However, the vast majority of people live outside the church's premises and the gates of the city. While they know the cross as an emblem, they know little about its message and meaning. The Good News of the cross of Christ was not given only to those in the church. In fact, the original command of our Lord Jesus Christ says, "Go and make disciples of all nations . . ." (Matthew 28:19).

The cross of Christ is not only the place of forgiveness, but it also is the place for justice. God showed both His perfect justice and His love on the cross. This means both the justice and love of God on the cross should find access into our human societies. In fact, the voices of Kanyandago and Sobrino are reactions against the silence and the impotency of the Christian churches to give a satisfactory meaning to a world full of suffering, social injustice, and poverty.

One of the most succinct definitions given about a human being is "body-soul-in community." If a human being is a "body-soul-in community," the cross of Christ has validity to everyone. As often indicated, the strict dichotomizing of the human being into two compartments, namely, the body and soul, was a Greek idea and not Hebrew idea. According to the biblical understanding, a human being is a unity. There is no division between the soul of a person and the body. The soul is the summing up of the whole personality.[14] In the twenty-first century we have come to understand in light of the biblical witness and our African context that a human being is not only the unity of body and soul. The body and soul do not exist in a vacuum. The person has a community that influences the body and soul. Therefore, a human being will fall short of being seen in totality unless the social system or community in which the individual lives is taken into consideration. Therefore, the cross of Christ, where the justice and love of God has been portrayed, should address all these aspects, including the social system.

THE PERSONAL ELEMENT

The reality of the atonement through which the personal reconciliation with God is effected because of the cross of Christ should not be underestimated by any means. The New Testament points to many living examples of times our Lord Jesus Christ and the apostles preached to individuals and led them to faith. The story of Philip the Evangelist and the Ethiopian eunuch mentioned in Acts 8 is only one example. The Ethiopian, the first African official to encounter the message of the cross, was reading from the song of the Suffering Servant, which is recorded in Isaiah 53.

He was led like a lamb to the slaughter, and as a sheep before her shearers is silent, so He did not open His mouth. By oppression and judgment He was taken away. And who can speak of His descendants? For He was cut off from the land of the living. (Isaiah 53:7–8)

As can be seen from the text, the message explained to the Ethiopian was the good news about Jesus, which was the message of the cross. As an expression of his acceptance of the message, the Ethiopian asked Philip to baptize him. (Cf. also Acts 2:38; Acts 17:30–34). For the apostle Paul, the message of the cross was his all in all. The cross was the summary of his witness of the Gospel. He knew nothing but Christ crucified. The message of the cross was his norm and yardstick not only to measure the teachings of others, but also as the most important signpost for his own teaching. The message of the cross was not something that Paul ingeniously devised, but it was revealed to him from God (Galatians 1:12). The cross is foolishness and a scandal to the world, but it is the power of God and the wisdom of God for those who are being saved.

The Christian's spiritual experiences, justification, peace, spiritual gifts, sanctification, and empowerment are the results of the cross. Christians live by identifying themselves with the death of Christ. Christians have died to the Law and sin when, through the Sacrament of Holy Baptism, they have died and been buried with Christ to join in His resurrection to new life. In the gift of Baptism, Christians live a life of faith grounded in the power of the death and resurrection of Jesus. Christians now live by faith the life of the resurrection as if in this very moment they rose from the waters of Baptism. If we believe that societies and communities have to be governed in justice, it is important to have individuals who are reconciled with the God of justice who revealed Himself in and through the cross. Knowing Him will give such leaders the sense and meaning of divine justice, which is justice par excellence.

This is important because, as our Lord said, it is difficult to reap justice from someone who has no sense of justice. If individuals are the cornerstones of communities and societies, those individuals who are equipped with God's justice will make a tremendous contribution to their constituencies. God's perfect justice is best understood and appropriated under the sacrifice of His Son on the cross. The cross, therefore, provides a powerful global witness and signpost to affirm God's justice in the world.

CARING FOR THOSE IN PHYSICAL NEED

The cross of Christ is the greatest and highest expression of love for sinful humanity. Our Lord Jesus Christ alluded to His self-giving love on the cross when He said, "Greater love has no one than this, that he lay down his life for his friends" (John 15:13). However, making oneself accessible to others and caring for others starts by attending to their needs. There seem to be different levels of suffering or crosses one can take on in our world communities. The greatest is self-giving. Our Lord Jesus Christ in the Gospels identified Himself with the sick, the poor, the disadvantaged, and the socially neglected. He fed the hungry and healed the blind, the lepers, and those suffering from various ailments. He accepted the socially ostracized groups, such as Zacchaeus and Matthew, the tax collectors; the sinful woman who washed His feet with her tears; and the Samaritan woman at the well. Jesus wept with those who wept, as can be seen from the narrative concerning the death of Lazarus (John 11:33–35). In short, Jesus carried the infirmities of all.

We in Africa want to live this kind of identification and witness. We know about preaching. We have heard verbal preaching many times. What we want and look for are those who are like Jesus Christ; those who are willing to identify and care for the sick, the poor, and the disadvantaged; those who are willing to bring about change. Jesus did not stay in an ivory tower or His "pastor's office" to prepare His homily for the coming Sabbath. Although I am not against this kind of preparation, it is important to stress that Christ went to the suffering people and participated in alleviating their problems. Such identification is a way to carry the cross. This is among the first levels of self-giving, and it reaches its climax when one lays down one's life for the helpless and the disadvantaged. We expect all missionaries and evangelists to do this, but it is what is lacking in most missionary and evangelistic enterprises. Today, becoming a missionary is like going to a picnic. The missionary comes from his home country not to identify but to be highly paid in hard currency so he may have an easy life in the field in which he works. In our African context we find that an ivory tower called the "mission compound" is built so the missionary can live a peaceful and undisturbed life away from the crowds and the disadvantaged.

We, as African intellectuals, are not doing any better. Although we have better access and possibilities to identify with our people, we are more clever in talking and writing rather than in sharing in the problems and suffering of our people. True cross-bearing requires genuine identification with those who are suffering so we may bring about a change. This undertaking assumes that the one who moves to stand and participate in the suffering of others is in a better or healthier condition. The movement from one's secure life to identify with the helpless and the least involves an element of cross-bearing (suffering). There is a more powerful witness of the cross in this living act of identification with the helpless and dispossessed than through merely sharing the spoken Word.

Almost everywhere in the world, people are looking for self-giving love, someone who will help them in their suffering and agony. There are many who live below the poverty line, especially in two-thirds of the world. They are homeless, hungry, sick, ignorant, naked, lonely, and in despair. We are living in Africa with AIDS patients in our communities and sometimes within our own families. Their orphans are on our thresholds. People displaced because of war and natural disasters such as drought and flood are among us. Those who literally beg for their daily bread are many. Those who can read and write are few. Is it possible to limit the message of the cross in such a situation simply to the verbal proclamation, "Jesus saves! He died for you!"? Definitely not! Jesus carried the cross by freeing people from their suffering and by walking with them in their needs. We, as living members of the body of Jesus Christ, His church, should be involved without any restraint in solving these practical problems. This means that we have to sacrifice our time, talents, and treasures to make this happen. It means that we must engage in self-giving and sacrificial love in the discipleship of the cross.

THE CROSS AND THE SOCIAL SYSTEM

Suffering that people endure socially is connected with their respective system of governance. A government that embezzles public treasures decreases the welfare of its citizens. Corruption, mismanagement, irresponsibility, dishonesty, segregation, ethnocentrism, racism, apartheid, and the like, when entrenched in the governing system, promote the suffering of the "others." Most of these systemic social evils have an element of selfishness. Selfishness and the cross are at variance. They are opposites. The cross is self-giving while corruption is self-aggrandizement. When established orders, whether civic or religious, use authority for their own selfish purpose, they promote the suffering of others. In objection to such a system, our Lord Jesus Christ spoke against the teachers of the law who embezzled from widows and did nothing out of a sense of justice, mercy, and faithfulness. The religious leaders of the time persecuted Jesus Christ not only for His benevolent deeds and miracles, which far surpassed theirs, but also because He vehemently opposed the showy and hypocritical system they had that did not address people's daily problems (Matthew 23:23). Our Lord disclosed the corruption, dishonesty, and unjust leadership of the Jewish ruling order. John the Baptist and Stephen followed in Christ's footsteps. They all paid with their lives for their opposition to an unjust leadership and for testifying to the truth, justice, mercy, and faithfulness of God.

In recent times Nelson Mandela was imprisoned for 27 years for his stand against Apartheid. Bishop Desmond Tutu raised a prophetic voice against the system. Many individuals in countries such as Uganda (during Idi Amin's regime), Ethiopia (during the Communist rule), and other African nations have paid with their lives by opposing the inhuman systems in their countries. These, however, are only a few examples. Systemic evil is rampant and stretches from the top to the bottom and from the center to the outskirts. This means that we Christians, disciples of the cross, have to stand against the systemic evil in our surroundings. We have to disclose these evils so justice, mercy, and faithfulness may prevail. This in turn may bring upon us the cross in its diverse modes: persecution, imprisonment, or even death. Despite what may come upon us, it is mandatory that we do not keep quiet when justice is overridden, the poor are trampled, and the innocent are sold. The theology of the cross in the African context demands such interference.

The cross of Christ, therefore, has a threefold relevance for us in Africa. First, it is the place where we are personally justified before God and have the hope of eternal life. Second, from our Lord's identification with the suffering and the disadvantaged, we get the impetus to do the same. Third, from our Lord's stand for justice, mercy, and faithfulness, we learn that we have an obligation to stand against injustice, corruption, and unfaithfulness in all its forms.

THEOLOGY OF THE CROSS VS. THEOLOGY OF GLORY

Theology of the cross (*theologia crucis*) and theology of glory (*theologia gloriae*) are two phrases used by Dr. Martin Luther to distinguish between true theology and false theology. According to Luther, the essence of true theology is the theology of the cross. In the same manner he distinguishes between true theologians and false ones. He wrote:

> That person does not deserve to be called a theologian who looks upon the invisible things of God as though they were clearly perceptible in those things which have actually happened. He deserves to be called a theologian, however, who

comprehends the visible and manifest things of God seen through suffering and the cross.[15]

While a theology of glory knows God from His works, the theology of the cross knows Him from His sufferings. Luther used *works* in a double sense. First, it meant God's work in creation, and second, it referred to humanity's good works intended to reach to God. When Luther used the word *sufferings*, he referred not only to Christ's suffering, but also to humanity's suffering. He makes the transition from the one to the other easily.

A theology of glory seeks to know God directly in His divine power, wisdom, and glory. The theology of the cross, on the other hand, finds God where He has hidden Himself: in His sufferings, weakness, and foolishness. In the theology of the cross, "God's power appears not directly but paradoxically under helplessness and lowliness."[16] According to Luther, God's gifts and benefits are so hidden under the cross that unbelievers can neither see nor recognize them; instead, they consider them to be only trouble and disaster.[17]

First, we should not forget that the theology of the cross about which Luther gives witness has a soteriological dimension. In this, Luther's theology of the cross is similar to Paul's theology of the cross. Any human attempt to know or please God directly, either by human ethical achievements or metaphysical speculations, belongs to the theology of glory. The way to know God and to receive forgiveness of sins is through faith in Christ crucified. Justification by faith alone for the sake of Christ crucified is not a matter to be negotiated. It is the Gospel (Galatians 1:8–10).

Having stated Luther's soteriological witness of the cross, how can we see the suffering we are going through in our world in light of the theology of the cross? Is God distant, unconcerned, impotent, or what? Not to mention what is happening elsewhere in the world, I will give some examples from Africa. Where is God when innocent children die with their mothers because of recurrent drought and famine, as has been the case in Ethiopia and the Horn of Africa? Where is God when innocent civilians are massacred because they belong to an ethnic group, as has been the case in the genocide in Rwanda? Where is God when flash flooding destroys farms, cattle, and life's earnings within an hour, as has occurred repeatedly in Mozambique. What about the nonstop war between Southern Sudan and Northern Sudan? After all are not the South Sudanese Christians? Does not God stand even for His people?

If we look at this suffering in light of the theology of glory—that is, God in His power, might, and glory—it may lead one to deny the existence of a caring and benevolent God. It is only in light of the suffering God, who came to the world in the person of Jesus Christ, that we can make sense out of such an existence. In fact our world, not only Africa, has witnessed a history of suffering century after century. There is no century in which suffering, either by epidemic, war, or natural calamity, has not been recorded. Are we certain that no such calamity—earthquake, war, or epidemic—will occur in the future? Are we so civilized that we can control natural and human catastrophic events?

How should we comprehend large-scale catastrophes that bring suffering to individuals, communities, nations, and the world at large? The suffering God, the God of the cross, can give us the answer. The God of the cross is not at all ignorant of the suffering of our world. Because He became a historical figure, bound to time and space, and because He Himself suffered, He experienced all the dimensions of human suffering. Not only that, He stands with His suffering people, whatever the nature of the tribulation. The Lord who has cried, "My God, My God, why have You forsaken Me?" (Matthew 27:46) stands close to all those who are in similar situations.

The Lord God, who has become a historical figure, bound to time and space in the person of our Lord Jesus Christ, does not view His suffering world as a spectator from the outside. He has suffered and still suffers together with His people on earth. The playlet entitled *The Long Silence* gives a dramatic and real presentation of human suffering in the world and God's place in this suffering. The setting is Judgment Day, and the people are arrayed before the throne of God. An animated discussion concerning God's ability to judge occurs. How can God judge the actions of individuals when He has not walked in their shoes? Finally, a representative group proposes that before God can be accepted as their judge, "he must endure what they had endured." The list of proposed tribulations includes illegitimacy, ethnic prejudice, injustice, torture, abandonment, and ultimately a horrible death. "And when the last had finished pronouncing sentence, there was a long silence. . . . For suddenly all knew that God had already served his sentence."[18]

The suffering of God in our Lord Jesus Christ makes it clear that God has not left us alone in our suffering. He Himself has passed through it and is still passing through it. Let it be clear that our Lord does not promote suffering, nor does He want its permanency. According to Scripture, suffering entered our world because of sin. Our present world is a world suffering from the result and effects of sin. This is reality. Our God dealt with our suffering world neither by ignoring it nor by denying it. Rather, He entered its life of sin and suffering so He could redeem it. And Jesus Christ has done that through His death on the cross and the resurrection.

THE CROSS AND DOUBLE RECONCILIATION

The cross of our Lord Jesus makes possible double reconciliation: vertical reconciliation with God and horizontal reconciliation with one another. Vertical reconciliation is effected when our conscience is made clean from the guilt of sin because of the blood our Lord shed on the cross. The author of the book of Hebrews, stating the power of the blood of Christ to reconcile us with God, writes:

> The blood of goats and bulls and the ashes of a heifer sprinkled on those who are ceremonially unclean sanctify them so that they are outwardly clean. How much more, then, will the blood of Christ, who through the eternal Spirit offered Himself unblemished to God, cleanse our consciences from acts that lead to death, so that we may serve the living God! (Hebrews 9:13–14)

The reconciliation with God becomes the basis for the reconciliation with one another. For the sake of the death of our Lord Jesus Christ, God did not count our sins against us. He forgave us. A forgiven person has the impetus to forgive others. In fact God forgave our sin though we deserved eternal punishment. If God forgave such an offense, should we not forgive one another? Therefore, God's forgiveness for the sake of Christ becomes the basis for reconciliation between human beings. As God made peace with us because of the cross of Christ, we can make peace with one another.

God's reconciliation with us for the sake of Christ and the peace thus made is especially relevant for Africa, where conflicts on ethnic, tribal, and national levels are rampant. The way God deals with us should be the norm for how we deal with one another. Each ethnic group, tribe, and nation can forgive the other for past offenses and can start a new relationship on the basis of justice. There should be willingness both by the offender and the offended to identify the causes for conflict. Once identified, the offense should be stopped and a proper compensation should be made. After the compensation there should be a resolve by both parties to live amicably in peace as equals and friends by maintaining the peace thus created. In this way the cross of Christ becomes not only the power for reconciliation, but also a model that human societies can imitate to solve conflicts.

THE CROSS AND ESCHATOLOGY

All human life culminates in death. As the apostle Paul said, "The last enemy to be destroyed is death" (1 Corinthians 15:26). All other suffering can be considered as "elementary or minor" deaths because the greatest and last of all the sufferings is death. Our Lord went through that greatest suffering. After death no person can be accused by the Law because that person no longer lives. Our Lord died our death so the Law may not have power over us to accuse us. "Christ redeemed us from the curse of the Law by becoming a curse for us, for it is written: 'Cursed is everyone who is hung on a tree' " (Galatians 3:13).

In this sense the Christian's life is an eschatological life. Although Christians live on this earth bodily, they also share an eschatological life, the life of the resurrection. The apostle Paul again says in describing this fact, "I have been crucified with Christ and I no longer live, but Christ lives in me. The life I live in the body, I live by faith in the Son of God, who loved me and gave Himself for me. I do not set aside the grace of God, for if righteousness could be gained through the Law, Christ died for nothing!" (Galatians 2:20–21). Therefore, the cross of Christ enables the believer to share the new life, the life of the world to come, the life of righteousness and the kingdom of God. This "realized eschatology," however, reaches its final and complete stage when one passes from this world of time and space to the next world. Not only human beings wait for the final and complete consummation, where the limitations of time and space cannot hinder. The whole creation is eagerly waiting for that day (Romans 8:18–22).

CONCLUSION

The cross of Christ has a multifaceted and holistic relevance on personal, communal, national, and cosmic levels. For those who have the eye to see and the sense to understand its meaning, over and beyond its apparent weakness, the cross gives the ultimate answer to the human quest. In fact it is the answer for understanding reality and our existence. It is through the cross of Christ and His resurrection that we can make sense of the present world and our own existence. The cross of Christ and His resurrection gives us hope amid suffering and a seemingly hopeless world (Romans 8:31–39). The theology of the cross gives us the motivation to work positively for righteousness, peace, and reconciliation. In short it is the heartbeat and center of our existence. The cross is the most important signpost for our witness in the twenty-first century. That is why the apostle Paul confessed, "For I resolved to know nothing while I was with you except Jesus Christ and Him crucified" (1 Corinthians 2:2).

NOTES

1. William Barclay, *The Gospel of Mark* (Edinburgh: St. Andrew, 1975), 360. Cf. also the study note on Mark 15:21 in *The New International Version Study Bible* (Grand Rapids: Zondervan, 1995), 1526.

2. "Cross," *The New International Dictionary of New Testament Theology* (ed. Colin Brown; Grand Rapids: Zondervan, 1975), 1:392.

3. Martin Hengel, *Crucifixion in the Ancient World and the Folly of the Message of the Cross* (Philadephia: Fortress, 1977).

4. Hengel, *Crucifixion*, 30–31.

5. Tokunboh Adeyemo, *Salvation in African Tradition* (Nairobi: Evangel, 1997), 33–35.

6. The Oromo's of the Adama Bosset area sacrifice to appease and pray to Wakayo, their god. After the animal is killed, its blood is sprinkled on the trunk of the tree, the green grass, and the people. Some of the meat is roasted to be eaten by the people after a little is burned as a sacrifice to *Wakayo.* Cf. Girmay Tekle, "Socio-Cultural Analysis of Adama Bosset District" (unpublished paper, July 2000).

7. John S. Mbiti, *Introduction to African Religion* (2d ed.; Nairobi: East African Educational Publishers, 1991), 63.

8. John Parratt, ed., *A Reader in African Christian Theology* (London: SPCK, 1987), 87.

9. Tetemke Yohanise Shonde, *The World View of Wolaita and Attempts to Contextualize the Gospel* (2000), 48.

10. An Ethiopian woman who was eight months pregnant was martyred by fanatic local people who belonged to the traditional Ethiopian Orthodox Church when she confessed Jesus Christ and became an evangelical Christian. This occurred in Amoute in the Gurage region. Cf. Shiferawu Zeleke, *The Martyrs of Amoute* (Bachelor of Theology Paper; Mekane Yesus Seminary, Ethiopia). The gifted Ethiopian solo singer Tesfaye Gabiso and his friends were imprisoned for seven years in the Yirgalem Prison in Southern Ethiopia because they confessed that "Jesus is Lord." These events took place under the Communist regime in Ethiopia during 1974–1991.

11. Hannah W. Kinoti and John M. Waliggo, eds., *The Bible in African Christianity* (Nairobi: Acton, 1997), 124.

12. Kinoti and Waliggo, *Bible in African Christianity*, 124.

13. Jon Sobrino, *Christology at the Crossroads* (Maryknoll: Orbis, 1978), 201.

14. "Soul," *Dictionary of New Testament Theology*, 3:680.

15. LW 31:52. Cf. WA 1:361f. See also Paul Althaus, *The Theology of Martin Luther* (Philadelphia: Fortress, 1966), 25.

16. Althaus, *Theology of Martin Luther*, 30.

17. Althaus, *Theology of Martin Luther*, 30.

18. John R. W. Stott, *The Cross of Christ* (Downers Grove: InterVarsity, 1986), 336–37.

FOR FURTHER READING

Adeyemo, Tokunboh. *Salvation in African Tradition*. Nairobi: Evangel, 1979.

Althaus, Paul. *The Theology of Martin Luther*. Philadelphia: Fortress, 1966.

Aulén, Gustaf. *Christus Victor*. New York: Macmillan, 1969.

Gruchy, John W., and Charles Villa-Vicencio, eds. *Doing Theology in Context: South African Perspectives*. Vol. 1. Maryknoll: Orbis; Cape Town: David Philip, 1994.

Hengel, Martin. *Crucifixion in the Ancient World and the Folly of the Message of the Cross*. Philadelphia: Fortress, 1977.

Kinoti, Hannah W., and John M. Waliggo, eds. *The Bible in African Christianity*. Nairobi: Acton, 1997.

Mbiti, John S. *Introduction to African Religion*. 2d ed. Nairobi: East African Educational Publishers, 1991.

Parratt, John, ed. *A Reader in African Christian Theology*. London: SPCK, 1987.

Stott, John R. W. *The Cross of Christ*. Downers Grove: InterVarsity, 1986.

———. *Issues Facing Christians Today*. 2d ed. London: Marshall Pickering, 1990.

8

The Witness of the Cross in Post-Marxist Russia

PAUL E. MUENCH

Boris Pasternak's novel about the Russian Revolution portrays important contrasts in one's understanding of Russia. Dr. Zhivago struggles with the brutal disruptions of war, searching to find peace and hope for the future. Life as he knew it disappeared, mangled in the bloody jaws not only of war, but of political eruptions. Zhivago is still Russian. He still lives in Russia. Yet he is a displaced person.

Komarovsky, a bureaucrat in czarist Russia, also struggles with the disruptions of war. He, too, wants peace and hope for the future. Komarovsky is still Russian. He also lives in Russia. However, unlike Zhivago, he is not a displaced person. Yes, Komarovsky now, after the revolution, lives in another part of Russia, but his position in life is much the same as it was before the revolution. His ability to manipulate the system, his ability to get what he wants from people, and his self-understanding are little changed.

After the revolution, Zhivago's whole world is changed. Komarovsky's whole world is much the same.

To discuss a theology of the cross in a post-Marxist Russia, we must be aware of the tensions that exist. What is a Marxist context? Is it the context envisioned in the idealism of Marx, or is it the reality of

Russia in the 1990s? Is Marxism only a veneer through which we can clearly see the realities of the Russian world?

Certainly the Marxist experience has changed the people of Russia. Yet upon closer examination, we find many Russian cultural values intact. Marxism used some of the values and opposed others, yet the core values are still much as they were before Marx. While we can be confident in the continuity of the Russian and Chinese cultures, we would misunderstand these people if we did not take into account the impact of Marxism on the people. Russia is still Russia; however, Russia has changed. Which world will we examine? Will we look at Zhivago's world? Will we look at Komarovsky's world. Is there a reality that combines both these worlds? When we ask outreach questions, the world of Zhivago and Komarovsky come together. Both are Russian realities.

Because of the limited length of this essay, the background and expertise of the writer, and the pioneering nature of the topic, this essay will focus on only a few issues crucial to outreach in modern Russia. These three foci will cycle us through the topic: (1) theology of the cross, (2) Marxism, and (3) Russian society. By cycle we mean that we will return to each of these topics several times until we bring them together at the conclusion. It is intended that this cycle will clarify the message a theology of the cross would communicate to the people of Russia today.

THE THEOLOGY OF THE CROSS

The theology of the cross talks of the hidden God who has chosen to reveal Himself on the cross. "The theology of the cross is a theology of revelation."[1] The cross is the focal point of this theology not only because it is the symbol of Jesus' suffering and death on our behalf, but also because it hides God behind suffering and reveals Him in the suffering of Jesus. God enters the concealment of humiliation, suffering, and death so He can be revealed.

> The hidden God is none other than the revealed God. God is hidden for the sake of revelation. Revelation is possible only in concealment, the revealed God as such must be hidden . . . Man hides his own things in order to deny them, God hides his own things in order to reveal them. . . . By this concealment he does nothing else than remove that which obstructs revelation, namely pride.[2]

When we attempt to find God anywhere but in the crucified Christ, we are relying on our human abilities to discover God. Any effort by humans to establish who God is and what God is places the

140

human being above God in rebellion. We can only know God as He reveals Himself. And God has chosen to hide Himself and to reveal Himself in the suffering and death of Jesus. It is only by faith, which God in His grace gives to us through Word and Sacrament, that we see the God of the universe dying for us on the cross.

MARXISM

To quickly get to the core issues of the theology of the cross in post-Marxist Russia, it is helpful to discuss Marxism as a faith system. Ninian Smart, in a book on world religions, includes Marxism as a religion. Smart says Marxism has a coherent set of doctrines, rituals, and institutions that invite adherence to this faith.[3] Marx never intended his writings to be a philosophy or a faith system. His social theory held that philosophy and religion would end. When society was on a firmer foundation because of the revolutions he predicted, it would no longer need either.[4] Although Marx never intended his writings to be a faith system, they quickly blossomed into a number of systems. Lenin was the dominant figure in Russia. Lenin based his "orthodoxy" on the writings of Engels and Plekhanov.[5]

At the heart of Marxism is dialectical materialism. Marx and his followers believe that no stage in history will be permanent because a contradictory force unleased by the dialectic will challenge the existing order and produce a new synthesis through structural change. This will continue until the final utopia, communism, is reached.[6] There is a tension in the Marxist faith between the inevitability of the dialectic process and the involvement of humans in bringing about the eventual utopia. The tension is similar to the tension between predestination and free will. To invite human participation, you must have free will. To have free will, determinism must be "dissociated from connotations of fatalism."[7] "Marx believed that communism would be the final historic stage, producing no antithesis as exploitation would have been ended and classes eliminated."[8] Although this process was to be inevitable, the individual who had faith could speed the process toward its destination.

Although the people of Russia can, in general, recite the creedal statements of Marxism, most people would have a greatly modified and simplified understanding of its promise. The mandatory memorization of doctrines and slogans produced in the faithful a glimmer of hope for the future. As real-life indicators erased evidence of positive change, hope faded. As hope faded, more and more Russians resented the Marxist sayings. The people of Russia hoped for real change. As the communist experience dragged on, it became increasingly evident to most people that there had been and would be little real change from the czarist rule. The promised utopia was not coming. Communism would bring no real change to Russian society.

RUSSIAN SOCIETY

While Prime Minister Boris Yeltsin was awaiting heart surgery, there was much speculation concerning who might be the next leader of Russia. To learn more about the people, I asked a number of my Russian friends to tell me which potential successor they would prefer. I found the responses interesting and surprising. I found the response of Valerie, who worked as my translator, especially interesting. His answer was typical of those I polled but different from the answer I expected. I felt I knew Valerie relatively well. In addition to being in the classroom together, Valerie and I traveled together to and from the seminaries at which I taught. This gave us much time to interact.

Valerie spent a year in the United States earning a master's degree from Concordia Seminary, St. Louis, Missouri. He enjoyed the time in the United States and appreciated the firsthand experience in the culture and language he studied. He returned to the United States several times to serve as a translator for Russian church leaders. However, English was Valerie's third language. He preferred to translate from Swedish to Russian. Valerie had also spent time in Sweden and often expressed a wish to immigrate to Sweden. This description of Valerie is meant to underline his interaction with and understanding of the world outside Russia. In fact, Valerie was not uncritical of Russia.

> When I asked Valerie of his choice for Yeltsin's successor, he replied, "General Lebed."
>
> "But, Valerie," I probed, "do you know the political philosophy of General Lebed?"
>
> "Yes, I do," he replied.
>
> Surprised, I pushed for clarification. "Do you know that General Lebed would model his regime after that of Pinochet, the dictator of Chile?"
>
> "Oh, yes, I know," replied Valerie.
>
> "Valerie, do you know that lots of people disappeared during the night when Pinochet was in power?"
>
> "Yes, I know. To be a strong leader you must do those things."

I was surprised by Valerie's choice of a potential leader and even more by his understanding of that choice. I assumed that his understanding of me, of Americans, and of Western peoples meant that he was assuming our worldview. This was a wrong assumption. Valerie's Russian worldview, though challenged and slightly modified, remained very much intact. If I wanted to understand Valerie, I would need to learn more about the Russian worldview.

Strong leadership and dictatorial leadership is all that has been known in the history of Russia. Attitudes about and acceptance of such leadership are embedded in the Russian worldview. This part of the Russian worldview helps us to understand that nation's openness to Marxism and how it was imposed by Lenin, Stalin, and their successors.

Another part of the Russian worldview important to our discussion is an understanding of Russian hermeneutics. While teaching an introduction to biblical hermeneutics at the Lutheran seminary in Novosaratovka, I was shocked by how quickly students would drift into allegorical interpretations. I know Christianity came to Russia from the East, bringing with it a more mystical approach. I know that the Russian Orthodox Church kept and strengthened this mystical tradition. However, none of my students had been members of the Russian Orthodox Church. And there had been 70 years of "secular" Communism to disrupt the dominating influence of the church. Why did allegory maintain such a strong grip on my students? As I wrestled with this, I rephrased the question. I asked, "How did my students learn to interpret almost everything allegorically?" This question guided me in a search for teachers. I found the teachers not in the traditional classroom, but in the political process.

During the Soviet era, at every level of society, leaders articulated the slogans of Communism. The idealistic projections of Marxism, however, would have soon died without some real movement, some accomplishments. Those leaders faithful to the Marxist dream were anxious to show results. Less faithful leaders used the dreams of Marxism to manipulate the people. Also some of the lower-level leaders repeated the rhetoric of the major leaders, fearing a loss of position and even life if they did not.

How did this teach allegory? As the Soviet regime aged, the rhetoric was increasingly out of touch with reality. More and more of the rhetoric was either simply not true or needed to be understood allegorically. When the leader proclaimed, "We have the highest standard of living in the world. We are on the way to utopia," the citizen had little choice as to how such statements should be interpreted. When you stand in line to buy bread, when the plumbing in your building hasn't worked in six months, when there are four families living in an apartment meant for only one family, it is difficult to interpret the leader's words literally.

However, those who listened soon learned there was meaning to the rhetoric. The literal meaning was not the key. The important meaning for day-to-day living was allegorical. By listening for key words and by listening to the tone and manner of the speech, the listeners learned important things about their freedom and safety. A certain style meant there would be a crackdown. It meant that until there were other indications you should be careful to follow literally all of the rules and expectations of the system. However, another set of words, gestures, and other nonverbal communication would indicate a period of fewer restrictions and more personal freedom.

Most Russians who heard the Soviet claims of the best standard of living and the greatest society realized the claims were not literally true. A few believed them to be projections. However, every Russian wanted to know what tomorrow would bring. Because the Soviet government controlled so much of life, clues to the attitudes of its leaders were important. Under the rhetoric about the good life in the Soviet Union, the people found, hidden in allegory, clues to indicate the current government attitude. As you grew up in the Soviet Union and were exposed to the rhetoric of the leadership, you were taught by your family and friends the allegorical method of interpretation.

THEOLOGY OF THE CROSS: MYSTICISM

Our discussion of the Russian tendency to interpret allegorically forms a natural bridge to the topic of mysticism. Allegory is an attempt to get behind the meaning of spoken words to find a deeper, higher, more significant meaning. Mysticism has a strong history in Russian society. If the theology of the cross is to have an impact in Russia today, it must have something to say to mysticism. Mysticism, however, is not simply a pre-Soviet phenomenon. One can certainly argue that there was a strong mystical tradition in the practice of Marxism in Russia.

To provide a background for our discussion of mysticism in Russian society, we will compare mysticism and the theology of the cross. Because of the societal and church influences of his time, Luther provides us with helpful insights because he also had to deal with mysticism. In addition, mysticism dominated much of monastic practice in the Middle Ages. If we are to talk about the theology of the cross in post-Marxist Russia, an understanding of the relationship of mysticism to the theology of the cross will be helpful.

We will not trace the many mystical influences surrounding Luther as a medieval monk. It is enough for our purposes to highlight the contrasts between the theology of the mystic and the theology of the cross. Although Luther does occasionally use allegorical interpretation, the mystic uses allegory almost exclusively. For example, when you compare the sermons of Luther to those of the leading mystic of the late Middle Ages, Tauler, Tauler's method is always allegorical.[9] The allegorical method of interpretation is a fitting tool for the mystic because the mystic is trying to find God in the innermost depths of the soul. Allegory allows the mystic to go beyond the obvious meaning of the words recorded in Scripture.

The mystic of Luther's time followed a prescribed method to bring about the birth of God in the soul. The mystic begins with a contemplation of the life and suffering of Jesus. However, in the next step, considered the "critical point" on the road to salvation, the mystic leaves behind what can be comprehended by normal human senses. It is also at this point that suffering and trials attack in full force. The mystic truly reaches this second stage when he no longer seeks advice or help from any human. He does not run away from himself but seeks God in his own soul.[10] Sufferings and trials are birth pangs. The third step, which can only be reached through complete resignation, is the birth of God in the soul. Tauler and other mystics thought highly of suffering and passivity while suffering. They considered this the short way (*via compendii*) to the mystical birth.[11] But for the mystic, there is even more. The final step is achieved when the mystic is submerged in God. There the human spirit, "the created nothing," submerges in the "uncreated nothing."[12]

Even the new piety (*devotio moderna*) of Thomas á Kempis does not go beyond the bounds of medieval mysticism. For Thomas á Kempis, the cross is humanity's way to God and not God's means to come to humanity.[13] The theology of the mystic is distinctly a theology of glory and is incompatible with the theology of the cross. "Luther rejects the speculative elements of mysticism."[14] The theology of the cross is the sharpest form of protest against mysticism. The theology of the cross is an antithesis to mysticism. The theology of the cross insists that God takes the initiative, God comes to human beings.

The problem with mysticism is that when we try to uncover the depths of God, we place ourselves in a position above God. If our efforts are able to bring us to an understanding of God, then God is not beyond us. When the mystic is reduced to "nothing," he becomes something because he finds the spark of the soul, he finds God. The theology of the cross knows of no such spark of the divine. The theology of the cross speaks of God's self-revelation, not of discovering the divine. "Revelation addresses itself to faith, not to sight, not to reflective reason.[15]

MARXISM AND MYSTICISM

It is well established that Christian values strongly influenced the conceptions that developed into Marxism-Leninism. It makes sense that people coming out of a long Christian tradition would borrow or attempt to transcend that tradition. Also Christians were among those who were most articulate and most capable of leading opposition to the Marxist movement. It makes sense that the movement would compare itself to Christianity. "Lenin Russified Marxism and developed the Bolshevik religion out of his country's influential nineteenth century Christian socialist mode of thought; themes of suffering, the Third Rome (as the spiritual heir to Rome and Constantinople) and the sacredness of the Kremlin were thus incorporated into the Soviet system."[16]

Although the Russian Communist leadership was always anti-Christian, it was also always interacting with Christianity and being challenged by the ideals of Christianity. This interaction is not difficult to trace, and sometimes it is quite apparent, even to the Communists themselves. Leon Onikov, a career activist and ideologist within the Communist Party of the Soviet Union, declared shortly before its political demise: "The ideas of socialism were first formulated by Jesus Christ in the New Testament."[17] Because there is a strong mystic tradition in Russian Christianity, it makes sense to look for such an influence in the Marxist experience in Russia. Arthur Jay Klinghoffer maintains there is a strong connection between the mystic tradition and Marxism in Russia.

> Bolshevism was similar to Sectarianism, a conglomeration of mystical Old Believer groups that split off from Orthodoxy beginning in 1666 plus denominations of non-Russian origin such as the Baptists and Jehovah's Witnesses. In fact, Fueloep-Miller goes so far as to claim that Leninism was actually Sectarianism cloaked in Marxist ideology as a means of concealing its religious nature.[18]

Because we in the West know little about the Old Believer groups in Russia, the connection to Marxism sounds farfetched. However, a comparison of beliefs quickly makes the claim more plausible.

> The Sectarians sought earthly salvation, stressed equality, opposed serfdom, and rejected private property. They believed that property would negate the spiritual struggle against the Anti-Christ and delay the millennium as man would become too materialistic. Their views surely helped predispose Russia to socialist values.[19]

The beliefs of the Sectarians were well known to Lenin through a close relationship with Vladimir Bonch-Bruevich. Bonch-Bruevich worked for a Christian socialist journal. He also traveled to Canada in 1899 with a Sectarian group known as the Dukhobors. Bonch-Bruevich asked Lenin and the Bolsheviks to make a special appeal to the Sectarians. He felt they were peasants poised to become proletarians.

> Bonch-Bruevich maintained that Sectarians were collectivist and millinarian, and hoped to defeat the tsarist Anti-Christ in preparation for an earthly Kingdom of God. He advised that the groups most susceptible to Bolshevik entreaties were the Dukhobors and Khlysty, both mystical sects, as well as the Jehovah's Witnesses and Neo-Shtundists. Lenin's resolution was approved, and Bonch-Bruevich was authorized to publish a journal directed at the Sectarians.[20]

Not only was the Russian Marxist movement similar to some goals of mystic groups, it also developed mystic practices of its own. The most obvious of these practices was the icon corner. Relics of Marxism—pictures of Lenin and Stalin and other artifacts—were displayed in the same way the Russian Orthodox faithful displayed icons of saints.

> "Lenin corners" appeared at military facilities, schools, museums, factories and apartment buildings as the Lenin cult got underway; this form of exhibition was reminiscent of saints' corners which presented items associated with these hallowed individuals. Displayed pictures of Lenin were highly stylized in terms of expression, pose and gesture as in saintly icons.[21]

The Polish philosopher Leszek Kolakowski describes the Marxist "religious" practices of the late Stalin period. He says, "All of the forms of popular religiosity were revived in a distorted shape: icons, processions, prayers recited in chorus, confession (under the name of self-criticism), the cult of relics."[22] Perhaps these outward practices only reflect the mystical nature embedded in Marxism. Marx believed in the basic goodness of humanity and, therefore, that it would be possible for human beings to evolve to perfection. Although Marx believed the utopian state of Communism was inevitable, he was not a fatalist. That is, Marx allowed for the participation of human beings in the process of bringing about the final utopia.

This "participation in salvation" ironically receives its most public expression in the deification of Lenin. "Fundamental to Russian culture was the Christian theme of enduring suffering on the road to salvation, which may be likened to Marx's interpretation of the working class' enmiseration."[23] Lenin was seen to be like the Starsky (mystics). He, through suffering, was reaching a higher state.

> As Lenin's health declined, a devotional cult claimed that he was robust. Furthermore, the term "Leninism" was coined in an effort to elevate his pronouncements; the communist party newspaper *Pravda*, in a passage imbued with Christianity, declared: "Lenin is the suffering for an idea; it is bleeding for the proletariat." In July 1923, a Lenin Institute was established to study his thought and, the following month, an economic exhibition included a "Lenin corner" filled with memorabilia which could be perused by visiting peasants. It was arranged similarly to icon corners in their homes. The eulogizing of Lenin had begun, but he was still clinging to life.[24]

RUSSIAN SOCIETY AND MYSTICISM

Although Russian society has undergone much trauma in its recent history, and the mystical influence of Leninism is no longer dominant, mysticism still has a strong influence in the life of most Russians. A mystical approach to life can be seen in religion, politics, family values, and most areas of Russian life.

While teaching a Bible class in the town of Sevolusk, about 11 kilometers outside of St. Petersburg, I had the opportunity to learn about Russian family life. Through visits to homes, Bible class discussions, and my seminary experiences, I came to see the strong mystical tradition in the lives of the Russian people.

A key turning point in the Bible class experience was a student-initiated discussion of the role of Mary in the life of faith. On the night we were scheduled to discuss the role of Mary in the church, one student brought a guest with some formal training in Russian Orthodox doctrine, a background of which I was unaware. This guest insisted our prayers were to be directed to Mary. He spelled out the process required to make ourselves acceptable to God. As this guest became increasingly vocal, I patiently witnessed to the fact that Christ has done everything for us.

During the next three weeks, when the role of Mary kept reentering the discussion, the class members asked primarily about what they needed to do to be saved. The student who had invited the guest was the most vocal and most insistent that Mary was more than a special human being. The class members were somewhat embarassed by the discussion because it was usually unacceptable to challenge a teacher. However, the discussion continued because (1) when I began the class, I had asked the students to evaluate everything I said on the basis of

Scripture. I suggested that this was necessary to find out whether I was really interested in them or was only an outsider who wanted to dominate them. (2) The students were also personally interested in the topic because of the prominent place given to Mary in the Russian Orthodox Church. (3) The students were fascinated (several personally told me) by my gentle but firm affirmation that we are saved by grace through faith in Jesus, the Christ. And (4) the students were genuinely curious about what this "faith in Jesus" approach meant in their life.

The climax to the discussion of Mary came in the third week. After a number of additional questions about faith, this woman who had been so vocal about Mary confessed that Jesus had saved her and there was nothing more required. Immediately, she relaxed, the class relaxed, and the focus changed. From that point, the questions shifted from the mystical "How can I improve?" variety to questions about faith. For these people, Mary seemed to embody the mystical "God needs my help to reach me" approach. Once it was understood and believed that Jesus has done it all, there was a different attitude toward Bible study.

The people in this Bible class were young couples in their 30s. My experience leads me to believe that their mystical approach to religion is typical of most Russian people. Certainly any Russians who call themselves Orthodox, and most Russians do, will tend to approach God as a mystic would. Orthodox tradition is steeped in mysticism. "For the Orthodox themselves, however, loyalty to Tradition means not primarily the acceptance of formulae or customs from past generations, but rather the ever-new, personal and direct experience of the Holy Spirit in the present, here and now."[25] As this quote from Bishop Ware indicates, contemporary Orthodoxy is still mystical. God's message to human beings comes from "inner revelation," not primarily from the external revelation of Scripture. Whether we label it mystical or intuitive, Russian decision-making is much affected by this approach. Deciding who is the best leader, deciding what is important for the family, and even making business decisions will be influenced by the "look within."

THE THEOLOGY OF THE CROSS AND SUFFERING

Suffering is an important issue to discuss as we attempt to understand the theology of the cross in post-Marxist Russia. The Russian mystic assumed suffering needed to be a part of the "search within." Suffering, perhaps through its central place in Russian cultural values, became a part of the Marxist view of life. Because God enters the concealment of humiliation, suffering, and death so He can be revealed, any discussion of a theology of the cross is already a discussion of suffering. In our discussion, however, we want to focus on human suffering and its relationship to the theology of the cross.

"Take up [your] cross and follow Me" (Matthew 16:24) is the saying of Jesus often used to justify human suffering. This passage is interpreted as an invitation to take on suffering as the means of following Jesus. Certainly the passage is an invitation to follow Jesus. However, the passage does not sanction suffering as the road to saving yourself. The whole context of Matthew 16:24 deals with Jesus' identity. Verse 16 of this chapter records Peter's confession, "You are the Christ, the Son of the living God." To further clarify His identity, Jesus tells His disciples about the suffering and death He will experience. Peter objects because, for him, suffering and death cannot be a part of the identity of the Messiah. The invitation to take up our cross may involve suffering, but the primary substance of the invitation is to be identified with Jesus. Forget about yourself. Identify with Jesus. This is the invitation.

Luther is adamant that voluntarily courting suffering is wrong.[26] Our suffering is of no benefit to God. It earns nothing from God. Therefore, it also has no inherent benefit for us. Suffering is pain. It hurts. Suffering came into the world because of sin. Suffering is not inherently a blessing from God. However, suffering can have a positive place in the life of the Christian. Suffering becomes positive not because the Christian suffers but because of what God does. Luther says, "God shows His mastery (*kunst*) by making something out of nothing, piety out of sin, life and holiness out of death."[27] Suffering has value only as God makes something positive out of it.

Trouble, temptation, and suffering come because of evil in the world. Through His suffering and death, Jesus brought about new life. Now, though suffering still is inherently a part of the evil in the world, it can bring about good things for the Christian. Christ intervenes in the life of His followers to make pain and suffering into a blessing. God often turns the evil of pain and suffering into a positive, faith-building experience for the Christian.

Life under the cross is often a life of suffering because in having been given the identity of Jesus, we are also opposed by the enemies of Jesus. The author of death and suffering now attacks the Christian because of the Christian's new identity. The cross of Christ and the cross of the Christian belong together because the Christian now has the identity of Christ.

MARXISM AND SUFFERING

Fundamental to Russian culture was the Christian theme of enduring suffering on the road to salvation, which may be likened to Marx's interpretation of the working class enmiseration. Dostoyevsky's works provide ample evidence of this cultural trait, and former American communist, Whittaker Chambers, maintains that endless suffering was so accentuated that it appeared to be a "secret virtue."[28]

For Marxism to have been successful at any period during its sojourn on Russian soil, it needed to deal with the issue of suffering. The transformation from czarist regime to Marxist regime was immerged in suffering. The magnitude of the suffering that was endured is difficult to comprehend. The transition to a collective society brought about unbelievable periods of disease and starvation. Without a metaphysical explanation for suffering, the Marxist regime in Russia would not have survived.

The Lenin cult received some of its momentum when Lenin was portrayed as a martyr for the people. The Communist party newspaper proclaimed, "Lenin is the suffering for an idea; it is bleeding for the proletariat."[29] The common people were encouraged to follow Lenin's model behavior. The people were to endure suffering patiently on the road to utopia. Their suffering was thought to speed progress toward the perfect society.

RUSSIAN SOCIETY AND SUFFERING

Suffering has been a relative constant in the life of the Russian people. Although greatly amplified during Soviet times, suffering is consistently a part of the Russian experience. Because there is not space to trace the history of suffering in Russia, a few descriptions will help us understand.

Suffering was imposed by the harsh climate, but much more suffering came through politics and war. The widespread oppression of the Mongol occupation was finally ended by the harsh and unpredictable Ivan the Terrible. Ivan's brutality was legendary. A part of his legacy is the secret police. From the time of Ivan to the present, Russian leaders have kept a strong and brutal secret police force. The Soviet KGB added only modern techniques to a system that already had been in place for more than 400 years.

The Soviet period, however, may be unique in Russian history because it provided little relief during its seven decades. It is hardly an exaggeration to say a river of blood flows through this period in Russian history. Russia suffered more than nine million casualties during World War I. The Bolshevik Revolution began even before World War I had ended. The internal struggles between those who deposed the Czar killed another two to four million people. "In the countryside, the Bolsheviks organized Committees of the Village Poor and sent out workers and soldiers from the cities to seize grain. Peasant revolts swept the countryside, and the civil war became a peasant war. . . . Over 7 million people died from hunger and epidemics; cannibalism spread."[30]

Lenin wrote a secret memorandum to his Politburo colleagues on March 19, 1922. He wrote with "brutal candor" about his plans to seize the valuables of the Orthodox church. Lenin called the opportunity "exceptionally beneficial" because the desperation of the situation could be used to the advantage of the new regime.

> It is precisely now and only now, when there is cannibalism . . . and corpses are lying along the roads that we can (and therefore must) carry out the confiscation of valuables with fanatical and merciless energy . . . No other opportunity but the current terrible famine will give us a mood of the wide masses such as would provide us with their sympathies or at least neutrality . . . Now our victory over the reactionary clergy is guaranteed . . . The trial of the Shuya rioters for resisting aid to the hungry (should) be conducted in as short a time as possible, concluding in the maximum numbers of executions. . . . If possible, similar executions should be carried out in Moscow and other spiritual centers of the country.[31]

The purges of Stalin are famous for the numbers of people executed or sent to suffer in Siberia. However, there was also other suffering. Although Stalin temporarily reined in the collectivization drive in March 1930, pressures on the peasants soon resumed, and a man-made famine spread. It reached appalling proportions in the Ukraine and the northern Caucasus in 1932. At least five million people died from hunger and attendant diseases. A Soviet demographer noted a population loss of more than seven million. In his memoirs, Nikita Khrushchev described how trains pulled into Kiev loaded with the corpses of people who had starved to death; railroad workers had picked them up along the route from Poltava. The rivers of the northern Caucasus carried thousands of bodies to the sea.[32]

The purges of Stalin come quickly on the heels of the famine. The suffering of the purges is different only because it also took many individuals who had been faithful to the Communist cause.

> It may be remembered that on December 1, 1934, a shot in the back had killed the Leningrad Communist Party chief, Sergei M. Kirov. The circumstances of the murder lent credence to the

probability that it was Stalin himself who had inspired the deed. Nevertheless, while "investigating" the crime Stalin had the secret police interrogate and torture an ever-widening circle of people. Of the members of the Central Committee of the Communist Party elected at the 1934 congress, more than two-thirds had perished by 1938. In the great purge trials, the towering figures of Lenin's time were forced to confess treasonous crimes, and most were executed. The commander-in-chief of the army, every officer who commanded a military district or an army corps, almost every division commander, and close to half of the 75,000 Red Army officers were arrested and shot. An estimated 19 million Soviet citizens died in the terror.[33]

The Stalin purges were interrupted by World War II. However, the suffering of the Russian people only continued. It is difficult to know the number of dead. At least four million soldiers died during the war, but there were also many other deaths. The siege of St. Petersburg (Leningrad) alone killed more than one million people.

Although Khrushchev began his rule by revealing some of the atrocities of Stalin, the Khrushchev regime was not without its periods of suffering. Particularly during the early 1960s, Khrushchev targeted the churches of Russia. From 1958 to 1966, Khrushchev managed to close 44 percent of the churches that had been functioning in 1958. This often included banishment of the clergy to Siberia.

I talked with many families during my travels while living in Russia. There are few families that were not directly affected by the tragedies. Nicolai's family is typical. His grandfather fought for Russia in World War I. When the Russian front collapsed and Russian soldiers returned home, Nicolai's grandfather expected to come safely home. Instead, he was arrested and shot for being a bourgeoisie. Nicolai's grandmother spent three days pulling apart piles of corpses until she found the body of her husband so she could give him a proper burial. Nicolai's parents lived through the great purge of Stalin. They knew of people who had disappeared from their community. There seemed to be no reasonable explanation as to who was taken and who remained. Each night they were fearful they would be the next to disappear. Nicolai was in grade school in 1953 when Stalin died. He remembers the desperate grieving he and his classmates felt at the death of the great and beloved leader of Russia. Nicolai remembers crying uncontrollably at the news of Stalin's death. "You see," Nicolai told me, "my parents never told me what happened to my grandfather. They never told me about the purges. Bit by bit and piece by piece I found out the truth over the next forty years."

And the suffering continues. There was much suffering as the Communist system came apart. In any other country there would have been mass riots and looting during the food shortages of the Gorbachev years. The Yeltsin years brought unbelievable inflation. Before the collapse of the Soviet Union, the Russian currency, the ruble, was valued as equal to the American dollar. (This was an artificial valuation maintained by the Russian government. However, the Russian ruble could buy the equivalent of an American dollar if Russian-made products were purchased.) If in 1990 a Russian had saved 20,000 rubles to purchase a new automobile but couldn't do so because there was no car available, inflation would have soon made such a purchase impossible, even if a car were available. By the time I arrived in Russia in 1996, the same 20,000 rubles would buy only a toaster. By the time I left Russia in 1999, the same 20,000 rubles would buy only a loaf of bread. Most Russians lost all their savings to inflation.

It might be argued that the Marxist philosophy was finally rejected by most Russian people because suffering became too common. In traditional Russian society suffering was glorified when it was thought to build character. Suffering was courted by those considered to be most spiritual because it was thought to be an important step on the road to redemption. During Soviet times, it became increasingly difficult to ignore the fact that suffering is simply the result of evil.

Russian Marxist ideology could so easily point to suffering as redemptive because the concept has a long history in Russia. The monastic tradition in Russia glorifies the experience of suffering as an important step on the road to enlightenment. "In general the type of a suffering just man, a kind of Christian Job, has flowered richly in Russia . . . It can even be considered as representative of all popular Russian piety at its best."[34]

The Russian people sought out those who suffered, expecting special advice and guidance. One example is Mikhail Bezrukov, a peasant who lived in the district of Ufa and died at the end of the nineteenth century.

> He . . . had been struck suddenly in the flower of his age by a paralysis, after exhausting himself in the field, and his body became covered with sores. He suffered terribly, was unable to move, and at the moments of sharpest pain would murmur against God. Then a moral change took place: he accepted his suffering, and little by little he became the shining centre of an intense religious life. Inhabitants of the village and people from the most distant places came to ask his counsel, and to seek his prayers.[35]

The voluntary sufferer was much admired by the people of Russia. Radical asceticism still existed in Russia in the nineteenth century.

> . . . cases of the renunciation of all the advantages of life, the renunciation of his social rank, family, fortune; but without entrance into the monastic life, for this was the rejection of all forms of life accepted and venerated by the world. There were then cases of total renunciation, where the holder of an honoured position would descend to the bottom of the social scale (so clearly stratified in Russia) and mix with simple people, with the poor among the non-priviledged classes, and would become one with them, even poorer than they, having no home, no means, no family, no position however, modest. Such people might become simple pilgrims without a place to sleep, or poor labourers who would divide their life between work and prayer.[36]

There is even a still more radical tradition. "Fools for Christ" was a title given to ascetics who thought it was not enough to renounce all material possessions of the world. "Fools for Christ," so as not to receive the admiration of people, faked insanity to achieve full surrender.[37] "The pilgrims, the 'idiots,' the 'fools for Christ' (*urodivi Khrista radi*) and the collectors of alms who would travel on foot all over Russia . . . how typical they are of the currents of religious experience in the vast ocean of the people's life!"[38]

And Russia continues to make the news because of suffering. *Parade Magazine*, in its January 28, 2001, issue, speaks of Russia in crisis:

> With the Cold War over, Russia doesn't routinely make the front page anymore. But if you thought all was well, think again. These statistics should give the whole world pause:
>
> • *Meditsinskaya Gazeta*, a medical journal, reports that just 10 % of Russian babies today are born healthy.
>
> • Alchohol-related deaths were up 43% in the last year. Among deaths of Russian men 20 to 55 years of age, 66% were alcohol related.
>
> • Russia has 146 suicides each day and a murder rate four times that of the U.S.
>
> • One million Russians become invalids each year.[39]

THE THEOLOGY OF THE CROSS
IN A POST-MARXIST SOCIETY

The cycle through theology of the cross, Marxism, and Russian society, with additional cycles examining mysticism and suffering, were limited and provide only a sketch of the situation in Russia. Yet even this sketch points to some important considerations for outreach in contemporary Russia.

Although to the outsider Putin may be stimulating some hope of stability and even a recovery of glory in modern Russia, the Russian people are more realistic. Their history, recent as well as distant, has implanted a thorough skepticism. This skepticism is not limited to political thought; it is pervasive. The suffering of the Russian people has been too real, too long, too recent, and too widespread. From leaders, sooner or later, comes suffering and loss. Promises of the good life, calls for patience, and patriotic appeals are dismissed as the usual manipulations of self-interested leaders. The Russian people, through their experiences, have developed a penetrating vision. They are able to look through the surface of most human schemes, usually finding them quite empty. This attitude of the Russian people, I believe, explains why there has not been a great surge in the number of Russians active in the churches. The peak of Sunday morning worship attendance occurred during the Gorbachev years, before the official end of Communism. Interest in and attendance at worship has been dropping since that time.

It is my opinion that a meaningful icon to the people of Russia would be the picture of Jesus praying in Gethsemane. Jesus knew the horror He faced. He understood the unmatchable pain that was coming. He was, however, willing to take this pain for the sake of humanity. As the disciples slept, Jesus was already experiencing the emptiness of betrayal. Jesus had no illusions about any glory in suffering. He prayed, "Father, . . . take this cup from Me!" (Luke 22:42a). Yet Jesus took up the cross. He identified with the Father. He affirmed the Father's plan. "Not My will, but Yours be done" (Luke 22:42b). Jesus' suffering in Gethsemane points to the fact that He was deeply committed to our human situation of sin. His suffering is taken willingly to overcome human sin and death. He stands with us and for us in suffering to overcome our suffering and to bring us God's peace.

Much of what has been revived or brought to Russia as Christianity is a theology of glory. Most Russians quickly find in these theological systems a human plan. The promise of a future utopia in exchange for current efforts or even current tolerance is nothing new. Making a "decision" for Christ is most often little different than the choice between a more active or less active part in the local political scene. The choice is made on the basis of immediate gains or losses. Can this leader get me what I want now? Church groups, whether Russian or imported, most often have outside contacts to support a system of giveaways. Pretending to buy into a system has for a long time been the price many people have to pay to receive basic help. It is probable that the decline in church attendance, among other things, is related to the decline in church-organized relief supplies permitted by the Russian government. As there is less interest in Russia from Western churches and as the amount of relief provided declines, it is predicted that church attendance will decline even more.

The Russian Orthodox Church is in a better position because of its long history in Russia. However, its traditional appeal through mysticism has been greatly weakened by the mysticism of the Communist leaders. The body is still in the mausoleum. The resurrection never happened. The experience with Lenin corners and Communist icons left most Russians with a reduced sense of the sacred.

Lutheran efforts have, unfortunately, suffered from the same ailments as other Christian groups. The theology of the cross has often been a clouded message. A Siberian Lutheran pastor provides, for me, the best example of proclaiming a theology of the cross. This pastor began his efforts near a Russian university in Siberia. His proclamation was apparently clear and compelling. Students responded to the message of Christ crucified. Many also became students of this pastor and learned to bring the message of salvation to others. This Russian pastor not only verbally proclaimed a theology of the cross, his entire life supported what he said. He trained Russian pastors using Russian resources to bring the message of Christ crucified to Russian people through Russian ways of communicating.

However, as often happens, because of the growing number of Christians attending the churches started through the work of this pastor, he was noticed. Because he was working in Russian ways, there was, in general, no major problem from the Russian government. The problems came from Americans who wanted to help. The pastor was diverted from his work of mission. While there was more money to do things, many glorious things, the message of Christ was blunted. The personal apprenticeship training gave way to U.S.-style training. Struggling and praying with Russian people to find Russian resources gave way to writing grant requests. Appeals for money clouded the message of repentance. The same young men who had copied the style of the Siberian Lutheran pastor as they learned the theology of the cross were now attempting to follow the Siberian pastor on the glorious path that brought cars, computers, trips to the United States, and subsidized salaries.

Because communication is more than words, the words of this Siberian pastor were drowned in the trappings of success. Although most would be unable to articulate what they were seeing, the Russians began to pull away from this reinvented Siberian Lutheran Church because it became just another manifestation of a theology of glory.

Some of the borrowed U.S. theologians have tried to blend the theology of the cross with traditional Russian mysticism.[40] Whether called theosis or deification, the effort is only a hovering mist. It is an effort to please the ancient monastic tradition by providing room for mysticism and at the same time pleasing those who have ecumenical debts to pay. The cloud raised by such a "mistical" theology is soon recognized by the Russians as a theology of glory.

The theology of the cross is never an imported theology. The God who created has come to live among His people. God knows the people, the language, the conditions of Russia. There, too, God has chosen to come via the manger and the cross. In His grace He considers the swaddling clothes of the Russian culture adequate for the baby in the manger. The message of Jesus is the message of a real historical happening for a real people in a real human context who really need to be saved from eternal damnation. As with any people, the Russian people only exist because God in His grace has kept evil from destroying them. In other words, the good in Russian culture is there only because God created that good. And as God chose to save us via the manger and the cross, He also has chosen to communicate that salvation to us through human forms of communication. In Russia this means through the Russian language and culture.

NOTES

1. Walther von Loewenich, *Luther's Theology of the Cross* (Minneapolis: Augsburg, 1976), 28.

2. Loewenich, *Luther's Theology of the Cross*, 30. Loewenich quotes from the Weimar Edition of Luther's works. Cf. WA 1:38.13ff.

3. Ninian Smart, *The World's Religions* (Englewood Cliffs: Prentice Hall, 1989), 25.

4. Neil McInnes, "Marxist Philosophy," *The Encyclopedia of Philosophy* (ed. Paul Edwards; New York: Macmillan, 1967), 4:173.

5. McInnes, "Marxist Philosophy," 174.

6. Arthur Jay Klinghoffer, *Red Apocalypse: The Religious Evolution of Soviet Communism* (Lanham, Md.: University Press of America, 1996), 16.

7. Klinghoffer, *Red Apocalypse*, 17.

8. Klinghoffer, *Red Apocalypse*, 16.

9. Loewenich, *Luther's Theology of the Cross*, 153.

10. Loewenich, *Luther's Theology of the Cross*, 153.

11. Loewenich, *Luther's Theology of the Cross*, 153.

12. Loewenich, *Luther's Theology of the Cross*, 154.

13. Loewenich, *Luther's Theology of the Cross*, 164.

14. Loewenich, *Luther's Theology of the Cross*, 156.

15. Loewenich, *Luther's Theology of the Cross*, 37.

16. Klinghoffer, *Red Apocalypse*, 4.

17. Klinghoffer, *Red Apocalypse*, 7.

18. Klinghoffer, *Red Apocalypse*, 47.

19. Klinghoffer, *Red Apocalypse*, 47.

20. Klinghoffer, *Red Apocalypse*, 47.

21. Nina Tumarkin, *Lenin Lives! The Lenin Cult in Soviet Russia* (Cambridge: Harvard University Press, 1983), 221–22, 244. This Lenin cult is very much alive and evident in the revival of paganism as a religion in Russia. Cf. Michael Bourdeaux, "In Sacred Groves," *Christian Century* (18 October 2000): 1036–37.

22. Leszek Kolakowski, *Main Currents of Marxism* (Oxford: Clarendon, 1978), 3:147.

23. Klinghoffer, *Red Apocalypse,* 44.

24. Klinghoffer, *Red Apocalypse,* 58.

25. Kallistos Ware, *The Orthodox Way* (Crestwood, N.Y.: St. Vladimir's Seminary Press, 1995), 48.

26. Werner Elert, *The Structure of Lutheranism* (St. Louis: Concordia, 1962), 469.

27. Elert, *Structure of Lutheranism,* 468. Elert quotes WA 24:576.19.

28. Klinghoffer, *Red Apocalypse,* 44.

29. Tumarkin, *Lenin Lives!,* 119–20, 132.

30. Nathaniel Davis, *A Long Walk to Church: A Contemporary History of Russian Orthodoxy* (Boulder, Colo.: Westview, 1995), 3.

31. Davis, *Long Walk to Church,* 3.

32. Davis, *Long Walk to Church,* 5.

33. Davis, *Long Walk to Church,* 11.

34. Nicholas Arseniev, *Russian Piety* (Crestwood, N.Y.: St. Vladimir's Seminary Press, 1975), 106.

35. Arseniev, *Russian Piety*, 107.

36. Arseniev, *Russian Piety*, 107.

37. Arseniev, *Russian Piety*, 110.

38. Arseniev, *Russian Piety*, 108.

39. Lyrid Wallwork Winik, "Russia in Crisis," *Parade Magazine* (28 January 2001).

40. Kurt E. Marquart, "Luther and Theosis," *Concordia Theological Quarterly* 64.3 (July 2000): 182–85.

FOR FURTHER READING

Arseniev, Nicholas. *Russian Piety*. Crestwood, N. Y.: St. Vladimir's Seminary Press, 1975.

Bourdeaux, Michael. "Paganism Revives in Russia: In Sacred Groves." *Christian Century*. 18 October 2000.

Davis, Nathaniel. *A Long Walk to Church: A Contemporary History of Russian Orthdoxy*. Boulder, Colo.: Westview, 1995.

Edwards, Paul, ed. *The Encyclopedia of Philosophy*. New York: Macmillan, 1967. Articles on Marxism and Orthodox Marxism.

Elert, Werner. *The Structure of Lutheranism*. St. Louis: Concordia, 1962.

Klinghoffer, Arthur Jay. *Red Apocalypse: The Religious Evolution of Soviet Communism*. Lanham, Md.: University Press of America, 1996.

Kolakowski, Leszek. *Main Currents of Marxism*. Vol. 3. Oxford: Clarendon, 1978.

Loewenich, Walther von. *Luther's Theology of the Cross*. Minneapolis: Augsburg, 1976.

Marquart, Kurt E. "Luther and Theosis." *Concordia Theological Quarterly* 64.3 (July 2000).

Smart, Ninian. *The World's Religions*. Englewood Cliffs: Prentice Hall, 1989.

Tumarkin, Nina. *Lenin Lives! The Lenin Cult in Soviet Russia*. Cambridge: Harvard University Press, 1983.

Ware, Kallistos. *The Orthodox Way*. Crestwood, N.Y.: St. Vladimir's Seminary Press, 1995.

Winik, Lyric Wallwork. "Russia in Crisis." *Parade Magazine* (January 28, 2001).

PART 3

North American
Themes for Witness

9

Postmodernism under the Cross

GENE EDWARD VEITH

The postmodern era began, according to architectural historian Charles Jencks, at 3:32 P.M. on July 15, 1972.[1] At that moment, the Pruitt-Igoe housing project in St. Louis, Missouri, was blown up. The gargantuan apartment complex—2,800 units in 33 identical 11-story buildings—had been built only 17 years earlier as part of the war on poverty. Social engineers devised the project as part of a scheme to provide low-cost housing to the poor, elevating their condition by allowing them to share in the fruits of twentieth-century progress. Internationally famous modernist architects designed the buildings, following the aesthetic tenet of "form follows function," creating a conglomerate of steel, glass, and masonry boxes, purged of old-fashioned decorative touches, as pure and unadorned as an abstract painting. The award-winning Pruitt-Igoe complex was a monument to human reason, to the ideal of human progress over the retrograde thinking of the past, to humanity's ability to solve its own problems.

Ironically, Pruitt-Igoe became something closer to hell on earth. The featureless, soulless housing complex became more of a warehouse for the poor. Criminals had free reign to terrorize their neighbors. The building's endless corridors became venues for drug-dealing, prostitution, and muggings. Fights, knifings, and murders became commonplace, terrorizing the honest tenants who could not afford to move elsewhere. Less dramatically, those who lived in Pruitt-Igoe had their spirits sapped by the drab, impersonal ugliness of their apartments and the complex as a whole. Soon the halls were filled with trash, routine maintenance was ignored, and the buildings—scarred by graffiti and vandalism—began to fall apart. After many attempts to make things right, including millions of dollars spent on renovations, the authorities decided the problems were unfixable and that they would do better to demolish the whole housing project and try something else. When the explosives were set off and the buildings collapsed, former residents cheered. Despite the architectural awards Pruitt-Igoe had won from modernist critics and the optimistic projections of social engineers, it proved unlivable. The same might be said of modernism as a whole.

On a more global scale, Thomas Oden defines the end of modernism and the birth of postmodernism in terms of other demolition jobs. Modernism was born, he says, with the fall of the Bastille in 1789; it ended and a new era began exactly 200 years later in 1989 with the fall of the Berlin Wall. The French revolution and the Communist revolution were both rationalistic projects to destroy the past and to rebuild society according to grandiose humanist ideologies. For all their liberationist rhetoric and their utopian planning, the French revolution devolved into the Reign of Terror and the reign of Napoleon. The Communist revolution manifested itself in gulags, the KGB, state murders on a nearly unprecedented scale, and the purging of every kind of freedom. Despite the vast power of a police state, Communism in the Soviet Union and Eastern Europe fell from within, collapsing like the Pruitt-Igoe buildings.[2]

The whole modern era, from the Enlightenment through the twentieth century, can be seen as a secular embodiment of the theology of glory. The postmodern era, in contrast, is a time ripe for the theology of the cross. Ironically, in the rubble of modernity, postmodernists have been feverishly building new theologies of glory, both in society and in the church. Nevertheless, it is only in the shadow of the cross that the Christian faith can address, with authenticity and credibility, the spiritual condition of a postmodern world.

THE MODERNIST THEOLOGY OF GLORY

If the theology of glory is oriented to certainty, power, and success, it well describes the faith of the modernists, even as they dismissed supernatural religion as unscientific and retrograde. Nothing, they assumed, was outside the scope of human reason. Nothing was beyond the achievement of human beings. Modern science opened up nature itself to rational scrutiny, and modern engineering put nature into the service of human beings. The human mind gloried in its capacity to know all things, on its own terms. Human potential was glorified, particularly the ability to transcend the perceived limits of the past. If the old myths had Prometheus, the titan who brought fire and thus civilization to mortals, chained to a rock while a vulture ate his entrails, the victim of the jealous, vengeful gods, then the myth of modernity, as articulated by Shelley, was Prometheus unbound. This time the titan would break the bonds of the past and throw off the strictures of the gods, including the God of the Bible.

Although Christianity lingered through the Enlightenment and the Victorian era, pundits such as Matthew Arnold, on the verge of the twentieth century, predicted that religion, in that heralded century of progress, would finally die out. Human beings did not need it anymore. Religious faith would be replaced by science, some said, or art or poetry or by a new religion based on the here-and-now, a religion whose only deity would be humanity itself.

Even the church felt the force of these claims, giving rise to modernist theology. Panicked, lest the predictions of the death of religion come true, and seeking cultural relevance, many theologians recast the Christian faith so it would conform with modernity. "Modern man" can only accept science and material reality, it was said, so Christianity had to be purged of its miracles and its belief in the supernatural. The business of the church would no longer be to convey salvation in the sense of eternal life in some realm beyond the dead. Rather, salvation would be translated into terms of the here-and-now: The church would help to improve society, saving people from poverty and unhappiness through programs to promote social justice and psychological therapy. The world would set the agenda for the church, and the agenda was that of secular modernity, with its utopianism, scientism, and rationalism.

Modernist theology was a theology of glory, denying dogmas of human limits, such as the doctrine of original sin, and rejecting teachings that could not be explained scientifically. The incarnation of God in Christ, His atoning death, His resurrection all had to be "demythologized" to fit the demands of the "modern mind." The Bible itself was subjected to rationalistic, scientific scrutiny, with scholars presuming to dismiss anything in Scripture that did not accord with the modernist worldview. Once they purged the Bible of its miracles, they offered judgments about "what the historical Jesus really said"—which turned out to be not much—and, with breathtaking reductionism and an audacious sense of certainty and scholarly hubris, eviscerated the Word of God as revelation and as authority.

In this climate, in which historical Christian doctrines could be revised at will, the theological differences between the various Christian traditions were considered old-fashioned and unnecessary. Unity was a prime value for modernists, whether in literary criticism or in the simple geometric repetitions of modernist architecture. Accordingly, modernist theologians founded the ecumenical movement to bring various denominations into unity, which would be achieved by political tactics, the minimizing of doctrine, and cooperation in the pursuit of social justice. The result, though, was that as the mainstream churches became increasingly like the secular world, they grew less visible, fading into the secularist background. However, the old spiritual needs—the crushing reality of sin and the desperate need for God's grace—persisted, or even intensified, but the rationalistic, culturally respectable modernist churches no longer had anything to say to anyone crying out for salvation.

The problem with all theologies of glory is that they are based on fantasies of self-aggrandizement rather than on the hard, cold truth. Ignoring the fact of their own sin and the way God hides Himself in weakness and what is despised, theologians of glory keep failing but, oblivious to the cross, keep constructing ambitious new ideologies and new monuments to their pride. The titanic pretensions of the modernists, like the ship of that name in the first years of the twentieth century—the technological marvel that "even God could not sink"—kept hitting icebergs. The utopian age began with World War I and the disillusionment of a generation. Then followed World War II and the Holocaust. Then the Cold War—the dread of nuclear war coupled with armed conflict in Korea and Vietnam—and then the wholesale reaction against what Western culture had become in the student protests of the 1960s.

Modernity did indeed achieve much in the way of eradicating diseases, increasing standards of living, and making possible untold wealth and pleasures. But it was as if, gaining the whole world, the modernists lost their souls. In the latter part of the twentieth century and into the new millennium, there was a reaction against the modernist theology of glory. Although the postmodernist sensibility might be seen as a sort of secularized version of a theology of the cross, it soon developed a theology of glory of its own.

THE POSTMODERNIST THEOLOGY OF GLORY

Today's postmodernists, in contrast to modernists, are suspicious of the possibility of objective, disinterested reason, insisting that even the empirical evidence of science is shaped by the perspective of the scientist. They are calling humanism into question. Some postmodernists are even taking apart the notion of the self. Postmodernist thinkers are smashing such sacrosanct icons of the modernist theology of glory as progress, socialism, and individual autonomy. The modernists' faith in progress, through science and social evolution, now seems naïve. Postmodernists tend to be cynical, ironic, skeptical of all overarching ideologies. They acknowledge the limits of the human mind. They apply the "hermeneutics of suspicion" to all philosophies, institutions, and artistic creations, seeing in them mere "constructions" in need of deconstruction.

Surely this epistemological stance makes impossible all theologies of glory and all their secular equivalents. It could also be an opening for the theology of the cross, which accounts for human weaknesses and offers a way out of the impasse.

One would think that the postmodernists' recognition that reason has its limits might call for a rediscovery of revelation. The rejection of modernist positivism could mean a new acceptance of a supernatural realm that transcends our limited perceptions. The inescapable sinister qualities postmodernists uncover in their hermeneutic of suspicion could help them understand the depths of original sin. The postmodernist admission of human weakness could lead them to a new dependence on divine grace. Their cynicism might lead them to despair of their own good works and become open to the Gospel of Jesus Christ, that is, to what He accomplished on the cross.

Indeed, an articulation of Christianity centered in the cross—as opposed to portraying Christianity as a rationalistic ideology, a means of cultural power, or a moralistic program—is likely to resonate most profoundly in the hearts of postmodernists. But if the cross is foolishness to the modernists (as to the rationalistic Greeks of St. Paul's time), it remains a stumbling block for the postmodernists. In fact what the postmodernists have done is to construct a new theology of glory. More than that, they have devised a way of thinking in which *every thing* is reduced to a theology of glory and in which a theology of glory is the only possible way of thinking.

Postmodernism counters the modernist penchant for objective truth by insisting that truth is essentially a "construction." Truth is not so much something human beings discover; rather, it is something human beings construct. Taking Kant to an extreme, postmodernists argue that while empirical data from the outside world does flood into our nervous systems, the mind structures that data by imposing meaning upon it. The particular meaning is conditioned by the perceiver's culture, history, self-interest, and will. The world experienced by twenty-first-century, white, affluent Americans is different from the world experienced by poor Americans or by tribal Africans or by second-century Hebrews. One's world, in this sense, is essentially a social construction.

Many postmodernist thinkers take this analysis a step further: Social constructions, they say—which account for a culture's moral code, its political structures, its religious beliefs, and all of its other institutions and artifacts—are determined by issues of power. The group in charge protects its privileges by imposing belief systems on those it plans to victimize. Ideas, works of art, codes of manners, laws, governments, and theologies are all high-sounding masks to hide the imposition of power. All culture is constituted, according to this analysis, to enable men to oppress women, whites to oppress blacks (or other racial hierarchies), and the rich to oppress the poor. We are now seeing even more radical critiques of culture, more paradigms of oppression: heterosexuals against homosexuals, human beings against animals, human culture against the natural environment.

This hermeneutic of suspicion, which interprets any cultural expression in light of some kind of oppressive power, derives, of course, from Marxist reductionism, which analyzed every social institution and work of art as an expression of class struggle. Although Marxism would surely be the supreme example of a modernist metanarrative, with its all-embracing ideology and its progressivist assumptions—a modernist edifice that, as Oden argues, collapsed with the Berlin Wall—it retains its allure for social radicals. The so-called "neo-Marxism," or, better, "post-Marxist analysis," adds other categories of oppression to that of economic class warfare. But this radical critique of culture casts down the utopias as well as the tyrannies. That Soviet Communism was oppressive few Marxists were willing to deny, but the neo-Marxists would have to see even the fabled achievement of the "workers' paradise," were it ever to have been achieved, as a mask for oppression. If culture, by its very nature, is oppressive, then there are no alternatives to oppression. If one group is always competing against the others for power, no kind of altruistic regime is possible. The only change possible, if this analysis of culture is correct, is which group is doing the oppressing. If there is no moral law that transcends the culture, then there is nothing, really, by which that culture can be judged. The end result is either the status quo or an alternative group in power that, in principle, would be no better. And the quest for power and its untrammeled exercise is the theology of glory unbound.

On another level, while postmodernists savage the humanism of the modernists, the constructivism of the postmodernists actually exalt human beings far more than the modernists ever dreamed. The modernists may have been rationalists, but the mind played the relatively humble role of observer of a vast natural order outside the self. According to postmodernist epistemology, though, human beings—whether as individuals or in cultures—construct truth. They also construct their own moral values. That is to say, theologically, they are their own creators. They are their own law-givers. Human beings, in effect, are deified, and—feeling no need for a redeemer because, in the absence of a transcendent law, they do not consider themselves sinners—they can bask in their self-bestowed glory. This deification is indeed different from the humanism of the modernists, which honored man (they talked that way then) for his humanness, his reason, his achievements, his works of art, and his civilization. Postmodernists, scorning the achievements of civilization, honor human beings not as men but as gods.

POSTMODERN CONSUMERISM AND THE CHURCH

The constructivist thinkers in the academic world generally imagine themselves to be social critics, yet their abstruse theories tally well with what is happening in the mass culture. In fact in taking the assumptions and the implications of the postmodernist thinkers to their inevitable conclusions, the popular culture is arguably more consistently postmodernist than is academia. It is this pop pomo whose theology of glory most influences the contemporary church, particularly among churches that used to be conservative.

Although postmodernists in academia make themselves out to be neo-leftists, the true fulfillment of postmodernism is in free-market capitalism. This is borne out both historically and theoretically. Socialism, in all its guises, was modernist in its pseudoscientific rationalism, its optimistic humanism, and its utopian expectations. The contemporary economy, in contrast, is laissez faire, supply and demand, entrepeneurial capitalism on a scale Adam Smith could never have imagined. This libertarian economy has brought unprecedented prosperity to the Western postmodernists. (Nations not sharing in this wealth are mostly laboring under premodern conditions or are casualties of economic power on the part of the postmodernist nations.) Postmodernism takes the next step of applying what is successful in economics to every facet of life. The new modes of thinking turn not only raw materials and manufactured goods but ideas, morals, and religion into mere commodities to be bought and sold.

Furthermore, the effect of the new technology is precisely to turn information into a commodity. Now that books, music, art, and other intellectual creations can be mass-produced, their value can be determined according to how they sell. In turn, publishers and studios choose what "products" they will make available on the basis of how much money they are likely to earn. Just as the survival of a television show depends not on its truth or its artistic quality but on the ratings it pulls in, the transmission of an idea depends less on its truth than on its attractiveness, that is to say, how pleasing it is to the greatest numbers. Neil Postman has shown how entertainment has become the governing value, from the nightly news to the classroom, from politics to theology.[3] Political discourse has gone from the day-long analytical debates of Lincoln and Douglas to the 30-second sound bite, which consists of constructing a positive image for your candidate and a negative image for your opponent. People today speak of "liking" a candidate rather than agreeing with the candidate's policies; "liking" or "not liking" certain ideas or moral positions rather than believing or disbelieving them; "liking" a church rather than agreeing with what it teaches.

This accords well with postmodernist theory. If truth is relative, a construction of the will, then ideas become a function of desire. People believe what they want to believe. Persuading someone is no longer a matter of appealing to reason or to any kind of objective criteria; rather, persuasion is a matter of manipulating and creating desires. The rhetorical model becomes that of advertising, that most postmodern of businesses: creating favorable images, starting fashions, and playing on the chords of consumer psychology. This consumerism is a theology of glory writ large, as everything is made to cater to the desires, the comfort, and the gratification of the buyer.

While academic postmodernism—with its feminism, indeterminate hermeneutics, and universalism—has influenced academic theology in mainline denominations, it is the postmodernism of pop culture—with its consumerism, commercialism, and market reductionism—that is exercising the strongest influence in contemporary Christianity. Ironically, it is the ostensibly conservative evangelical churches, those that resisted modernist theology, that have become most open to this kind of postmodernism. Modernist churches disdained the supernatural, but postmodernist churches, having rejected reason, have no problem accepting the supernatural, even when it borders on the irrational. They will, however, have little interest in objective doctrines or theology, tending to subjectify the supernatural, preferring experiences to beliefs and personal theological constructions to creedal authority.

Traditional evangelicalism has always had an experiential focus, a theological openness, and the understanding of conversion as an act of the will—characteristics that, while in conflict with modernist intellectualism, fit well with the postmodern climate. In the past, though, evangelicals understood themselves to be in tension with the world, refusing to conform to the dominant secular culture. Today, U.S. evangelicals, despite the subcultures they tend to erect, are more willing to embrace cultural conformity, imitating the musical styles, the status symbols, and the communications media of the pop culture. They have also developed a sophisticated marketing consciousness, showing a willingness to tailor their message, their worship, and their theology to the consumer demands of the religious marketplace.

This has resulted in the sophisticated marketing strategies for building large churches known as the Church Growth Movement. In this way of thinking, the success of a church is measured by its numerical growth. Attracting large numbers of people is the goal, and any obstacles to this growth—an over-demanding theology, historic liturgies, ecclesiastical music styles, and church traditions in general—must be eliminated. Instead, growing churches will respond to the "felt needs" of the religious consumer, providing practical and therapeutic guides for successful living, culture-friendly contemporary worship and music styles, and a more open-ended theology that allows for individual preferences. Specific church practices are shaped by sophisticated demographic studies and market research, all designed to make church attractive to the "unchurched," as well as to the Christian church-shopper.

The Church Growth Movement specifically cultivates a theology of glory.[4] Its emphasis on tangible success through numbers, its assumption that human efforts and marketing strategies bring people into the kingdom, and its grandiose power churches reflect an ecclesiology of glory. Many such churches also teach a theology of glory. Instead of proclaiming the Law and the Gospel, many Church Growth pastors, bolstered by opinion polls that show laypeople prefer "practical" sermons, are preaching sermons that set forth biblical principles for successful living ("How to Avoid Stress at Christmas"; "The Bible's Steps for Financial Success"; "The Power of Positive Thinking"). Whereas the theology of the cross is expressed in sermons that destroy human sufficiency by showing our lost condition under the Law and revealing the free salvation—to which we contribute nothing— in the Gospel of Jesus Christ, these "practical" sermons build up the listeners' self-sufficiency. According to sermons like these, God's Law, as found in the Bible, is easily kept. One simply has to follow the biblical principles and family worries, money problems, and other trials of life will disappear. You will be happy all the time.

Robert Schueller's theology of positive thinking, a staple of many megachurches, goes so far as to define faith as this positive mental attitude (turning Christ's Beatitudes into the "be-happy-attitudes"). In practice, this means faith in oneself rather than faith in Christ. People can actually change their circumstances by thinking positively, thus overcoming financial problems, bad health, and negative situations by the sheer force of their mental attitude. In postmodernist language, they can construct their own realities. They can live in their own theologies of glory.

THE POSTMODERN WAY OF THE CROSS

Despite all the megachurches created by the Church Growth Movement, the total number of Christians in the United States has not really grown since that movement became popular during the past few decades. Rather, the number of Christians has declined slightly. The problem with theologies of glory is that they do not really, in the crassest pragmatic terms, work well, at least for long. Postmodernists who imagine themselves creating their own realities ultimately must confront realities they did not construct: failure, guilt, disease, death. Churches that promise health and wealth, pop psychology, and consumer gratification to their parishioners eventually seem shallow, phony, and manipulative, once suffering strikes.

But if the church is not growing in the United States, it is growing in other parts of the world. In 1950, there were some 834,000 Christians in China. Today, there are 85 million. There are a hundred times more Christians in China than there were before Communism. The church in China is the fastest growing church in the world, and it is growing not by accommodation to the culture but in the face of intense persecution. Jonathan Chao, a Chinese Christian, describes the standard treatment meted out to leaders of house churches:

> When a leadership gathering or training center (usually a farmer's home) is discovered, the police send truckloads of officers to encircle a courtyard-house complex so that no one escapes from the gate. After taking the names of everyone present, the officers take them to the police station, where each person is interrogated by two to three police officers in isolation for several days, sometimes for twenty-four hours straight by three shifts of interrogators. During the interrogation, house church leaders are often slapped, beaten, kicked, or stricken by 2,000-watt electric rods. Then a fine of 2,000 to 5,000 Renminbi (People's currency) (RMB) is imposed on such an individual. This is equal to one to two years of a farmer's annual income. Those who fail to pay the fines are sent to Educational Labor camps for eighteen to thirty-six months of hard labor. . . . Church leaders as new "inmates" are often beaten and humili-

ated by the "king of the cells." One elder was put next to the urinal and forced to drink his own urine, mixed with detergent and his own excretions. Many other forms of persecution are intended for the believer to give up his faith and ministry.[5]

Yet the church grows? How is that possible?

Chao actually credits the sufferings and persecutions of the Chinese Christians for the growth of their church. He offers seven reasons why this might be so: "First, persecution deepens a Christian's spiritual life." During the torments, he says, Christians find themselves depending on Christ, who meets them in their sufferings.

> Those who have gone through imprisonment testify how they experienced the joy of close communion with the triune God. When they are released, they seldom talk about the tortures that were inflicted upon them. Rather, they talk about how they were drawn closer to the Lord. A spirit of meekness, humility, and joy characterize their transformed personalities. When they preach Christ to others, they preach a Christ whom they have come to know experientially, a Christ for whom they suffered, and a Christ who saw them through their darkest hours.[6]

Second, Chao says, "persecution can purge the believer of his inward sins and conform his faith in Christ." It also has practical consequences. His third reason has to do with the way breaking up the house churches and scattering their members serves to multiply them and spread them throughout the countryside. His fourth reason is the constant infusion of new blood as old pastors, once arrested, are constantly being replaced by younger pastors. His fifth reason is that persecution forces Christians into close solidarity with one another, leading to a tight but fluid organizational and communication structure.[7]

Chao's sixth reason is that "persistent state persecution has turned the Church in China into a church of persistent prayer." He tells of the custom of rising at 5 A.M. and praying for two hours every morning. "Sometimes the only thing they can do is pray; the only help they can expect is from the Lord." And he tells about how God answers those prayers in ways that are often spectacular—the death of their persecutors, the Joseph-like rise to influence of some Christians within the prisons, the spread of the Gospel throughout China. Finally, "the testimonies of those who have suffered long under persecution have become a source of inspiration to the growing Church in China. Their faithfulness spurs the younger leaders to continue in their footsteps; their convictions are passed on to the subsequent generation of church leaders." Today, Chao says, "the state's determination to subjugate the independent house churches . . . and the house churches' determined resistance to that pressure through prayer and enduring suffering is like two armies engaged in warfare. One side uses brute force, the other resorts to God's spiritual power." And the persecuted church is winning. "The ongoing expansion of the Church in China has already passed the point of the state's ability to control it. There are already more Christians than party members, some of whom are turning to Christ."[8]

Something similar, of course, happened in the great period of the church's growth in the West, when the early church was cruelly persecuted by the Roman Empire, resulting in that empire's evangelization and conversion. It seems that the church is at its best when it faces cultural hostility, that it is strongest when it is weakest, when it follows the way of the cross.

This is not to say that when the church bears the cross it will grow as it is currently doing in China. Churches are sometimes small, weak, and struggling—yet Christ is present, though hidden, with all His gifts, in Word and Sacrament. Whether the postmodern centuries will bring a revival of Christianity, its increasing marginalization, or even overt, China-style persecution, the cross means that Christ will never leave His church.

Indeed, there is another way of being postmodern. If the modern era is over, one may become a relativist or a jaded consumer. Another alternative is to go back before the modern era and to bring what is of value in the past into the contemporary context.[9] This is evident in the neopagan revival, but it is also evident in the rediscovery of classical, confessional Christianity. Casualties of postmodernism, burnt-out cases from megachurches, young people raised on the shallowness of pop culture are looking for something authentic, something real, something beyond themselves. They do not trust the arid rationalistic reductionism of the modernists—and for good reason. They are suspicious of phoniness, rhetorical manipulations, and power plays. They are sick of theologies of glory. They are ripe for the theology of the cross.

NOTES

1. Charles Jencks, *The Language of Post-Modern Architecture* (London: Academy Editions, 1984), 9. For additional details, see Peter Hall, *Cities of Tomorrow* (Cambridge: Blackwell, 1996), 235–39.

2. Thomas Oden, *Two Worlds: Notes on the Death of Modernity in America and Russia* (Downers Grove: InterVarsity, 1992).

3. Neil Postman, *Amusing Ourselves to Death: Public Discourse in the Age of Show Business* (New York: Penguin, 1986).

4. See *For the Sake of Christ's Commission: The Report of the Church Growth Study Committee* (St. Louis: The Lutheran Church—Missouri Synod, 2000).

5. Jonathan Chao, " 'Success' under the Cross: The Example of the Persecuted Church in China," *Modern Reformation* (May/June 2000): 41.

6. Chao, " 'Success' under the Cross," 41.

7. Chao, " 'Success' under the Cross," 22.

8. Chao, " 'Success' under the Cross," 42–43. See also Wayne Martindale, "Christianity and Culture: The China Challenge," in *Christ and Culture in Dialogue: Constructive Themes and Practical Applications* (ed. Angus J. L. Menuge et al; St. Louis: Concordia Academic Press, 1999), 145–66.

9. This is what Thomas Oden calls for in his book *Two Worlds* and elsewhere. See also Gene Edward Veith, *Postmodern Times* (Wheaton: Crossway, 1994), 224–34.

FOR FURTHER READING

Carson, D. A. ed. *Telling the Truth*. Grand Rapids: Zondervan, 2000.

Connor, Steven. *Postmodernist Culture: An Introduction to Theories of the Contemporary*. Oxford: Basil Blackwell, 1989.

Groothuis, Douglas. *Truth Decay: Defending Christianity against the Challenges of Postmodernism*. Downers Grove: InterVarsity, 2000.

Myers, Kenneth. *All God's Children and Blue Suede Shoes: Christians and Popular Culture*. Wheaton: Crossway, 1989.

Oden, Thomas. *Two Worlds: Notes on the Death of Modernity in America and Russia*. Downers Grove: InterVarsity, 1992.

Postman, Neil. *Amusing Ourselves to Death: Public Discourse in the Age of Show Business*. New York: Penguin, 1986.

Veith, Gene Edward. *Postmodern Times*. Wheaton: Crossway, 1994.

10

A Pastoral Perspective
from the Cross
on the Bioethical Revolution

RICHARD C. EYER

ETHICAL RELATIVISM AND BIOETHICS

Although the word *bioethics* has appeared in journals and news headlines for several decades, most people still have to ask for a definition, even for a spelling of the word, in conversations outside professional circles. I recently hosted a conference entitled "Genetic Interventions" and worked with an agency to record the various presentations. I used the word *bioethics* frequently in our conversations. After weeks of negotiating arrangements, the highly successful, intelligent CEO of the company suddenly asked me, "What is *bioethics* anyway?" It took a good deal of explanation and illustration before he could comprehend what his company would be recording.

The following definition of *bioethics*, therefore, might be helpful to the nontechnical professional:

> Whereas ethics might be understood to be about the morality
> of how we ought to live together, bioethics deals with the
> ethics of making choices available to us as a result of break-

throughs in medical technology: genetic engineering [and cloning, human embryo and fetal tissue research, reproductive technologies], the withholding or withdrawal of treatment in illness, physician-assisted suicide, and euthanasia.[1]

If the word *bioethics* defies easy definition, the revolution accompanying it has nevertheless transformed our world for better and for worse. A woman, advised by her obstetrician, may choose to have an ultrasound examination to see visually how the child is developing. If it appears there is anything wrong with the developing child, abortion is always available. This is an issue in bioethics that has been with us for some time.

From the early 1970s and the debate over abortion to more recent discussions of physician-assisted suicide and euthanasia, hostilities and politics have made reasonable discussion of ethical concerns virtually impossible. Bioethics as the study of ethical questions relating to both secular and religious concerns has been stalled for lack of clear direction from either traditional or New Age proposals. For years Jack Kevorkian, a pathologist in Michigan, had been using what he called a "suicide machine" to accommodate the killing of people worn down with discouragement by their disease. The "machine" was nothing more than several bottles, tubes, and needles hooked up to the person who desired to die. At a given moment the person would open the flow of various drugs and within minutes the individual would be dead. Although the technology for this method of physician-assisted suicide was not sophisticated, the issues raised added to the plethora of bioethical issues already beginning to glut the agenda. The solution to the Kevorkian problem regarding physician-assisted suicide came when he was found guilty of murder and incarcerated. But the resolution was a legal, not an ethical, one. The debate about assisted suicide and euthanasia continues.

Although the blame for controversy concerning issues in bioethics is often placed on the complexity and rapidity of technological changes, paralleling these, and quite apart from them, has been the declining influence of traditional Judeo-Christian morality. Perhaps one of the most obvious changes that occurred in the 1960s was the introduction of the birth control pill. This small technological innovation revealed the fragile nature of moral conviction by removing the consequences of promiscuity and revealing the lack of moral character in those who only refrained for fear of pregnancy rather than out of respect for chastity as a moral virtue. The pill may be seen as the turning point of morality as displayed in issues involving reproductive technologies. In fact, it is the children of the parents who saw the pill as liberation that are enamored with the possibilities of reproductive technologies today. The parental generation seems to have lost not only its virginity through promiscuity, but also its moral compass for other critical areas of life that now flounder for lack of moral direction.

The reasons for the breach in the relationship between technology and traditional morality in ethics is not obvious. It is not clear, for example, that the relationship between the two involves cause and effect. Changes in traditional moral understanding, today culminating in ethical relativism, preceded the rise of technology. Moral decline more likely can be attributed to replacement of the Judeo-Christian story with the story of individualism and autonomy spawned in the eighteenth century and Nietzschean attacks on the Christian faith in the late nineteenth century. The twentieth-century phenomena of multiculturalism and rising affluence have prepared the soil for social revolution and continued attacks on traditional morality. More recently, medical technologies have added complexity to the bubbling pot of moral confusion and have posed what are actually old moral questions in new ways that we are no longer able to identify or address. The easy way out is to deny morality altogether. The claim of recent generations is that there are no objective moral answers. Many who have held traditional moral beliefs have been intimidated by this assertion and have surrendered to the assault of ethical relativism.

Ethical relativism claims there are no objective moral principles and that right and wrong are relative to the culture or to the person making the decisions. What Louis Pojman[2] identifies as the diversity thesis claims that because of the diversity of moral rules that appear to exist in different societies, it is difficult to conclude that any one, single, true morality exists. On the heels of this diversity thesis, the dependency thesis draws the conclusion that because of the diversity of moral rules in various societies, a person's morality is, therefore, dependent on the society in which she or he lives. However, upon deeper investigation it has been shown that though societies vary in the outward expression of moral convictions, the underlying principles are often similar to the traditional moral beliefs of most people. It has also been found that adherence to what appears to be one's own cultural beliefs of right and wrong still appeals to the objective standards of justice when one violates those standards, giving evidence to the belief that some moral principles, such as justice, are shared by all societies.

But much superficial reasoning has undermined belief in absolute truth and objective morality. Consequently, as old moral issues arise in new bioethical formats, we are no longer clear where to draw the line to identify what is morally acceptable and what is not. Controversies in bioethics flourish with seemingly little hope of resolution, and the conclusion drawn is that each person has to decide for oneself what is morally right or wrong "for me."

Therefore, as the technology revolution is taking place in the twenty-first century, so is the way we think of ethics. Ethics has come to rest almost exclusively on matters of moral taste for the individual and publicly on matters of utilitarian benefits to society. To ensure what might now be called the virtues of ethical relativism, privacy and informed consent, bioethics has been moved into the judicial sphere, where rights rather than the right is paramount. *Ethical* has now become synonymous with *legal* and *procedural*. This has led to the development of an ethic based on principles that are severed from the Judeo-Christian worldview, an ethic of rights defined by the courts. But such principles as the right to privacy and the right to informed consent do not address, as does the Judeo-Christian worldview, the deeper meaning of who we are and what we ought and ought not to do. The new interpretation of ethics and the accompanying judicial guarantee of rights is supposedly based on the U.S. Constitution, which, it turns out, ensures an interpretation of liberty that today appeals to the basest instinct of sinful human nature: self-interest. But this guarantee of liberty does not address the questions of what is objective right and wrong. In fact, ethical relativism and principlism of this sort merely denies that there *is* any objective right and wrong, hence the discontent in society concerning the failure to address the growing number of bioethical questions.

There is a sense, however, in which the ethical relativist comes closer to the truth than many of us would like to admit. Pojman, speaking against ethical relativism, says that "moral differences have their roots in worldviews, not in moral principles!"[3] Whereas the ethical relativist may take this to mean that ethics is merely relative to one's worldview, the Christian champions the belief that having the right worldview leads also to discovering the right moral principles. Because the Christian worldview proposes that moral principles are discovered rather than created, there is no question of relativism in truth. The Christian worldview provides individuals with a moral vision accessible most clearly through divine revelation. But the Christian claim is that God's vision for the moral life can be discovered by means of reason or natural law for those who are not Christians. The bioethical revolution challenges Christians and non-Christians alike, both by revelation and by reason, to claim a moral vision that will enable human beings to flourish in this world.

THE CROSS AND BIOETHICS

The foundation of the Christian's worldview is the cross of Christ. Whereas the cross is first the sign of our justification before God, the cross also prefigures our sanctification. Justification and sanctification are both the work of God: the Son winning our salvation for us and the Holy Spirit working it out in our lives. The unwillingness of human beings to live under the grace of God sometimes leads us, mistakenly, to limit the significance of the cross to our justification, turning sanctification into the work of human beings, albeit the redeemed human being. But the Word of God does not draw such tight parameters around the grace of God and the cross of Christ, limiting them to the arena of justification. From the beginning, God has attempted to work holiness in the lives of His people despite sinful human nature. God has chosen to work through human weakness, suffering, and ultimately the cross of Christ to reveal enough of Himself for us to know that it is God and not we who bear the credit for being holy people who live holy lives. The cross, understood as inclusive of the sufferings of Christ and His people, is the sign of our salvation, applicable in this life (for sanctification), as well as in the world to come (for justification). If we are made one with God in Christ's death on the cross, we are also made one with God in holiness of living.

Holiness is not attained by moral living; it is attained through the forgiveness of sins. Forgiven and standing in the presence of the holy God identifies us as one with God. To be one with God in His holiness is to be holy also. Therefore, the life we live to God is the life of holiness, worked in us by the Holy Spirit, resulting in what the world calls "moral living." Although we sin daily, we return to the one who said, "I am the door," and we knock daily. Confident of the forgiveness of sins, we stand at the door as a son before his father, asking the Holy Spirit to work in us His holiness of living through the Word of God that we hear and the body and blood of Christ that we eat and drink.

Luther put the matter of seeing the Holy Spirit at work in our lives clearly when he wrote, "God can be found only in suffering and the cross."[4] This theology of the cross, as Luther coined the phrase, also provides us with a lens through which we might see God as present and at work in the dilemmas of life. The theology of the cross enables us to accurately perceive aspects of the moral issues in the bioethical revolution. The theology of the cross enables us as Christians to see beyond the scope of our own comfort and advantage in ethical decision-making and reveals to us the perspective of God, who works through suffering among His holy people so they might live holy lives. In reference to bioethics, this is not to say that God gives us all the answers to all the questions we might ask. To go down that road is to move from the theology of the cross to what Luther called the theology of glory, in which the answers to our dilemmas become more important to us than God Himself. We can appreciate Paul's application of the theology of the cross when he elaborates in 1 Corinthians 1: "God chose what is foolish in the world to shame the wise; God chose what is weak in the world to shame the strong; God chose what is low and despised in the world, things that are not, to reduce to nothing things that are, so that no one might boast in the presence of God" (vv. 27–29 NRSV). Paul's point is that there is purpose in God choosing the way of the cross and suffering as the pathway of our salvation.

The theology of the cross does not answer all the theological questions that might be raised in bioethics, but it does address the larger picture of our spiritual life in facing them. That is, there are other themes in the Scriptures, such as being made in the image of God and its relevance for our thinking about genetic engineering; or the paradigm of marriage as a sign of Christ and the church and its relevance for our thinking about reproductive technologies; or the incarnation of Jesus Christ and its relevance for our thinking about abortion. On the other hand, it is clear that the theology of the cross is more directly applicable, for example, to such issues as illness and dying, life-and-death decision-making, and responding to the proposals of physician-assisted suicide and euthanasia.

But the greatest significance of the theology of the cross is its spiritual meaning in all ethical decision-making in which sinful human nature and the righteousness of God conflict. Before we can begin to examine the issues in bioethics, we must first find our peace with God in Christ and lay down our sin of hubris and our naïvete of self-inflated importance. Hubris shows itself in the attitude that there is nothing we will soon be *unable* to do, and self-inflated importance shows itself in the attitude that there is nothing that *should* stand in the way of our doing it.

A PASTORAL PERSPECTIVE

The word *pastoral* has become an adjective applicable to any attempt, by clergy or laity, to support another human being who is in need of spiritual care. Pastoral care in a hospital setting has become synonymous with hospital chaplaincy. Today chaplains in a hospital, nursing home, or elsewhere may or may not be ordained. Chaplains may have formal theological training or they may not. Some are called by God, both ordained or otherwise commissioned, and are accountable through the church. Others are certified by agencies that have little connection with, or accountability to, the church but that represent the cultural interests of the spiritualities of our times. Although the need today is great for professionally trained, ordained clergy (representing and accountable to the church) who can engage physicians and other healthcare professionals as peers in discussions related to bioethics, it is also true that we need spiritual care provided by others in the fellowship of believers who speak the Word of God and pray with people in Christ's name. Those who have the theological background for helping the faithful find their way through the maze of ethical dilemmas posed by a highly technological healthcare system are a blessing to the church. Those who can sit patiently at the bedside and listen to those who suffer also bear God's presence in the name of Christ.

Pastors need to be winsomely engaged with professionals who present to people the medical choices of contemporary technology. But as strange as it may seem, physicians generally know less than clergy about the underlying ethical issues. Physicians know what can be done medically with technology, but they have little advantage over clergy when it comes to knowing ethically what should be done. Unfortunately, modern medical ethics does little more than protect the rights of the patient to privacy and informed consent. Although one cannot generally engage a physician in an extended theological discussion in a moment of medical crisis, a point when decision-making is urgent, it is necessary to engage spiritually those involved in an ethical crisis. That is, before practical decision-making can occur, one needs to help parishioners, doctors, and nurses prayerfully lay aside all hubris and self-importance in taking upon themselves those decisions that only God can rightly decide. This can be done either in a moment of crisis or in an extended conversation in which the pastoral caregiver sets the stage for the family meeting with a physician or nurse, inviting them to pray before making a decision.

The theology of the cross puts our spiritual life in perspective. None of us is in charge of our own lives or the lives of others in the sense that we are ever free to choose from any and all choices placed before us. Much of spiritual support is a matter of drawing the parameters around the choices that are compatible with Christian faithfulness. The theology of the cross reminds us that our lives belong to God the Father who created us, the Son who redeemed us, and the Holy Spirit who sanctifies us. Contrary to the cultural emphasis on "choice" as the highest good, Christians are first to remind themselves that their lives are not their own to choose to do with as they wish. Ours is always a choice made within the context of what it is to be a son or daughter of our Father in heaven. The twenty-first century world needs to hear again the words "You are not your own; you were bought with a price" (1 Corinthians 6:20) and hear that as Good News not bad.

THE BIOETHICAL REVOLUTION
AT THE FOOT OF THE CROSS

To understand how the theology of the cross works in an issue of bioethical concern, the following scenarios might be helpful.

> James is faced with the news that he has been diagnosed with terminal cancer. The physician is honest enough to say that no treatment will change the outcome of the disease and that James probably has about six months to live. Because James has been in some discomfort for several months already, he asks the doctor about relieving the pain he has been increasingly feeling. Although he is assured that there are pain medications, he is also told that these medications may cause him to feel drowsy and unable to concentrate on his work as a newspaper writer. It is suggested that he leave his job. James believes that his writing is what makes his life worth living and confides in a friend that if he cannot work, he will take his own life.

> Three months later, James finds that he does indeed need to leave his job because the pain is increasing and he has been missing many days of work. One morning he leaves a message for his doctor that he feels the need for double the amount of pain medication previously prescribed and hints that he will use it to overdose and end his life. The physician picks up the hint and, believing James has to decide for himself whether he wants to live or die, complies and writes the prescription as requested. At the end of that week, having overdosed, James is found dead at home in his bed. He is the victim of cancer and of what is clearly a form of physician-assisted suicide.

The theology of the cross, had James heard it, could have addressed his dilemma. It tells us that God comes to us in our times of weakness, suffering, and dying to reveal Himself. As Jesus experienced fear and agony the night before His death and was comforted by God so He could endure the ordeal (Mark 14:32–38), so James might have received the same comfort and strength. James might have turned to God daily before his death for comfort, but he took his life in what he thought to be the final solution.

What was defeating for James was not his cancer but the loss of that which gave his life meaning, namely, his newspaper writing. But in such times of loss and disappointment caused by suffering, each of us needs to face the deeper question of a greater fulfillment that makes life worth living. When illness attacks the foundations on which we have either deliberately or inadvertently built our lives, it is essential that we ask ourselves whether such foundations are solid enough to support us to the bitter end. God was willing to stand with James in suffering and dying, but James never hoped to find God there. Had he lived in such hope, he would have had opportunity to discover the thing that his love of writing only symbolized: the Word made flesh on the cross. Those who learn to let go of their lives in times of suffering find comfort. Those who grasp their lives tightly in their own hands often find that their hands become the means of their self-destruction. The theology of the cross is the hand of God that holds us in His peace and protection in times of weakness, suffering, and dying.

In another scenario we see the theology of the cross address the disappointment and grief of childlessness.

> Allen and Sarah were passing through the childbearing years rapidly and still had no children. They were both Christians and had prayed for God to give them a child for many years. Both Allen and Sarah had been through infertility testing. It had been discovered that Allen had barely viable sperm while Sarah had scar tissue blocking one of her fallopian tubes, probably the result of an infection she had contracted from another man before she had met Allen. The doctor felt they could still conceive a child with the use of reproductive technologies.

> In a visit with the endocrinologist they were told that among the several options available to them, they would most likely benefit from in vitro fertilization and the use of donor sperm. Although there was no guarantee of a successful, full-term pregnancy, the chances were good that they might conceive and bear a child. But after several months of disappointment with unsuccessful attempts, Sarah began to become bitter and resentful toward Allen. Allen responded by blaming Sarah for not being able to conceive. Their marriage suffered greatly and they cancelled further attempts at the clinic. Six months later they filed for divorce.

Like James, Allen and Sarah were not guided pastorally by a theology of the cross as they suffered first anxiety and then anger at not being able to overcome infertility. The issue Allen and Sarah had never faced along the way was how to live with loss. Through the months of attempting pregnancy, in their desperation, they had come to believe that their fulfillment and self-worth rested on their ability to have a child. In the end, they neither conceived a child nor attempted to adopt one. Bitterness and blame toward each other prevented them from standing at the foot of the cross, where life's fulfillment in a fallen world is found. Had they been able to suffer the loss of fertility and lose their lives in God during this ordeal, they might have found their lives in a way they had never known, though they were Christians. In the end, they had neither children nor each other, and they were confused, disappointed, and angry at God for their loss. Dietrich Bonhoeffer, in a Nazi prison, wrote that finding God in our loss is the deliverance we need to live life in fulfillment despite suffering.

CONCLUSION

The theology of the cross is the Christian's foundation for the pastoral care of those living in a world challenged by the twenty-first century bioethical revolution. The cross both addresses our relationship to God and points us in the direction of holy living in response to that relationship. Four aspects of the theology of the cross come to mind with regard to the bioethical revolution.

1. The theology of the cross puts our relationship with God in holy perspective, reminding us who and whose we are. We have a holy origin, created in the image of God, and a point of holy return, the Day of Resurrection. Between our origin and our return stands the cross, our redemption. Whatever new worldview may emerge from an attempt, successful or unsuccessful, to rearrange the basic structure of the human genome, it will fall short of the truth that defines our existence for this world and the next. Human beings, created in the image of God, are more than the sum total of their genes. Further, whatever aspirations geneticists may have for the human genome, it risks being conceived and carried out in the shadow of the tower of Babel and the hubris of humanity. God will not be laid aside for what a person thinks she or he can become without Him. This is a warning to those who do evil in the name of good. The promise to those who do good is that God has set boundaries for the Evil One and will watch over His children as a faithful shepherd guards his sheep.

2. The theology of the cross addresses the deeper mystery of life that is spiritual and not merely scientific. Promises of a longer, more fulfilling, life through technology is a half truth; science can produce neither fulfillment nor immortality. Treating disease, comforting the suffering, caring for the weak and frail through technology, these are the works of God in and through humanity. But no human endeavor can give meaning to a life that God has not already given. And no solution to overcoming the barrier of death can be found anywhere other than at the cross. The cross is the

sign of the new life that is ours in Christ. All human attempts to find fulfillment through material means to the exclusion of the one who hung on the cross will ultimately be shown to be merely distraction from the fulfillment. Surely we are blessed by the gifts of God that come to us through technology, but it is not the gift that makes life fulfilling; rather, it is the Giver of gifts.

3. The theology of the cross reminds us that in a world that places its hope in material things, even high-tech things, there also will be disappointment and judgment. With every sign of what some call progress, science seems also to introduce new dilemmas for which we have no solutions. For example, reproductive techniques that enable formerly infertile couples to have children also move us from the intimacy that procreation requires to the commodification of children in which the paradigm becomes the making of products for eager customers, married or unmarried. Also, as a result of genetic sex selection, we may well find that we have created a social imbalance with which future generations will have to cope. The judgment against us for what we have become capable of doing may come only when God calls us to account for the hope that has been lost to us. Our unwillingness to commend our wants and wishes to the will of God and our making for ourselves idols of technology that never satisfy will come under the judgment of God.

4. The theology of the cross addresses our spiritual life and provides us with a theology on the basis of which to evaluate attitudes toward and uses of the new technologies. When we have come to see that God works not always through what we set out to do, but also through the failures of our efforts and the pains we suffer for it, then perhaps we will be ready to learn the limits God sets to our works. This is not to say that good can come from evil. And it is certainly not to paraphrase Paul when he asks, "Should we continue in sin in order that grace may abound?" (Romans 6:1 NRSV). It is to say that we should examine our attitudes toward the new sciences in success and in failure. With the advent of new technologies, there is a great deal of hype and speculation about what we might do and its results. Whether we actually accomplish a tenth of that for which we hope, the greater challenge is to face up to those attitudes that accompany our efforts. What new paradigms will be accepted in attempting what we attempt? What moral inhibitions will be set aside "for the betterment of humanity"? What will we intentionally overlook in how we treat people "for the sake of research"? What will our attitude toward

the human body embody? Even if we fail to achieve with technology that for which we have great hopes now, our efforts will change our attitudes toward life for the future. The theology of the cross keeps us focused on God and not on ourselves, reminding us that we are creatures, not the Creator. Humility must grow in proportion to the capability of our technologies so, in gaining the world, we do not lose our souls.

The bioethical revolution of the twenty-first century may emerge as an era that changes history. But that change will also change us as a people. As the holy people of God, called to live holy lives, we have much to offer the world. As the world starves for meaning, we bring Good News of great joy in Christ. It is a good news for heaven and earth, for our justification and our sanctification. Our challenge as the people of God is to greet change with open arms, confident in the Lord. Not all change will benefit humanity or be faithful to the calling with which God has called us, but we have no reason to retreat in fear or ignorance. God has revealed to us the mysteries of the kingdom with which we can face the mysteries of life.

NOTES

1. Richard C. Eyer, *Holy People, Holy Lives: Law and Gospel in Bioethics* (St. Louis: Concordia, 2000), 7.

2. Louis Pojman, *Ethics: Discovering Right and Wrong* (4th ed.; Belmont, Calif.: Wadsworth, 2002).

3. Pojman, *Ethics*, 6.

4. LW 31:53.

FOR FURTHER READING

Bonhoeffer, Dietrich. *Ethics*. Edited by Eberhard Bethge. Translated by Neville Horton Smith. New York: Collier, 1986.

Eyer, Richard C. *Holy People, Holy Lives: Law and Gospel in Bioethics*. St. Louis: Concordia, 2000.

Eyer, Richard C. *Pastoral Care under the Cross*. St. Louis: Concordia, 1994.

Meilaender, Gilbert. *Bioethics: A Primer for Christians*. Grand Rapids: Eerdmans, 1996.

———. *The Limits of Love*. University Park: Penn State University Press, 1987.

Schulz, Gregory. *The Problem of Suffering*. Milwaukee: Northwestern, 1996.

Veith, Gene Edward. *Postmodern Times: A Christian Guide to Contemporary Thought and Culture*. Wheaton: Crossway, 1994.

Walther, C. F. W. *Law and Gospel*. Translated by Herbert J. A. Bouman. St. Louis: Concordia, 1981.

11

The Witness to the Cross in Light of the Hispanic Experience

ALBERTO L. GARCÍA

The crucified Christ is a powerful symbol in the popular religiosity of Latin Americans and U.S. Hispanics/Latinos. There is no doubt that the figure of the anguished, suffering Christ is also a significant religious symbol in Spain. One of the most moving Spanish visual images of the crucifixion is the painting by Diego Velázquez (1599–1660). *El Cristo de Velázquez* has been immortalized by the Spanish philosopher and writer Miguel de Unamuno (1864–1936) in his philosophical work *The Tragic Sense of Life in Humanity and the People.* Unamuno saw Velázquez's Christ "as the highest catholic artistic expression . . . at least Spanish . . . where Christ is always dying without ever dying to give us life."[1] This gory image of Christ has been considered one of the most popular religious symbols inherited by Latin America from Spanish Catholicism. Georges Casalis, a Latin American theologian, criticizes this omnipresent image of the suffering Christ in the popular art and culture of the Southern Cone: "When the people pray before those images or venerate them, as they become inscribed in their spirits throughout a life of a subjected pedagogy and passive practice, it is no doubt that the people find there their destiny, and worship or accept those images with a masochistic identification."[2]

We need to add to these images the processions of Holy Week as they are staged in many parts of Latin America and in some Hispanic Catholic parishes in the United States. Ignacio Ellacuría, former rector of the Central American University, and one of six Jesuit priests killed by Salvadoran troops in November 1989, saw as one of the most important images for witness in Latin America the portrait of "the crucified people."[3] Ellacuría's depiction of the Latin American people as the crucified people corrects, in a sense, the masochistic interpretation offered by Casalis concerning the people's identification with Jesus' suffering. The Latin American and U.S. Hispanic/Latino experience of the crucified Christ may be seen from a different perspective. It cannot be merely interpreted as a fatalistic or masochistic symbol of human existence. It has to do with an incarnational and soteriological understanding of how the experience of Jesus' crucifixion becomes an important signpost in the reading of the Hispanic religious experience.[4]

This essay will unfold, therefore, the incarnational and soteriological reality of the cross in light of the U.S. Hispanic experience. We must take seriously the insights of Ellacuría in light of the catholic evangelical biblical teaching of the incarnation and soteriology. The fact is that the witness of the cross in light of the Latino experience must take seriously the experience and identification of Latinos with the crucified Christ. Our language about God in light of the cross is incarnational and relational. It takes into consideration the community's hopes and aspirations. I believe that the image of the crucified Christ is at the center of our reading and witness of Scripture. We need to hear the voice of the crucified Christ in humility. It is only in this *cross*-cultural reading and witness that we can take the next step to live the unconditional love of Jesus.

The catholic evangelical teaching of justification by faith through grace may be applied in this reading of Scripture. It is grounded on the theology of the cross that calls all our human sinful situations into question. It destroys our theology of human works. It calls idolatrous our rationalizations and our rejections of "the other" as God's creatures. The cross, however, calls also the messenger of God's Word, as well as the hearers, into repentance and new life as the living voice of the Gospel creates this miracle. This miracle of reconciliation creates a new community in Christ. This is at the center of Paul's witness of the cross:

> For I resolved to know nothing while I was with you except
> Jesus Christ and Him crucified. I came to you in weakness and
> fear and with much trembling. My message and my preaching

> were not with wise and persuasive words, but with a demon-
> stration of the Spirit's power, so that your faith might not rest
> on men's wisdom, but on God's power. (1 Corinthians 2:2–5)

This is the same kind of witness that Luther emphasizes in his Heidelberg Disputation when he puts down our idolatrous readings of God's
creation and calls believers to know God in light of the crucified Christ:

> He is not worth calling a theologian who seeks to interpret the
> invisible things of God on the basis of the things that have
> been created. (Thesis 19)

> But he is worth calling a theologian who understands the visi-
> ble back side of God through the revelation present in suffering
> and the cross. (Thesis 20)[5]

This witness of the cross puts down our false sense of security that
is grounded in the greatness of our sinful acts. It is a prophetic witness
that is not blind to the idolatry present in all cultures. However, it is a
witness that is done in light of the crucified God. It is grounded in
God's incarnational love for each and every culture. This love requires,
therefore, that we become attentive to the wounds and anxieties of the
foreigner, the stranger, and their communities. To speak of the forgiveness of sins that we have in Christ and the reconciliation that we have
with God and humanity outside of this incarnational love of the cross
is an offense to the witness of the cross. The witness of the cross
requires, therefore, that we understand the context, the culture, and
the human drama of the people to whom we minister with the Gospel.
It is necessary to understand in an incarnational manner the U.S. Hispanic experience of *mestizaje,* popular religiosity, and festive hope to
render a faithful soteriological witness of the cross. It is only then that
we can become theologians of the cross to our Latino/a brothers and
sisters in North America.

This is an important witness that we cannot neglect. There are
about 35.3 million Hispanics/Latinos living in the United States at the
beginning of the twenty-first century. The 2000 census data shows a
61.2 percent growth in the Hispanic population during the last
decade.[6] If we were able to count accurately the usually undercounted
Latino population, I believe the number would be closer to 39 million.
U.S. Hispanics will become in a short time the most numerous ethnic
group in North America. The Roman Catholic Church estimates that
more than half of its membership in the United States is Hispanic.
Please note that I am using the words *Hispanic* and *Latino* as equivalent
terms that presently unite Hispanics in the United States. We are also
proud of our distinct heritage as Mexican, Mexican Americans, Puerto
Ricans, Cubans, Guatemalans, and so forth. In this essay, I will pay par-

ticular attention to the U.S. Mexican and Mexican American religious and cultural experience because these groups comprise more than 64 percent of the U.S. Hispanic population. However, the other Hispanic nationalities share in one form or another similar experiences of *mestizaje*, popular religiosity, and festive hope.

MESTIZAJE

In 1986 I was struck by the devotion of Guatemalan *mestizos* to a dark-skinned *mestizo* crucified Christ at the cathedral in the main square of Guatemala City. This *mestizo* Christ was strategically located in the back of the church at a side altar that points to the Palacio Presidencial, the center of political power. There are many altars in this cathedral; however, they attracted few devotees. I was amazed that on a common Monday afternoon there was a small group of men and women praying to this *mestizo* Christ. In Guatemala and Mexico there are great processions during Holy Week that take place outside the church in reverent devotion to a *mestizo* suffering Christ. The figure of a *mestizo* Christ is the accepted iconographic image in the Latin American and U.S. Hispanic religious experience. In fact this picture offers a vivid contrast to the figures of Christ preferred by Northern Europeans. In my office I have a picture that was given to me that depicts a blond, long-haired Christ. It was painted by a French artist. This Christ is laying hands on a darker complexioned Peter. At home I have a picture of a *mestizo* Christ. This is a picture I bought years ago in Mexico during my student days in Texas. The artist's name is Arturo, and he painted a picture of a bloody *mestizo* Christ with a crown of thorns. It depicts great human suffering. I have this picture in my study at home because I identify with it. I want to offer some reasons why this *mestizo* Christ is an important image to understand the Hispanic/Latino experience of *mestizaje*. I am not here to cast a "dark" Christ against a "white" Christ. However, we cannot understand the Hispanic religious experience unless we understand the experience of *mestizaje*.

During the introduction of this essay, I pointed out that one of the predominant images for believers in Latin America is the symbol of a suffering people in identification with a suffering Christ. The figure of the crucified Christ has been misunderstood as a passive symbol of suffering and defeat. This may be the case in many situations. However, it is also a symbol of the one who "became flesh and made His dwelling among us" (John 1:14). In my readings of Isaiah 49–53, I find that the "servant of the Lord" is one who is "despised and abhorred" because He stood on behalf of His people. The servant suffers because He identifies with the suffering of His people to overcome it. The exodus points also to the same sympathetic God who is in the midst of His people's sufferings (Exodus 3:7). Many Latin Americans and U.S. Hispanics find God identifying with their suffering and human situation. The suffering of the people is, therefore, a witness that God stands on behalf of His community. Their suffering is not merely a passive suffering; it is the kind of suffering that Christ wants us to take on behalf of others (Matthew 10:38–39). This was also the way of discipleship proclaimed by St. Paul (2 Corinthians 4:10–12).

The presence of suffering in our lives is not a masochistic wish to suffer. It is, rather, a life lived in conformity to the incarnational love of the cross. This is the kind of reading that Virgilio Elizondo and Jon Sobrino argue that we must make of the crucified Christ.[7] There is no doubt that some Latinos see the cross as a symbol of defeat. However, the cross in the Hispanic experience is a clear signpost, a symbol, of God's active presence with us and for us. It is a clear sign that God in the person of Jesus Christ came to stand with His people in their entire human drama. We cannot give a witness of the forgiveness of sins unless we also affirm this holistic message of the Gospel. God came to bring His people into His community of love. Central to this proclamation is that Jesus Christ came to call the lowliest and the most despised to be members of His community. This signpost of the cross cannot be understood apart from the reality of *mestizaje* in the U.S. Hispanic reality.

The U.S. Hispanic human experience is a borderland experience. This experience points to the reality that we are never part of the mainland North American culture. Most U.S. Hispanics consciously know, whether we are poor or rich, that we belong between two cultures. We are bilingual, but we do not belong to a specific culture. This is the reality of our existence as Cuban Americans, Mexican Americans, and so on. This borderland experience has been documented by most U.S. Hispanic theologians. This problem of identity is at the heart of our U.S. Hispanic/Latino reality. Elizondo, the dean of U.S. Hispanic/Latino theology, reflects on this important situation in light of his Mexican American identity:

> The deepest suffering of the *mestizo* comes from what we might call an "unfinished identity," or better yet, an undefined one. One of the core needs of human beings is the existential knowledge that regardless of who I am socially or morally, I am. The knowledge of fundamental belonging—that is to be French, American, Mexican, English—is in the present world order one of the deepest needs of persons. When this need is met, it is not even thought about as a need; but when it is missing, it is so confusing and painful that we find it difficult to even concep-

tualize it or speak about it. We strive "to be like" but we are not sure just which one we should be like. As Mexican-Americans, we strive to find our belonging in Mexico or in the United States—only to discover that we are considered foreign by both. Our Spanish is too Anglicized for the Mexicans and our English is too Mexicanized for the Anglos.[8]

This reality of *mestizaje* is not merely a psychological or ethnic problem of Latinos. *Mestizaje* is the result of historical transgressions. The history of the people of the world is full of *mestizajes*. However, it is impossible to offer an incarnational witness of the cross among U.S. Hispanics apart from their experience of *mestizaje*. I am summarizing this history, reflecting primarily on the history of Mexicans and Central Americans. This is not to say that other Hispanic/Latino groups do not share a similar painful history. The history of Puerto Ricans, for example, also carries a painful history of *mestizaje*. In fact, the two pastorates that I have served have been mostly among Puerto Ricans in Chicago and Hollywood, Florida. Puerto Ricans are not even acknowledged to have an existence under the name Puerto Rican American, yet they live a borderland existence in their own land.

Mestizaje is the key cultural experience that explains Hispanic religiosity and spirituality. What makes a person "Hispanic" or "Latino/a" is not race or a particular country of origin; rather, it is the Spanish language, the culture, and the traditions that have come about from the "mixture" (*mestizaje*) of several races and cultures of people. *Mestizaje* is characterized by the mixture of human groups of different races that determine skin pigmentation, shape of eyes, and bone structure. In the case of the U.S. Hispanic reality, this *mestizaje* is the result of two conquests. The Iberian Spanish conquest led to a mixture with Indian blood with that of African slaves brought to the New World. As Elizondo observes, "It is a fact of history that massive *mestizaje* giving rise to a new people usually takes place through conquest and colonization."[9]

The Hispanic people were formed through this *mestizaje*. Churches need to be sensitive to the fact that *mestizaje* has occurred through the imposition of a different culture and a different way of life, including religion, upon the Hispanic people. The Bible and the cross were used, in fact, as instruments of conquest. This is why during the visit of John Paul II to Peru, Amerindians descendants from Atahualpa, the Inca chief conquered by Pizarro, presented the pope with a Bible inscribed with the following words:

> John Paul II, we the Amerindians from the Andes, have decided to take advantage of your visit to return you the Bible, because during the last five centuries it has not brought love, peace or

justice to us. Please take your Bible and return it to our oppressors because they need its moral teachings more than we need them. Since the arrival of Christopher Columbus to our land, the culture, the language, the religion, and the values that belong to Europe have been imposed on Latin America by force. The Bible came to us as an instrument of the colonial transformation imposed by force. The Spanish sword that attacked and killed the Indians, night and day, became the cross that afflicted the native soul.[10]

It is important to note that in this process of *mestizaje,* the Roman Catholic conquistadores built altars in the most sacred places of worship of the Aztec and Mayan Indians. It was a way for the Spaniards to substitute and supplant the most important religious symbols of a culture with their own religious symbols. A people's fundamental religious symbols provide their ultimate identity because these symbols mediate for them the absolute. In the case of a conquered people, new symbols, new language, and a new way of life are imposed by the conquerors and are presumed to be superior.[11]

The second conquest that contributed to the *mestizaje* of U.S. Hispanics has been described as the "Nordic-Protestant Conquest."[12] This conquest is the history of Northern Europeans imposing their ideals of cultural superiority over conquered people. Europeans who came to North America seeking religious freedom and a better life for themselves also exhibited a purist way of thinking. As early as colonial times, laws were passed that prohibited racial mixture between the immigrants and the native people in America. In fact a large number of Protestant colonizers considered it to be their divine mission to eliminate the "savages" from their territory. This work was believed to be equivalent to destroying the power of sin and Satan. The Anglo-Saxon American had strong feelings of divinely ordered superiority over other ethnic groups in the United States. Their work in the development and progress of the young nation reaffirmed this sense of superiority in their vision of freedom. There is no doubt that, at the time of their writing, the Declaration of Independence and the U.S. Constitution guaranteed the principles of equality and freedom. This vision of equality and freedom, however, was guided by a sense of "manifest destiny" to bring a better way of life to the uncivilized people of the Americas. This led many colonizers to move into the northern territories of Mexico. It is interesting to note that, in most cases, this expansion occurred through illegal immigration into Mexican territories and had no regard for Mexican laws. Elizondo describes sadly this first encounter of the two cultures:

From the very first encounters, the Anglo-American immigrants looked upon the Mexicans (for them, all the Spanish-
speaking) with disdain. The Mexican was brown, *mestizo*, Spanish speaking, Roman Catholic. The North American was white,
pure-blooded (racial admixture was contaminated), English
speaking, Protestant. And the Mexican had a different worldview from that of the aggressive, land-hungry, power intoxi-
cated Anglo-American Indian-fighter. The Mexicans were
labeled inferior, lazy, deceitful, superstitious, incapable of
assimilation.[13]

The North American colonizers used the Protestant Bible in this
second conquest as an instrument to "rescue" individuals from their
communities. It was used as an instrument of cultural expansion to
integrate individuals into the religion and culture of the pioneers.[14]
The colonizers promoted cultural genocide by denigrating the value of
the native peoples' communities and cultures. The "empty cross"
became also the symbol of these Protestants who brought their apparent civilization and *mestizaje* to the Southwest.[15]

This history is also marred by the expansionist vision of President
James Polk (1795–1849), which resulted in the U.S.-Mexican War. The
official act that ended this war was the Treaty of Guadalupe Hidalgo,
which was signed by the people of Mexico and the United States on
February 2, 1848. Mexico—which ceded the states of California, Ari-
zona, and New Mexico, as well as large sections of Colorado, Nevada,
and Utah—gave up 525,000 square miles for a mere $15,000,000. This
treaty was signed with the condition that the people of Mexico who
inhabited these acquired territories could (1) continue to practice their
religion, (2) receive an education in Spanish, (3) continue to own their
properties, and (4) become U.S. citizens.[16] These promises were not
kept.

Negative connotations of *mestizaje* persist today in North America. In the 1960s one could find signs in San Antonio, Texas, that read:
"Mexicans and dogs not allowed." Even today, based on the color of
their skin or their accent or their way of life, Hispanics are harassed by
police in many parts of the country. During the year 2000 Cinco de
Mayo celebration in Milwaukee, close to a hundred Mexicans were
arrested or cited simply for carrying Mexican flags in their cars in a joyful parade through the South Side. A Hispanic judge at the scene was
mistreated when she complained to a police officer because of his mis-
treatment of two Mexicans without cause. Apologies and a dismissal of
the charges came later. In 1999 the Mexican community of East Los
Angeles experienced a painful defacing of at least nine images of the
Virgen de Guadalupe on murals along César Chavez Avenue. Her image

had been painted over with white paint. In one mural her image was covered with red and the number 666 had been painted on her face.[17] Although my family and I are Cuban Americans, we have suffered similar experiences.

Today U.S. Hispanics find themselves in the United States as strangers and foreigners. The painful reality of *mestizaje* becomes even more painful for Mexicans who experience this reality in their own land. Our witness of the Gospel has not taken seriously, in most cases, the U.S. Hispanic experience of *mestizaje*. Missionaries doing evangelistic work among Hispanics in Mexico, Central America, and the United States often begin by criticizing their "syncretistic practices," their "obsessive attraction to human suffering," their "deep devotion to Mary" (in particular to the Virgen de Guadalupe), and their Roman Catholic insistence on "good works" rather than "grace."[18] We should begin, however, with an incarnational witness of the cross. In this manner we can maintain a faithful catholic evangelical witness and at the same time understand and take into account the reality of *mestizaje* within the Hispanic experience.

Elizondo is the first to suggest that we read the reality of *mestizaje* in light of the Gospels. Rather than accepting this reality as a negative experience in which we pitch Hispanics versus Anglos, or *mestizos* and blacks against whites, we need to read our *mestizaje* in light of the Gospels. This reality is truly attentive to the incarnate God who came into the world on our behalf. This reality hopes for a new creation in light of the proclamation of the kingdom of God. It reads our history in light of Jesus Christ, who lived among us as "the prophet from Nazareth in Galilee" (Matthew 21:11).[19]

One of the fatal mistakes that we make in our witness is not to consider the radical nature of the incarnation in relationship to our salvation. Luther began always with the human nature of Jesus in his theological reflection: ". . . Christ must be apprehended as Man, before he is apprehended as God: and the cross of his humanity must be sought after before we know the glory of his divinity."[20] In Philippians, Paul underscores that Jesus actually took the human form of a servant (Philippians 2:7) on the way to the cross. The author of Hebrews points to Jesus as our high priest because He was "tempted in every way, just as we are—yet was without sin" (Hebrews 4:15). We tend to forget the radical confession of our witness in light of the Council of Chalcedon (451): Jesus Christ is truly God and truly man in one person. We overlook the implications of His humanity. The Gospels reveal Jesus as sharing in reality our humanity in truly human terms.

Often in theological discourse the word *incarnation* implies an abstract concept. In this way of thinking, we can acknowledge that

God the Son became incarnate to live a perfect life on our behalf. However, we do not fully comprehend the impact of the fact that Jesus, in His human nature, was truly "tempted in every way . . . yet was without sin." Jesus shared the same psychological and physical experiences that we experience because of His human location in a sinful world. He was not sinful, but He lived as a true human being in a sinful world. Jesus' incarnate presence with us was also impacted by His social human relationships. He is able to sympathize with all our weaknesses because of His humanity. I see here His sympathy extended without hesitation to our social and human relationships. This is the radical nature of the incarnation. The beauty about the Spanish language is that the word for incarnation is not an abstract term. *Encarnación* means what it says, "He took *en* (in) *la carne* (the flesh) our human drama" (John 1:14). This is why it is so common among Hispanics to name their sons Jesús. Our father, grandfather, uncle, or son may have been named Jesús because in our Hispanic reality we find that Jesus walked and lived as one of us in a real family and community. The name Jesús is called out many times in our communities not as a curse but as a realization that Jesus walks with us in our daily lives.[21]

It is important to consider also the role of the Holy Trinity within our human situation as we acknowledge the experience of *mestizaje*. We tend to isolate the trinitarian reality of Jesus Christ from His incarnate life in history. A natural point at which we include the trinitarian reality in our salvation history is the biblical narrative of creation. The trinitarian God in the relationship of the persons created human beings according to His image (Genesis 1:27). God created humanity as male and female—a family. To offer a message of salvation that speaks of the restoration of our relationship to God but then ignores our relationships within our human community negates the incarnational reality of our God. The picture of Jesus as the prophet from Galilee allows us to take the Hispanic reality of *mestizaje* seriously in light of the trinitarian reality of the incarnation. It also impacts in a powerful manner our witness of the cross.

In the Gospels we read how Jesus comes from Nazareth in Galilee (Mark 1:9). His first sermon about the kingdom of God is proclaimed in Galilee (Mark 1:14; Matthew 4:17). Jesus' inaugural address in which He reveals His mission took place in a Galilean synagogue (Luke 4:14–19). Most of His trusted apostles came from Galilee (Matthew 4:18–21). His first miracle, turning water into wine, occurred in Galilee (John 2). In His final entry into Jerusalem, Jesus is identified without doubt as "the prophet from Nazareth in Galilee" (Matthew 21:11). The women from Galilee are the ones who followed Him into Jerusalem to care for His needs. They also are the first to hear the good news of the resurrection, and they run to tell His disciples the great news (Matthew 27:55–56; 28:5–7). Jesus goes to Galilee after His resurrection. It is there that He gives His Great Commission to His disciples and to His church to "make disciples of all *ethne*," that is, all ethnic groups, tribes, and races in the world (Matthew 28:19–20).

There is no question that Jesus was a Jew, but he was recognized as a Galilean Jew. He lived, in a sense, a hyphenated existence as a human being in His specific historical and geographic situation. In his denial of Jesus, Peter could not hide the fact that he was from Galilee. He was set apart because of his accent: "Surely you are *one of them, for your accent* gives you away" (Matthew 26:73; *my emphasis*). Jesus' followers were identified as His disciples because either they also spoke with such distinctive accents and/or lived their distinct human lives as people from Galilee. What is, therefore, the significance for our witness of the cross that Jesus was identified as a prophet from Galilee?

Jesus' important relationship to Galilee has received little attention in the past. However, I believe that we cannot bypass this specific geographic locus and Jesus' identity as a Galilean Jew when we offer a global witness of the cross. Galilee was, in reality, an outer region, a borderland, far from the center of Judaism in Jerusalem. It was also a crossroads of the great caravan roads of the world. It was a region of mixed people and languages. Roberto Goizueta observes that: "Galilee was often viewed by first-century Jews as a 'Jewish enclave in the midst of unfriendly gentile seas.' "[22] This area was indeed a frontier for the great empires in their struggles. The cities of Sepphoris and Tiberias, for example, were administrative centers of Hellenistic-Roman culture. Jewish worship in Galilee was affected by the influences of Hellenistic-Roman culture and political domination. Richard Horsley argues that "[i]t is possible, perhaps even likely, that some Jews considered themselves faithful even while they utilized what would be classified as pagan or Graeco-Roman symbols as a matter of course in their everyday lives."[23] Those multicultural centers of affluence were viewed with suspicion by the Jews in the Galilean countryside. Nevertheless, the Jewish traditions of the peasants in Galilee were also different from those practiced in Jerusalem. Let me point out some of those significant differences:

> Galilee was heir to the traditions of the Northern Kingdom: the Torah was important, also the circumcision, but they did not affirm the written and oral Torah as interpreted by the Judean Israelites, the Jerusalem retainer class and the Temple aristocracy. Galilee was home to popular legal and wisdom traditions. Galilee was also ambivalent about Jerusalem, the Temple, the priestly aristocracy, and their dues and tithes.

The population at Galilee would have been composed of non-Judean Jews with distinctive yet shared Jewish traditions with Jerusalem. It is also possible that some of the population in the region must have been Gentiles in their ethnic and cultural heritage. Israelites and Gentiles shared in Galilee adjacent homes, courtyards, perhaps even a house or cooking area.[24]

If we take the incarnation seriously, we need to take seriously also that Jesus was a Galilean Jew. In this context, we need to understand that the Jews of Judea looked down on the Jews from Galilee. The Galileans were considered ignorant of the rules of the temple and impure in many ways because of their daily contact with pagans. They were not considered capable of speaking "correctly" because of their mixture with other cultures. The Galilean Jews were, in fact, regarded as inferior and impure by their own relatives from Judea. They were looked down because of their *mestizaje*.

In light of Jesus' identity as a Galilean, the scandal of the incarnation and crucifixion becomes even more poignant as we observe how Jesus chose to bring His message of reconciliation to the whole world (2 Corinthians 5:19). His message of reconciliation in light of the trinitarian reality of community and His incarnate ministry as the prophet from Galilee includes welcoming those despised by the dominant culture. Jesus' message of repentance and freedom to the captives begins with His offer of the kingdom to the Galilean Jews (Matthew 4:17; Luke 4:18–19). He empowers them also to bring this message of reconciliation and new creation to the whole world in the Great Commission. In this light, we can read the "genealogy of Jesus Christ the son of David" as good news that impacts and includes *mestizos* as heirs of the kingdom (Matthew 1:1–16), for example, Tamar, Boaz, Obed, and Jesse.

Jesus' exhortation to His Galilean disciples to go first to the house of Israel also becomes more empowering (Matthew 10:6). It includes the witness of Galilean Jews to Judean Jews. Jerusalem must hear the message from those who were considered to be living a borderland existence as *mestizos*. This is the paradoxical nature and the scandal of the cross. Jesus, the prophet of Galilee, goes to Jerusalem as a true prophet of all the Jews (Luke 13:33). The message of the cross has to impact first those who consider their own family to be aliens and foreigners in their own land. It is a call, therefore, to lead the strange community into a new reality and a new day under the message of the cross. This is the impact that Jesus brings with His parables concerning His eschatological banquet (Matthew 22:1–17). Jesus' eschatological call to a new hope, a new creation, is given in the power of the Sacrament of Holy Baptism: "Therefore go and make disciples of all nations, baptizing them in the name of the Father and of the Son and of the Holy Spirit" (Matthew 28:19). Paul declares also in Ephesians that we live the power of the cross that unites us in the reality of our Baptism (Ephesians 2:11–18; 4:3–5). However, this witness of the cross becomes a mockery unless we take seriously the reality of popular religiosity in the U.S. Hispanic experience.

POPULAR RELIGIOSITY

U.S. Hispanic popular religiosity is in essence a popular Catholic religiosity. As such, it may cause some Protestant or evangelical Christians to disdain this important aspect of the Hispanic psyche. In fact, the Protestant Reformation in light of Scripture attempted to put down the popular religious beliefs in Europe.[25] Luther, Zwingli, and Calvin were united at least on this use of Scripture. The Protestant principle of *sola scriptura* was applied against superstitions, adoration of saints, and relics. This aversion to popular religiosity is also evident in Protestant evangelistic work in Latin America. This quest for biblical truth, however, was also mediated by the Enlightenment's quest for rational truth instead of superstitions. This was also the case for the Catholic Reformation in its attempt to pursue a more educated Christianity. Some elements of popular religiosity were permitted in the post-Tridentine church only as a practical strategy against Protestantism. Orlando Espín has argued in a convincing manner that the Tridentine reforms did not have an impact in Latin America.[26] The distances were too great, communications almost impossible, and the native (and later African) populations to be evangelized were enormous.

In light of this history, there are three courses open for our reading of the popular religiosity of Hispanics. First, we may read this popular religiosity as syncretistic. Using a linguistic approach, we may say that the *signifiers*—God, Christ, the Virgin Mary, the saints—were accepted as the symbols of the people's faith. However, they were accepted on the basis of a shift in the corresponding code of *signification*. The Christian symbols were read in light of corresponding ancestral religious significants. Christianity was interpreted according to the values and meanings offered by the ancestral faith. Cristián Parker, as well as other Latin American cultural anthropologists, find in this popular religiosity of the people a way to survive in light of their cultural reality.[27] There is no doubt that these syncretistic practices have occurred in Latin America and the Caribbean. Syncretism is a complicated business because followers of a popular religion in a second and third generation may become quite angry and disturbed when elements foreign to Christianity are pointed out to them.[28]

Second, the tendency for Protestants and evangelicals, in light of this syncretistic reading of popular religiosity, will be to offer a witness of the cross through a process of transculturation. This witness of the cross rejects the other culture and imposes the missionary's culture on the hearers out of fear of heterodoxy. However, this approach ignores the incarnational dimension of the Gospel. Third, we might engage in a process of inculturation. In this point of departure, the message of the Gospel is offered in the most appropriate form possible within the specific culture so the people will be able to understand and assimilate the message. This is the approach followed by many contemporary missiologists.[29] I find this approach wrestles seriously with the Gospel in relationship to the cultural context. However, the practice of inculturation may be compromised by syncretism in an effort to support the particular values of a culture in a way that ignores the good news of the Gospel. I believe that this happens when a natural theology predominates over a theology of the cross in the process of inculturation. The Gospel message becomes ineffective if our method of inculturation does not offer the Gospel as God's means of transformation and reconciliation.

In other words, the planting of the Gospel is more than the affirmation of the important values of our *mestizaje*. It is a call to a new creation, a new hope, in light of the cross. This hope can only be ours in light of the incarnational and soteriological vision of the cross. God's people are called to repentance and a new day in this power of the cross (Mark 1:15). I find that in the witness and experience of the cross we can acknowledge seriously the popular religiosity of U.S. Hispanics and not fall into syncretistic practices. This requires that we understand popular religiosity and what it signifies to U.S. Hispanics in light of the cross.

A Latino/Hispanic popular religiosity is not merely the "folk," or "popular," religiosity of the people. It is better understood as "the faith of the people."[30] U.S. Hispanic Roman Catholic theologians make great efforts to ground their Christian faith in Scripture and also in true Roman Catholic style, in the written post-apostolic tradition. However, they find in the "faith of the people" an intuitive awareness, a *sensus fidelium*, that is able to interpret "whether something is true or not vis-à-vis the Gospel" or whether "someone is acting according with the Christian Gospel or not" or whether "something important for Christianity is being heard."[31] This is to say that the faith of the people can sense that God as creator honors and values their situation of *mestizaje*. Also it is intuitively understood that Jesus Christ's love for His people in the Gospels cannot be ignored or placed aside in God's acts of creation. This faith of the people is grounded in *lo cotidiano*, that is, in the daily experiences of the people in their homes and communities.[32]

Elizondo, former rector of the San Fernando Catedral, San Antonio, Texas, and founder of the Mexican American cultural center, points to the "faith of our *abuelos* and *abuelitos*," that is, the faith of our grandfathers and grandmothers, as the key component that defines a Hispanic/Latino community.[33] We must take seriously *la familia* if we are to offer a faithful incarnational witness of the cross. The family is the cradle of the Latino/Hispanic religiosity. *La familia* is what primarily shapes a Hispanic person's personal, social, and religious values. The family, not the individual, is the main focus of social stratification. The fundamental religious values that shape a Hispanic/Latino sense of wholeness are taught by the grandparents and parents. The grandmothers and mothers in particular teach the presence of God in everyday life situations.

God is present in a real way in the everyday life of a Hispanic family. Our language about God is relational and spoken in light of the community's hopes. Our parents teach us early in life to pepper our everyday speech with *"Dios te bendiga"* ("May God bless you"); *"Hay Jesús"* ("God be with us"); *"Vaya con Dios"* ("May God be with you"); and *"Si Dios lo permite"* ("If it is God's will"). There is no compartmentalization of the sacred and secular worlds in this way of life. This is affirmed in the homes of many Hispanics who keep a "family altar" in the master bedroom or living room in much the same way that Anglo Lutherans display Albrecht Durer's *Praying Hands*. I have found that Hispanics will maintain these altars even after affirming the catholic evangelical faith. These altars often contain statutes of Jesus, Mary, and the family saints. We could look at these altars and say: "You are worshiping false idols." Or we could affirm the "faith of the people," their hopes and dreams in our sinful human world, in light of the cross. This is, I believe, what Paul did when he visited Athens. He observed their objects of worship. He affirmed the altar of the "Unknown God" by proclaiming whom this God was, the creator of all, the one who died and rose for humanity (Acts 17:23).

To honor the *mestizaje* of the U.S. Hispanic community, we need to explore at least the two predominant foundational symbols to the U.S. Hispanic popular religiosity. They are the Virgen de Guadalupe and the crucified Christ.

La Morenita, the Virgen de Guadalupe, is the manifestation of Mary as the *mestizo* virgin of Guadalupe at Tepeyac in 1531. Tepeyac was an important shrine for the worship of the Aztec goddess of war, Tonantzín. Cultural anthropologists have read the Virgen de Guadalupe as a syncretistic image that has helped the people of Mexico survive in a new identity and hope despite their *mestizaje*.[34] An evangelical catholic Christian could certainly be turned off by what appears to be a syncretistic practice. The *Nican Mopohua* narrative of the virgin apparition is written in *Nahuatl,* the language of the people. The language and symbols used, such as numerology and roses, are important to the Aztec culture.[35] However, this narrative is definitely about an apparition of Mary as a *mestizo* virgin who affirms the reality and worthiness of the *mestizo* people. She manifests herself as a humble and pure virgin who brings God's acceptance and love of the *mestizo*. They are most worthy in God's eyes. The virgin appears to Juan Diego, a poor *mestizo* faithful, who was considered inferior in God's eyes by the Spanish bishop. To Juan Diego, in his own native language of Nahuatl, Mary reveals God's intention to build a temple in her name as a place of refuge for the oppressed and dispossessed.

The image of a pure *mestizo* virgin is an important affirmation. The conquest of the people was brought about through the rape of their mothers by the white conquistadores. Now a *mestizo* woman, a pure virgin, brings to the new people honor rather than dishonor. She speaks to Diego in loving, motherly, and humble terms, relating that he, not the bishop, is the carrier of God's gift of affirmation to His people. Mary affirms a place of refuge and honor for a people forged in conquest out of white and Indian blood. Jeanette Rodríguez describes quite admirably what is offered to U.S. Hispanics through La Guadalupana. She writes:"Guadalupe's message of love and compassion, help and protection, cannot be frozen into a mere devotional experience. Rather the message has to do with the affirmation of the people. Her image is a carrier of eschatological hope . . ."[36]

The Virgen de Guadalupe is the most significant figure in the popular religiosity of the Mexican community. We should note that it was only after the narratives of the apparitions of the Virgin of Guadalupe took hold in the popular religiosity of the people that the Catholic church in Mexico experienced tremendous growth among the *mestizo* population. The history of Latin America and the Caribbean point to similar narratives of apparitions of Mary in which she affirms the people.[37] Some of the narratives have had more impact or are more popular than others. None are as well known or have had the impact of the Virgin of Guadalupe. How do we provide a message of the cross that is truly liberating to our human and social conditions of sin in light of the Guadalupan narrative? How do we do this without falling into Mariology or syncretism?

Several Roman Catholic theologians, such as Elizondo and Orlando Espín, have interpreted the image of the Virgin of Guadalupe as a more powerful symbol than just a Marian apparition. They see it as a revelation of God's trinitarian presence through the power of the Holy Spirit working in history.[38] They read it in light of pneumatology. I agree with them that pneumatology, the doctrine of the work of the Holy Spirit, is important to a living witness that is attentive to a Hispanic/Latino popular religiosity. The meaning of redemption, however, cannot be read only in light of God's affirmation of His creation. We would confess in this manner the Second Article of the Apostles' Creed in light of the First Article. Both articles belong together. The message of the cross is what should guide our reading of God's unconditional love in creation (1 Corinthians 1:21–25). It is in light of the cross that we should understand the gifts of the Spirit and provide a living witness to the power of God in our wounded communities. Elizondo's poignant affirmation of Jesus' Galilean ministry and Espín's earlier attempts to ground the "faith of the people" in the datum of Jesus' incarnation and cross come closer to this catholic evangelical witness of the cross.[39]

While we as catholic evangelical Christians cannot support a devotion to Mary, we need to remember that one of the most important images for Luther is the one of the servant mother Mary, who in humility proclaims God's love and affirmation of His people.[40] In the Magnificat, Mary embodied for Luther a humble servant of God's unconditional love in Jesus Christ. In fact Mary underscores for Luther a theologian of the cross who affirms the paradox of calling worthy what is unworthy and unworthy what is considered worthy through human eyes. Mary affirms a theology of grace that reveals our unrighteousness yet God's affirmation of His people under the cross. It is in this light that we can read the narrative of La Guadalupana and affirm the "faith of the people." The narrative reflects God's affirmation and healing of the helpless vis-à-vis the disdain of the powerful. It is in this realization, Luther observes, that we live the joy of the presence of the Holy Spirit.[41]

Probably the most universal symbol of Hispanic religiosity is the symbol of the crucified Christ. In particular, from my personal experience as a U.S. Hispanic and as a pastor among Hispanics, *Viernes Santo*, Good Friday, is an important date in the popular religiosity of U.S. Hispanics. I have already made reference to how this symbol sometimes is read as an impotent and masochistic symbol rather than as a powerful symbol that recalls God's affirmation of His people. Students of the Reformation know that Luther's theology of the cross affirms the way of discipleship in affirmation of the neighbor and of all humanity. From a Hispanic perspective, I have found in the theological work of the Pentecostal theologian Samuel Solívan a similar vision in his attempt to follow what he calls an "orthopathos."[42] Solívan grounds his theology in the authority of the Word. However, he finds that orthodox theology has often pursued propositional truth without engaging and affirming the suffering of the helpless and dispossessed. Also he is critical of those who pursue an orthopraxis because many have failed to engage the real meaning of Christ's transformative love for others. Only in the engagement of Christ's incarnational and soteriological relationship with others, an "orthopathos," are we able to understand the profound meaning of the popular religiosity of U.S. Hispanics.[43] It is when we are engaged in this incarnational relationship with Jesus that we are able to live the scandal of the cross that is articulated so well by Elizondo:

> Why is the "scandal" of the cross as necessary for salvation today as it was for Jesus? Because the cross continues to reveal the impurity of the pure and purity of the impure, the innocence of criminals and the crime of the innocent, the righteousness of sinners and the sin of the righteous, the wisdom of the foolish and the foolishness of the wise.[44]

This is what Luther understood as the way of the cross in his Heidelberg Disputation.[45] Luther did not separate orthodoxy from orthopraxis. The righteousness of God is completely realized in Christ's condemnation of our human pride (sin) and in His affirmation of the sinful and helpless through a life of faith. Similarly, the life of a Christian is one of active discipleship for others on the way of the cross. Luther affirms: "For one becomes a theologian by living, by dying, by being damned: not by mere intellectualizing, reading and speculating."[46] It is in light of this theology of the cross that we can read also other popular religious symbols in the life of U.S. Hispanics.

Harold Recinos underscores this active vision of the crucified Christ in the telling of the parable of the rich man and Lazarus in Luke 16:19–31.[47] This narrative is a powerful popular religious symbol among exiled Salvadorans in the city. It expresses for them that the despised ones are affirmed by God. They have a name and a future. The rich man is nameless, but Lazarus is loved by God in his human condition. God is active in this parable to transform the fate of the helpless and destitute. In other words, Lazarus is a symbol of Christ's incarnate presence. He stands as an active disciple of the cross, and God honors him for his stand of faith. The Christ that died for our sins and rose for our justification is the incarnate Christ that never abandons His people.

Elizondo and many Protestant theologians have affirmed that U.S. Hispanics cannot deny their popular religiosity as a way of life. It is imbedded in our psyche because of our families and culture. This is why I must share an autobiographical note concerning my family's popular religiosity. My middle name is *Lázaro*. I was named by my father after San Lázaro, who is, along with La Caridad del Cobre, the most popular saint in Cuba. San Lázaro is, in essence, the Lázaro of the parable in Luke 16. Many Cubans give and have given devotion to this popular saint. This is why when I became a Lutheran, I tried to change my middle name to Luther, an action that visibly disturbed my father. I had the good sense to respect my father's wishes, and later he became a catholic evangelical by affirmation of faith. During his last years, I remember how he would recite Romans 3. He had a faith similar to mine. He understood clearly the concept of justification by faith alone, which is why I could not understand why until the day of his death he had a statue of San Lázaro in his car. I also remember that one of the last shrines we visited in Cuba was El Rincón. This shrine, dedicated to San Lázaro, was the site of a ministry to those who had suffered with leprosy. Several times after his death, I dreamt of my father as a Lázaro-like figure, pointing to La Habana. This may sound ridiculous and even unevangelical to some, but in my unconscious mind there is a profound religious symbol that is rooted in the popular religiosity of my family. Lázaro was one who stood in his poverty, helplessness, and exile and was loved by God. He symbolizes that God walks with us on the way home. He affirms our struggles and humanity and gives us hope against all hope.

This is the kind of popular religiosity that sustained my father through poverty and discrimination. This is the faith that I inherited as meaningful and valid. It is the kind of faith that has given me healing and wholeness in the name of Christ. It is, in my humble opinion, the kind of faith that is not contrary to an affirmation of the incarnational reality of the gift of justification by faith. This faith experience is also sought and expressed in other forms and ways in the Latino Protestant experience of popular religiosity.[48]

Hispanics, however, also underscore the celebration of life amid their struggles. It is in this celebration of festive hope that we can find a witness to the eschatological and sacramental dimensions of the cross. It is also in light of this festive hope that we can find some practical applications of the witness of the cross in the U.S. Hispanic reality.

FESTIVE HOPE

Anyone acquainted with Hispanic culture knows that one of the blessings that Hispanics share is their capacity to celebrate. This capacity to celebrate, however, is not frivolous and carefree. Fiestas in the Hispanic experience are not just "parties." They are solemn religious or public celebrations of important events in the life of the community. I would like to offer some suggestions of how our fiestas serve as religious points of contact for the witness of the cross. Roberto S. Goizueta has summarized quite admirably some of the important characteristics and functions of "fiestas" in the life of the faithful. Fiestas in the U.S. Hispanic experience offer: (1) an expression of *communitas*; (2) human life lived in the subjunctive; (3) the confluence of play and work; and, therefore, (4) they are a form of liturgical action.[49]

Latinos in the U.S. Hispanic experience celebrate their sense of community. Fiestas allow U.S. Hispanics to celebrate their "essential we." When U.S. Hispanics celebrate a certain patron saint, this is not a mere celebration of a particular individual, it is a celebration of their identity as a family. In the Hispanic experience, a person's "saint day" is more important than his or her "birthday" because most Latinos were named after a favorite, or patron, saint of the family. My first name is Alberto. I was named after my maternal grandfather, who was named after Alberto de Sicilia. My saint day is August 7. While in Cuba, my saint day was always a time that my grandfather and I and my whole family celebrated together our common bond. When I became a Lutheran and it came the time to celebrate the "saint day" again, I told my grandfather that I did not wish to do this because I did not believe in worshiping saints. My grandfather was deeply disturbed and disappointed, and my action took something special away from our relationship. My grandfather was my godfather, and during my childhood he took seriously the joyous task of taking me to church with the family. The theology of the cross must affirm these relationships. We must express a theology of the cross that affirms this popular religiosity while remaining faithful to our confessional faith. This imperative becomes critical in achieving wholeness in our Christian walk.

Baptisms and weddings also bring extended families closer together. It is during these religious acts in which the secular and religious arenas unite that we celebrate our sense of being a community. It is during the preparation and celebration of weddings and baptisms that godfathers and godmothers form a common bond. The word *godfather* in Spanish is *compadre*, that is, one who "coparents" with the parents of the baptized. These celebrations are like sacramental acts because the community joins as one in these ceremonies and fiestas.

These celebrations are always a celebration of life. They are not empty festivities because Latinos celebrate and respond to the presence of God's love. Central to these acts of communal celebration is the fact that we celebrate life amid our sufferings and sorrows. This is why in Latino popular Catholicism the cross is commonly at the center of the celebrations.[50] The celebration of *Viernes Santo* (Good Friday) cannot be viewed, therefore, as a morbid celebration. It is, rather, a celebration of the giver of life amid the sufferings and absurdities that are faced in life. *Las Posadas*, for example, a narration of Mary and Joseph's journey to Bethlehem, becomes an event in which the community lives and remembers their rejection as immigrants, but it is also a remembrance of God's presence and care in the journey.[51] This is why the public acting out of the *Posadas* and the *Via Crucis* are important events in the celebration of U.S. Hispanic spirituality.

These celebrations, however, are also opportunities to live life in the subjunctive. A verb in the subjunctive mood, by Webster's definition, is used to express "supposition, desire, hypothesis, possibility, etc. rather than to state an actual fact . . ." The subjunctive mood, for all practical purposes, is obsolete in the English language. However, it plays an important role in the Spanish language. I also believe that it plays an important role in our festive hope.[52] When Latinos come together and celebrate, they are, in essence, creating a space for possibilities in their life of pilgrimage and borderland existence. These religious celebrations and fiestas allow the participants to celebrate the present in light of the hoped for future. This understanding is central to our witness of the cross.

When we celebrate the Eucharist, we celebrate the Lord's real presence, but in this walking together we also celebrate new possibilities for the future. We celebrate real authentic community and the liberating presence of the Spirit in a world where the wolf does not yet sit with the lamb (Isaiah 11:9). The Eucharist always reveals a not-yet-realized future. I believe that the agape meals celebrated in the New Testament are also indications of this real-yet-hoped-for eschatological community. Yet we know how those celebrations were carried out in the subjunctive from the conflicts that took place in the New Testament church (1 Corinthians 11:17–27). The agape feasts were celebrated only as temporary possibilities for community. They were also marked by the disdain of the powerful toward the least.

This festive hope celebrated in the subjunctive is manifested especially in unique celebrations such as *El Día de los Muertos,* the Day of the Celebration of the Dead. This is also an important date in the history of the Reformation. Catholic evangelicals celebrate All Saints' Day on the same day. We know that Luther posted his Ninety-Five Theses on the Eve of All Saints' Day, October 31. He desired to lead the people of his day to the freedom of the Gospel in light of God's grace. November 1 is also one of the most significant family dates among the U.S. Mexican population. In this Day of the Celebration of the Dead, beautiful altars are built in honor of the dead. Pictures of the departed ones, as well as of Jesus, Mary, and the saints, are placed on the altars. Special bread for the dead is baked, along with sugar candy made to resemble a skeleton. In Mexican folklore the dead have a sweet tooth. *El Día de los Muertos* is the day that Mexicans and other Hispanics remember their dead and celebrate life. Also in this celebration of life and family, present life situations are seen as temporary. This is a day to laugh at problems in the hope for a better future. It is a celebration of festive hope in the subjunctive.

If we analyze this celebration, we will discover also the third dimension of the fiesta, "the confluence of play and work." It takes a lot of work to create such fiestas. The Easter Triduum celebration, as Goizueta observes, encompasses three days. These are not escapist, random celebrations (as in postmodernism) or work directed in a mechanical way to create something productive for society (as in modernism). The people work together to affirm the values of the community. These celebrations are affirmations of the community and the people's hope amid sufferings and a borderland existence. The witness of the cross and the celebrations of the sacramental acts of Baptism and the Eucharist support, I believe, the values underscored in these celebrations.

How may we offer, therefore, celebrations of festive hope in light of the Hispanic reality and the witness of the cross? I have some suggestions in light of our confessional witness.

1. We should celebrate All Saints' Day Latino style. I am not suggesting masses for the death. I am suggesting agape meals, fiestas, and displays in remembrance of loved ones in light of our Baptism. The non-Hispanic community must join and affirm these acts of celebration with the Hispanic community.

2. I suggest the celebration of a person's birthday or the celebration of the day of her/his baptism with their families and the community of faith. The special celebration of *La Quinceañera*, the welcoming of the young daughters who turn 15 as valid and accepted adult members in the family and the community of faith, is an important celebration for the church.

3. Holy Week should be an important time to celebrate through liturgical acts Maundy Thursday, Good Friday, and the celebration of Easter as it was experienced by the Galilean disciples.

4. The faith community should celebrate Ash Wednesday at the beginning of the Lenten season with the imposition of ashes. It should also celebrate *Las Posadas* during the Advent season through congregational and community participation. Such celebrations contribute to the vision of festive hope in light of the way of the cross and the affirmation of the faith of the people.[53]

All these celebrations need, however, the participation of our greater community of faith. So we can give an incarnate witness of Jesus, who "was delivered over to death for our sins and was raised to life for our justification" (Romans 4:25), we must live with the *mestizo* people of God the discipleship of the cross in a real sacramental community. We must experience together the real expectation of God's eschatological kingdom in our festive celebrations. As we walk together, we live, we pray, and we hope together as the children of God. We sing joyful songs in this loving act just as the prophet Isaiah sang and hoped with his people, the people of God—*nuestra familia* (Isaiah 11:1–12).

NOTES

1. Miguel de Unamuno, *Del Sentimiento Trágico de la Vida en los Hombres y en los Pueblos* (Madrid: Espasa-Calpe, 1971), 79.

2. José Miguez Bonino, *Jesús: Ni Vencido Ni Monarca Celestial* (Buenos Aires: Tierra Nueva, 1977), 120.

3. Ignacio Ellacuría, "The Crucified People," *Systematic Theology: Perspectives from Liberation Theology* (ed. Jon Sobrino and Ignacio Ellacuría; Maryknoll: Orbis, 1996).

4. Ellacuría, "Crucified People," 264–67. Cf. also Luther's comments on 1 Peter 1:10–12, LW 30:23: "For just as faith, the name, the Word, and the works of Christ are mine by reason of my belief in Him, so His sufferings are also mine . . . Christ's sufferings are fulfilled . . . every day until the end of the world."

5. Martin Luther, *Early Theological Works* (ed. James Atkinson; Philadelphia: Westminster, 1961), 290. Thesis 20 is my translation from WA 1:362.1–2. It takes into consideration Atkinson's translation.

6. Cf. "City population lowest since 1940," *Milwaukee Journal Sentinel* (9 March 2001), 14A. These statistics are based on the 2000 U.S. census report.

7. Virgilio Elizondo, *Galilean Journey* (Maryknoll: Orbis, 1983), 41. I believe, however, that Sobrino and Elizondo must incorporate in this incarnational reading the impact and power of the atonement. I find that God's reconciliation in Christ in light of the atonement offers a powerful and faithful biblical signpost for affirming God's people. See my earlier essay in this book, "Signposts for Global Witness in Luther's Theology of the Cross," in which I make some critical comments on the relationship of the atonement to the incarnation in light of Luther's theology of the cross.

8. Virgilio Elizondo, "*Mestizaje* as a Locus of Theological Reflection," in *Beyond Borders: Writings of Virgilio Elizondo and Friends* (ed. Timothy Matovina; Maryknoll: Orbis, 2000), 162–63. This is a reprinted essay that was originally published in 1983. David T. Abalos, *Latinos in the United States* (Notre Dame: University of Notre Dame Press, 1986), is a perceptive sociological work that explores how this problem of identity has unfolded in the U.S. Hispanic reality. See also the essay by

David Maldonado Jr., "Doing Theology and the Anthropological Questions," in *Teología en Conjunto: A Collaborative Hispanic Protestant Theology* (ed. José David Rodríguez and Loida I. Martell-Otero; Louisville: Westminster John Knox, 1997), 98–111. Maldonado identifies how, in the U.S. Hispanic experience, Mexicans, Puerto Ricans, and Cubans share different perspectives but the same reality concerning identity. Roberto S. Goizueta, in *Caminemos con Jesús: Toward a Hispanic/Latino Theology of Accompaniment* (Maryknoll: Orbis, 1995), 1–17, reflects on this reality of *"mestizaje/exile"* in light of his Cuban American experience. As white, educated Cubans, we are not exempt from this borderland experience of *mestizaje*. I concur with Goizueta in light of my Cuban American experience within church and society.

9. Elizondo, *"Mestizaje* as a Locus of Theological Reflection," 161.

10. As quoted in Vitor Westhelle, *Voces de Protesta en América Latina* (Chicago: Lutheran School of Theology, 2000), 31 (*my translation*). Cf. Jean-Pierre Ruiz, "The Bible and U.S. Hispanic American Theological Discourse," in *From the Heart of Our People: Latino/a Explorations in Catholic Systematic Theology* (ed. Orlando Espín and Miguel H. Díaz; Maryknoll: Orbis, 1999), 100–05. Professor Ruiz gives a summary of the conquistadores' abuse of the Bible. He narrates in particular how the Scriptures and the cross were used as instruments of oppression by Pizarro against Atahualpa.

11. Cf. Justo L. González, "The Religious World of Hispanic Americans," in *World Religions in America* (ed. Jacob Neusner; Louisville: Westminster John Knox, 1994), 111–29, for a general overview of this *mestizaje* and conquest. Cf. also Enrique Dussel, *The Invention of the Americas: Eclipse of "the Other" and the Myth of Modernity* (New York: Continuum, 1995).

12. Elizondo, *Galilean Journey*, 13. Elizondo provides a powerful summary of this "Nordic-Protestant Conquest" in pages 13–18.

13. Elizondo, *Galilean Journey*, 14.

14. Cf. Vine DeLoria, *Custer Died for Your Sins: An Indian Manifesto* (New York: Avon, 1969), 106.

15. Tomás Atencio, "The Empty Cross: The First Hispano Presbyterians in Northern Mexico and Southern Colorado," *Protestantes/Protestants: Hispanic Christianity within Mainline Traditions* (ed. David Maldonado Jr.; Nashville: Abingdon, 1999), 38–40.

16. Atencio, "Empty Cross," 15–16. I will not discuss here the Spanish-American War of 1898, which occurred under the expansionist vision of President William McKinley (1843–1901) and ended with the Treaty of Paris (December 10, 1898). This treaty made Puerto Rico an acquired territory. The history of Puerto Rican migrations to the United States is a direct result of this second phase of the Nordic Protestant Conquest.

17. Patricia Gonzales and Roberto Rodriguez, "Column of the Americas," *Universal Press Syndicate* (22 October 1999).

18. A recent article by Linda K. Barrow, "An Evangelical Surge: Mission in Mexico," *Christian Century* (28 February 2001): 22–25, shows sadly

how the influence of North American missionaries have contributed
to the degredation in Mexico of the image of the crucified Christ
and the meaning of the Virgen de Guadalupe. Cf. Elsa Tamez,
"Cristología latinoamericana a la luz de los nuevos sujetos del que-
hacer teológico," *Vida y Pensamiento* 20.1 (2000): 91–104, for a summary of key themes that the witness of the cross must take into consideration in the *mestizaje* of the Latin American reality.

19. See in particular Elizondo, *Galilean Journey*, chapters 4–9, pp. 37–125.

20. Henry Cole, trans. and ed., *Select Works of Martin Luther* (4 vols.; London: T. Bensley, 1924–1926), 3:184. The citation is from Luther's
Operationes in Psalmos, which is in WA 5.

21. Luis G. Pedraja, *Jesus Is My Uncle: Christology from a Hispanic Perspective* (Nashville: Abingdon, 1999), 1–38.

22. Roberto Goizueta, "A Christology for a Global Church," in *Beyond
Borders*, 154. Goizueta draws from the work of Douglas Edwards, "The
Socio-Economic and Cultural Ethos of the Lower Galilee in the First
Century," in *The Galilee in Late Antiquity* (ed. Lee I. Levine; New York:
Jewish Theological Seminary of America, 1992).

23. Goizueta, "Christology for a Global Church," 153. Goizueta relies on
the study by Richard A. Horsley, *Archaeology, History, and Society in
Galilee: The Social Context of Jesus and the Rabbis* (Valley Forge: Trinity
Press International, 1996).

24. Goizueta, "Christology for a Global Church," 153–54.

25. Cf. Justo L. González, "Reinventing Dogmatics: A Footnote from a
Reinvented Protestant," in *From the Heart of Our People*, 217–29, an
excellent treatment of the challenge of "popular religiosity" to
Protestantism and the official Roman Catholic Conciliar theology. I
follow here his insights on this topic.

26. Orlando O. Espín, *The Faith of the People: Theological Reflections on
Popular Catholicism* (Maryknoll: Orbis, 1997), 1–10.

27. Cristián Parker, *Popular Religion and Modernization in Latin America*
(Maryknoll: Orbis, 1996), 12–13.

28. Andrés I. Pérez y Mena, "Understanding Religiosity in Cuba," *Journal
of Hispanic/Latino Theology* 7.3 (February 2000): 29–30.

29. Cf., for example, Manuel M. Marzal, Eugenio Maurer, Xavier Albó,
and Bartomeu Meliá, *The Indian Face of God in Latin America* (trans.
Penelope R. Hall; Maryknoll: Orbis, 1996). All the writers are Jesuit
missiologists. See in particular the reflections of Eugenio Maurer concerning Tseltal Christianity. The Tseltal are descendants of the Mayas
and live primarily today in the state of Chiapas, Mexico.

30. Cf. Orlando O. Espín, "Tradition and Popular Religion: An Understanding of the *Sensus Fidelium*" in *Mestizo Christianity: Theology from
the Latino Perspective* (ed. Arturo J. Bañuelas; Maryknoll: Orbis, 1995),
149–52; and Goizueta, *Caminemos con Jesús*, 1–46.

31. Espín, "Tradition and Popular Religion," 149–50.

32. Orlando O. Espín, "An Exploration into the Theology of Grace and
Sin," in *From the Heart of Our People*, 124–30.

33. Elizondo, *Galilean Journey*, 28–29.

34. Cf. Parker, *Popular Religion and Modernization in Latin America*, 15.

35. See Jeannette Rodríguez, "Sangre Llama a Sangre: Cultural Memory as a Source of Theological Insight," in *Hispanic/Latino Theology* (ed. Ada María Isasi-Díaz and Fernando F. Segovia; Minneapolis: Fortress, 1996), 122–33. Rodríguez has provided an excellent narrative of how the Virgin of Guadalupe in the story uses the language and symbols of the people to express how God affirms them in their reality of *mestizaje*.

36. Rodríguez, "Sangre Llama a Sangre," 133.

37. Miguel H. Díaz, "We Walk-with Our Lady of Charity," in *From the Heart of Our People*, 153. Cf. Parker, *Popular Religion and Modernization in Latin America*, 14–15, for a list of the most important recognized regional devotions of Mary.

38. Espín, "Exploration into the Theology of Sin and Grace," 137–41.

39. Elizondo, *Galilean Journey*, 91–114; Espín, "Tradition and Popular Religion," 162–63

40. Martin Luther, "The Magnificat," LW 21:300–01.

41. Luther, "The Magnificat," LW 21:301.

42. Samuel Solívan, *The Spirit, Pathos and Liberation* (Sheffield: Sheffield Academic Press, 1998), 66–88.

43. Goizueta, *Caminemos con Jesús*, 68–69. See also Alberto Lázaro García, *Theology of the Cross: A Critical Study of Leonardo Boff's and Jon Sobrino's Theology of the Cross in Light of Martin Luther's Theology of the Cross as Interpreted by Luther Scholars* (Ph.D. diss., Lutheran School of Theology, Chicago, Illinois, 1987).

44. Elizondo, *Galilean Journey*, 41.

45. See n. 5 and my contribution in this book on Luther's theology of the cross.

46. Martin Luther, *Operationes in Psalmos* (1519–1521), WA 5:163.29–30: "Vivendo, immo moriendo et damnando fit theologus, non intelligendo, legendo aut speculando."

47. Harold Recinos, "The Barrio as the Locus of a New Church," in *Hispanic/Latino Theology*, 186–87.

48. Cf. Edwin Aponte, "*Coritos* as Active Symbols in Latino Protestant Popular Religion," *Journal of Hispanic/Latino Theology* 2.3 (February 1995): 52–65. Aponte identifies "*coritos*," spiritual songs, as serving in the same manner as African American spirituals: They affirm the hope of God's people amid oppression and suffering.

49. Roberto Goizueta, "Fiesta: Life in the Subjunctive," in *From the Heart of Our People*, 90–96.

50. Goizueta, "Fiesta," 91; Elizondo, *Galilean Journey*, 42; Atencio observes ("Empty Cross," 58) how important the cross and the remembrace of Christ's sacrifice is for the identity of the Indohispano as a community in New Mexico. It is because of this importance that it is impossible for some Hispanic Catholics to think that Hispanics could be Protestant. Cf. also the work of Eldin Villafañe, *The Liberat-*

ing Spirit (Grand Rapids: Eerdmans, 1993), 12. He incorporates, in light of his Pentecostal faith, the important experience of fiesta within the Hispanic reality of suffering.

51. Elizondo, *Galilean Journey*, 37–38.

52. Goizueta, "Fiesta," 93–94.

53. Cf. Elizondo, *Galilean Journey*, for more examples of important celebrations; Cf. Gilbert Romero, *Hispanic Devotional Piety* (Maryknoll: Orbis, 1991), discusses several of these important celebrations, connecting them to Scripture.

FOR FURTHER READING

Bañuelas , Arturo J., ed. *Mestizo Christianity: Theology from the Latino Perspective.* Maryknoll: Orbis, 1995.

Elizondo, Virgilio. *Galilean Journey.* Maryknoll: Orbis, 1983.

Espín, Orlando O., and Miguel H. Díaz, eds. *From the Heart of Our People: Latino/a Explorations in Catholic Systematic Theology.* Maryknoll: Orbis, 1999.

———. *The Faith of the People: Theological Reflections on Popular Catholicism.* Maryknoll: Orbis, 1997.

Fernández, Eduardo C. *La Cosecha: Harvesting Contemporary United States Hispanic Theology.* Collegeville, Minn.: Liturgical Press, 2000.

Goizueta, Roberto S. *Caminemos con Jesús: Toward a Hispanic/Latino Theology of Accompaniment.* Maryknoll: Orbis, 1995.

González, Justo L. *Mañana: Christian Theology from a Hispanic Perspective.* Nashville: Abingdon, 1990.

Isasi-Díaz, Ada María, and Fernando F. Segovia, eds. *Hispanic/Latino Theology.* Minneapolis: Fortress, 1996.

Maldonado, David Jr., ed. *Protestantes/Protestants: Hispanic Christianity within Mainline Traditions.* Nashville: Abingdon, 1999.

Matovina, Timothy, ed. *Beyond Borders: Writings of Virgilio Elizondo and Friends.* Maryknoll: Orbis, 2000.

Pedraja, Luis G. *Jesus Is My Uncle: Christology from a Hispanic Perspective.* Nashville: Abingdon, 1999.

Recinos, Harold J. *Who Comes in the Name of the Lord? Jesus at the Margins.* Nashville: Abingdon, 1997.

Rodríguez, José David, and Loida I. Martell-Otero, eds. *Teología en Conjunto: A Collaborative Hispanic Protestant Theology.* Louisville: Westminster/John Knox, 1997.

Romero, C. Gilbert. *Hispanic Devotional Piety.* Maryknoll: Orbis, 1991.

Solívan, Samuel. *The Spirit, Pathos and Liberation.* Sheffield: Sheffield Academic Press, 1998.

Villafañe, Eldin. *The Liberating Spirit.* Grand Rapids: Eerdmans, 1993.

12

The African American Experience and the Theology of the Cross

JOHN NUNES

From the outset it is conceded—if not celebrated—that there is not merely one African American experience, nor is there a single school of expertise on this cultural group. Theological opinions and constructive intellectual options abound in the highly variegated study of black religious life in the United States. In fact, a sign of a maturing culture is its emergence beyond one, monolithic critical interpretation of its past or one prescription of a course of action for its future. This should not be surprising. In their lifetimes, few expected Professor Lionel Trilling to adhere to the same cultural perspective as the Rabbi Jehiel Jacob Weinberg, despite their common Jewish ancestry. From at the least the 1980s forward, commensurate with the renewal of black conservatism, alternate voices have offered refreshing viewpoints on the black experience in the United States.

These divergent voices do, however, have a lineage of dialogue. A classic example is the debates between the cooperative self-sufficiency of Booker T. Washington[1] and the protest radicalism of W. E. B. Du Bois.[2] The third millennium A.D. will witness evolving notions of what it means to survive and thrive as a person of African descent in the United States. This will occur especially as other subcultures of the African diaspora living in North America are incorporated into the burgeoning African American family: namely, West Indians, Afro-Hispanics (Dominicans et al.), and especially recent immigrants from the African continent. Recognizing and anticipating this widening sense of the so-called African American experience, this essay will attempt to go beyond merely one methodological or sociopolitical viewpoint.

Few deny the unique challenge of being black and Christian in the United States. Some have called it a double consciousness; others consider it a providential appointment; still others consign it to the treacherous trash heap of being a sellout. Dr. Samuel Proctor offered this compelling, compassionate, and comprehensive view:

> We face the challenge of being both Black and Christian at the same time, bearing our own burden of oppression while helping others to be relieved of theirs; we are faced with drying our own tears of frustration and failure while drying the tears of others; here we are struggling to overcome our own estrangement and marginality while trying to create a blessed community out of [the] polarization, tribalism, and xenophobia that surround us. We are indeed the wounded healer. We are the victims of wanton hatred while calling others to selfless love. We are falling under the weight of our own crosses while being called on to help shoulder the cross of someone else. Black and Christian! We are called to teach our brothers to be positive, constructive, and nonviolent, while they are the victims of denial, benign neglect and violence.[3]

Dr. Proctor clearly articulates that the sense of identification is connected to community and to the cross. This has been the historic expression within the African American church.

An ecclesial trend in many African American communities in the late twentieth century has been the emergence of a new theology—likely a new expression of an old heresy, though such exploration is not within the scope of this essay. Simply, the content and confession of popular black Christian spirituality has veered toward a theology of individualism and glory at the expense of the preaching of the cross for the sake of the community. In times past, many black churches were stereotyped as preaching an irrelevant fire-and-brimstone, pie-in-the-sky, by-and-by religion. The upside of this emphasis was plain: In "Black preaching, Jesus must die, be buried, and then be resurrected. . . . The whole of the Black experience can be understood in preaching, biblically and theologically, by identifying with what happened to Jesus."[4] The theology of the cross has been central to the Christian black experience in the United States.

A CONTEMPORARY CRISIS OF THE CROSS

The religion *du jour,* however, that is now the rage in many black communities urges the use of faith to obtain material favor, one's long-deserved piece of the American dream. No longer primarily eschatological (or "in the sky"), this novel American pie piety redefines saving faith as a positive attitude in the psyche of the believer rather than a gift given and worked by the Spirit through the Word. Many things are promoted in this highly psychologized faith, from self-improvement to increased popularity. Felt needs dominate and drive this style of ministry that is prescribed in quick tips and easy steps. Peter's warning jumps to mind (2 Peter 2:3). It admonishes truth-compromising leaders with stern correction, especially those engaging in what the Greek literally calls "plastic words" (*plastoi logoi*), that is, linguistic forgery, fake, fabricated, manufactured language, deliberately designed to deceive. To make my point, permit a hyperbolic "cut and dry" statement: At one extreme is a message of greed often euphemized as blessing. At the other pole is the message of the cross. Greed demeans the victim. The Gospel of the cross first gives meaning to being victimized, then offers and applies salvific victory. The sign of the cross signifies the invasion of Christ's victory over the terrible triad of sin, death, and the devil.

In the African American community the rise of these therapeutic models is relatively recent. They tend to avoid and evade the realities of sin and evil by calling, in Luther's words, "evil good and good evil." Rather than by calling it as "[a] theologian of the cross calls the thing what it actually is."[5] Such "success" methodology is not merely antithetical to the theology of the cross, it actually militates against those God most desires to save (Matthew 9:13; Luke 4:18–21; Luke 19:10)—the poor, the systematically oppressed, the chronically feeble, the inordinately fearful, and the vulnerable. Toward these this spiritual seduction appears targeted. The dissembling of truth occurs in the very naming of Jesus, often fervently. This Jesus, however, is not the personal Savior, historical Redeemer, or dominical Lord, but more like a formulaic incantation, a magical leverage for paying bills supernaturally or possessing a millionaire faith for business success or maximizing latent potential. Christian living, according to this scheme, seems defined as primarily organized around an individual's drives, dreams, desires, and delights.

THE ROOTS OF THE CROSS

From slavery until recent times, black people in the United States have most strongly identified with the presence and promise of God's love in suffering. This corresponds with Martin Luther's Heidelberg Disputation of 1518. That is, God is hidden in suffering under the cross—*tecta cruce*. But God does not intend His hidden character to imply an invitation to speculation about His nature and purposes. Rather, the face of God is evident, revealed on the cross. Here, God makes Himself known in His preferred manner: the weakness, shame, and foolishness of the cross. But even here we only see the back parts of God, *posteriora dei.*

One observer suggests the theological practice of African Americans is "crypto-Lutheran," referring to the manner in which these human chattel slaves connected their suffering with the sufferings of Jesus Christ. Finding God's love not in triumphant, overwhelming power and glory but at the cross. "God's love is most hidden in Jesus' suffering and death on the cross. God's love is most hidden where the world and its theology of glory least expects, or wants, to find it."[6] Innately, these people knew that, in all their suffering, God, too, suffered, and in the suffering of God, seen most evidently in Jesus, compassion and saving love would be conferred (see Isaiah 63:9).

It is likely the extraordinary expansion of the black middle class that has prompted movement toward a more individualized preaching of human achievement and material success. Lincoln and Mamiya note that this growth from a petit bourgeoisie to a viable black middle class was accompanied with the internalization of "the major American middle-class values of individualism, privatism, pragmatism, conspicuous consumption, and upward mobility."[7] Human care needs, community crises, and justice issues are more easily sacrificed on the altar of preoccupation with privatized "mighty victory" faith. In an attempt to nudge toward a more biblical, cross-centered, prophetic speaking—as contrasted with the theology of glory—this essay will focus on the roots of theology done by African Americans, leading to the public theology of the civil rights movement. In this activism, Martin Luther King especially balanced social concern (the scandal of segregation) and Christian personalism (the therapeutic necessity of human dignity and worth).

A SUNG THEOLOGY OF THE CROSS

Black theology in the United States begins with suffering and minor key moaning: the "torture tombs of slave ships," the experience of branded servitude, lynching, church-burning, non-suffrage, Jim Crow, second-class citizenship. Their way of speaking about God (*theos logos*) begins as a sung theology, feelingly expressed by weeping exiles in psalms of deep lament, yearning for home, for Zion, for Africa. It is

Lent-like, shaped to relate directly to the crucified and hidden God (*Deus crucifixus et absconditus*). It is also doxological, that is, praise rending. It encompasses the pain of a persecuted people who cried many tears, bled much blood, and crossed many rivers with many gods. "Deep river, my home is over Jordan. . . . Oh, don't you want to go to that gospel feast, that promised land where all is peace?"[8] Thanks be to God, through the Gospel He lavishly outpoured His saving peace on these people.

It was precisely amid implacable suffering that these people came to define themselves in Torah and in Christ, in exodus and freedom in Christ. The African American spiritual says, "Sometimes I'm up. Sometimes I'm down. Sometimes I'm level to the ground, but I still say glory hallelujah."[9] In the theology of the cross, glory is located in the midst of, and despite, suffering and outward circumstances. Albeit this sound of "glory hallelujah" praise was muted, stifled, and silenced by a Babylon-like social experience in the United States, as the spiritual says, "Sometimes I feel like a motherless child, a long, long ways from home."[10]

Yet the theology of the cross succeeded in embedding a deep, durable faith within African Americans. The first slave of African descent landed on American soil in 1619 at Jamestown, Virginia. A half century later, a man named Emmanuel was the first documented Baptism of an African in a Lutheran church, occurring in New York in 1669. Now these people "arguably are the most religious people in the entire world. . . . Ninety-four out of every 100 blacks in the U.S. express the belief that Jesus is God or the Son of God. The comparable proportion for whites is 82 out of 100."[11]

Because of a suffering and injustice similar to the forced servitude and marginalization endured by God's people, Israel, at the hands of the despotic Pharaoh, black people seized the Scripture's exodus story as normative and descriptive. With a mighty hand and an outstretched arm, God became their liberator, leading His chosen people (African Americans) out of Egypt. Geographically, "Egypt" was taken to mean the slave states, and existentially, it was represented by the experience of bondage and racism. The driving core conviction of God's providential care for Israel was preached as precedent and promise of divine help despite circumstances. In his study of the antebellum sermon, David T. Shannon observes that the sermons of that era "present the basic biblical theme of divine presence in the midst of oppression and suffering as a basis of hope."[12]

Historically, African American popular spirituality has viewed the cross as a place (Calvary) and as a symbolic base to represent the metaphysical battle between God and evil. The cross becomes a theological sign and the believer's symbol of hope. Historical theologian Albert Raboteau observes, "In their oppression the slaves found it natural to identify with the sufferings of Jesus, who was depicted in the spirituals as an ever-present and intimate friend."[13] The successive verses of this anonymous slave spiritual pose a series of rhetorical questions: "Were you there when they crucified my Lord? Were you there when they nailed him to the tree? Were you there when they pierced him in the side? Were you there when the sun refused to shine? Were you there when they laid him in the tomb? Were you there when they laid him in the tomb? Oh, sometimes it causes me to tremble, tremble, tremble. Were you there when they laid him in the tomb?"[14]

The identification with the cross extends even to popular literary culture and the African American arts. Marvin B. Tolson (1898–1966), the son of a Methodist preacher, published "Dark Symphony" in 1939. It won a national poetry contest sponsored by the American Negro Exposition. But it was the poem's publication in the *Atlantic Monthly* that won Tolson critical acclaim. In this work he connects directly with the experience of African American suffering and the suffering of Christ. Listen to the human passion and Christ's Passion in this excerpt. The live recording of Tolson reading this section reveals his righteous inquiry in pugilistic tones:[15]

> Oh, how can we forget
> Our human rights denied?
> Oh, how can we forget
> Our manhood crucified?

UNITY UNDER THE CROSS

Some have colloquially commented that at the foot of the cross all ground is level. The cross of Jesus Christ, appropriated by faith, indeed serves as a unifying symbol for the church and the world. Stanley Crouch is a relatively lone voice. As an astute cultural critic he has resisted the temptation toward bashing Christianity in the interest of critical race theory. On the contrary, he affirms the positive, civic, unifying role of this faith even within the context of black suffering, which he connects to the suffering of Jesus on the cross.

Instead of expressing their submission to white people by embracing Christianity, as black nationalists always claim, African Americans actually recognized the extraordinary insight into human frailty that runs throughout the Old Testament and the fact that the New Testament contains perhaps the greatest blues line of all time— "Father, why Thou forsaken Me?" In essence, the harsh insights of the Bible were perfectly compatible with the cold-eyed affirmation of the blues, and from that spiritual and secular foundation an indelibly American sensibility evolved, one perfectly suited for the demands of this society. The result was an incredibly long line of achievement that predates institutionalizing any narrow nationalism that would segregate the world and education into eurocentric or afrocentric, and it is the best argument against all forms of prejudice.[16]

Yet not all are prepared to grasp the culturally specific contributions of this theology of the cross for the sake of the church catholic. The controversial African American hymnal project involving the LCMS and the ELCA resulted in the development and production of the exemplary supplement *This Far by Faith: An African American Resource for Worship* (TFF). This book contains illustrations of the sung theology within this culture—remarkably intact, preserved by oral tradition, through many years of forced illiteracy.

Another feature from TFF is the "Way of the Cross." It is recommended for use especially on the Fridays in Lent. It consists of eight evangelical stations of the cross—accordingly demythologized of nonbiblical content. An opportunity is given in the service notes for stations to

> . . . be made outside the church walls as a public witness. Outdoor stations may be made at significant locations in the immediate neighborhood where healing is needed and where associations between the contemporary struggles of life and the events of Christ's suffering can be made (for example, sites where crimes have occurred, abandoned buildings, or other places of human struggle).[17]

The inclusion of this ritual and this exhortation toward public performance demonstrates the expectation that the symbol of the cross still carries an allusive sense of the sacred in the African American urban community. Not without cultural significance is the biblical ascription of African ancestry to Simon of Cyrene, who was compelled to help Jesus carry His cross (Matthew 27:32; Mark 15:21; Luke 23:26).

MORE THAN EITHER/OR

When Lutherans engage in Gospel-based pastoral care, *Seelsorge*, their action is motivated by Word and Sacrament and directed in two general areas: individual healing (spirituality, individual forgiveness, personal faith maturation) and public healing (marginalized groups, body of Christ needs, and justice issues). Too often and tragically, these are set off as antithetical, as either/or efforts; that is, one cares *either* about counseling individuals *or* about advocating for oppressed people. Sometimes more conservative believers reduce sin to personal action and moral failure while more liberally inclined believers de-emphasize individual accountability, reducing sin to the systemic, social, and contextual. This adversative view negatively affects necessary ministry, missing the truth of God's Word: Humanity is best ministered to when taken as a whole. Or, as Dr. Benjamin Mays[18] (1894–1984) once sagely remarked, "The strength of the wolf is in the pack and the strength of the pack is in the wolf."

In God's eschatological city we see the consummation of God's preferred vision: wholly integrated living. John's apocalyptic vision of Revelation 22 reports that between the main street and the river is the life-giving tree with leaves giving healing to all nations. " 'The tree of life' is for all people of all nations who are written in the Lamb's 'book of life.' "[19] This healed life encompasses the totality of human needs— spiritual, physical, and emotional—without disintegration of the individual and without segregation within society. Vastly different is what we witness in our contemporary world. We live in an idolatrously materialistic, self-interested society, increasingly distanced by this sin from God's goal. The manner of human relations appears to be spiraling in a deathly direction, along an accelerating path. Rather than growing in unity, many churches reflect the same scars of division seen in society as a whole—and sometimes even more. The catastrophe of human disunity is magnified whenever divisions are not doctrinally based—for which there may be biblical rationale—but merely mirror the socioeconomic forces in society that pull people apart according to culture, ethnicity, and relative financial status. When differences arise not because of grace but principally because people are of a different race, God's people have missed the mark.

Despite the apparent ultramodern sophistication of Western society, primitive traits remain. There are vestiges of a cave mentality even amid a technologically advanced computer society. The pernicious persistence of racial segregation is an example. Recent reports from the United States Census Bureau indicate that between 1990 and 2000, racial segregation among children worsened.[20] At the same time the nation is growing multitudinously more ethnic, the problem of the color line continues to segregate, as predicted by W. E. B. Du Bois one hundred years ago. Pockets of resistance have grown deeper and wider in some cases. This may be caused by the widespread fascination with ego needs and self. Check any bookstore and you'll discover shelves chock-full of New Age, self-help, personal maximization books. This rage is often at the expense of social healing. What about Christian bookstores? What about local churches?

Even the spiritual therapy of some churchly preaching and teaching has become highly privatized. Growing churches (or at least those churches increasing numerically) sometimes measure spiritual life "in terms of personal happiness, earthly success and appearance, worldly wisdom and human glory."[21] It cannot be denied that financial blessing is one gift of God, but when these pursuits gain equivalency with scriptural kergyma and the center of a church's confession, it is an ethos of greed that has prevailed. Churches that emphasize human-centered, outward, "for-show" success tend to suppress the heart of God, which was exposed at the cross. They also tend to humiliate those trapped in chronic struggles, patiently endured but never cured in this life. Thus churches for which the foremost pursuit is personal happiness are most often at cross-purposes with a biblical theology of the cross. Churches primarily bent on nurturing their members' psycho-spiritual growth tend to back away from preaching and teaching on tough topics. Prophetic messages are too unsettling. Unpopular implications of faith active in love remain unspoken or, worse, are swept under the rug as if they do not exist. In an ethnically and fiscally homogenous gathering of folk trying to find personal happiness, few really dare to expose the still weeping open wound of race relations. In a world of limited time, tightly budgeted money, and finite resources, personal development comes first, leaving no time for any movements or marches or other people's problems. In the fast-paced twenty-first century, personal priorities get first and utmost attention—like Bible tips to compete with and beat professional peers to the top of the ladder or perpetrating a self-congratulating façade of illusionary service without excessive personal sacrifice. In this personal development shuffle, Gospel-centered human care ministry loses. The way of the cross is abandoned.

But the way of the cross is equally misunderstood if it is allowed to serve as an excuse for failure in ministry and the life of faith. We misrepresent the theology of cross if it becomes a crutch: "At its nadir, the theology of the cross can deteriorate into a basin for the depressed, a holding tank for masochists and lazybones, an unaccountable void for bad stewards." A common urban application of this rationalizing opens those in urban ministry to the temptation to "fall for failure and consider it success because, as the great ones have said, 'history is cruciform' and all must come to naught."[22]

THEOLOGICAL PERSONALISM AND SUFFERING

A good thing to do when lost is to return to the last identifiable place or state of being not lost, if ever one existed. In her new book *In Therapy We Trust*, Eva Moskowitz points us in a direction worthy of exploration. Among the consequences of our obsession over self-fulfillment, Moskowitz suggests the following:

> The other main problem with the therapeutic gospel is that the emphasis on individuals and mental healing often comes at the expense of considerations of the larger public good. There is clearly a civic cost to our obsession with the psyche. In the late 20th century, while we worried about self-esteem, the children in America who died from gunshots outnumbered the American soldiers who died in the Vietnam War. Internationally, the contrast is even bleaker. Starvation, illness, and warfare ravage the world while we obsess about anxiety, shyness, and denial. We must somehow shift our outlook so that we may be socially responsible.[23]

Obsessions aside, Moskowitz notes a prior era when a therapeutic model (defined by personal consciousness and human concern) merged with social activism (an expression of altruistic, community concern) in a healthier, more balanced, manner. She cites the 1960s civil rights movement. A force for holding together personal good and the public good was inherent in that era's personalism.

An excellent resource that uncovers the roots of this strain of personalism is John J. Ansbro's study of Martin Luther King.[24] Personalism is an idealistic movement not only in the sense of optimistic pursuit of a positive end (though it is that), but as an ideal in the formal philosophical sense. Here, reality is related to the rational sphere. "Theological personalists" (to employ this emerging term) hold a pattern of contemplation and action framed in an environment of integrity and equity that honors personal worth while aiming to redeem social conditions.

Proclaiming a universal, objective justification is nonnegotiable. The central *kerygma*—that Christ died for all irrespective of status or background or social condition—is the church's lifeline. Preaching the Gospel moves us toward a community in which all cultures are respected, all people are regarded as worthwhile, and all nations have value because God so loved the whole cosmos that He gave His only Son as the Savior. This is "theological personalism"—the truth that all people and cultures, by virtue of their creation by God and the objective reconciliation won by Christ, are the proper focus of the church's mission.[25]

This is a core Christian conviction. "Unafraid of charges of individualism," a theologian the stature of no less than Wolfhart Pannenberg "has advanced the unfashionable theses that one of the greatest contributions of Christianity to humanity has been the sense of individual dignity."[26] But this contribution never aims for any individual's dislocation from the wider fellowship or disconnection of personal goals, mission, vision, values, and vocation from the body of Christ. Rather, it inheres a reciprocal faith-strengthening benefit: the faith of the whole flock in each sheep and the faith of each sheep in the whole flock.

Shortly before his death Dr. King again articulated this symbiotic sense of group action and individual value. His assassination interrupted participation in his second march on Washington, the poor people's campaign. King remarked: "I feel this movement in behalf of the poor is the most moral thing—it is saying that every man is an heir to a legacy of dignity and worth."[27] The civil rights movement represents an ideal historical reference with societal action motivated by a high understanding of human worth. The individual life is hidden with Christ in God (Colossians 3:1).

Many believers, congregations, and church-based entities have formally recognized this theological personalism. Lutheran Services of America (LSA) is the umbrella organization for ELCA and LCMS social ministry agencies. It is the largest nonprofit entity in the United States. LSA has embraced this theological personalism as a core value: "Our social ministry organizations are keenly aware that respect for the dignity of every person is a profound and unassailable principle of biblical faith."[28]

Early in the civil rights movement, even from within the confessionally conservative LCMS, leading orthodox voices spoke out against segregation. The love of God shown in Jesus Christ on the cross inspires the church to carry out the mission of love in truth and spirit. God's pure gifts are available to everyone. Ordinary people become recipients of extraordinary goodness and kindness. No one is excluded. When Christ is Lord, we see Jesus and His love in every person. There are no exceptions. That is the Lutheran Christian way.

Every individual is a creation of the Father. Every individual is an intended recipient of the redemption won by Christ. The sainted Concordia Seminary, St. Louis, Missouri, professor Martin Franzmann warned that though race-based divisions might be a pervading standard in the world, "these lines of division simply fade away in the church; they are wiped out by the great and overruling fact of Christ."[29] As we hide ourselves with Christ in God, distinctions disappear, and Christ increasingly appears.

OCCASIONAL THEOLOGY

There are occasions when speaking out is not an option for Christians. There are circumstances that cry out for an address. There are false answers that demand questioning. There are systems that require the voices of the conscious for the sake of the voiceless. As Dr. A. L. Barry, the sainted former president of the LCMS, has remarked, "The church must proclaim God's moral law to the world, against all fashion, pressure and opposition."[30] A Christian witness takes the form of street corner demonstration and academic dialogue and news media participation. Christians must speak out or risk the triumph of a Nietzschean "will to power" and a Faustian "might makes right" (following the example of Mephistopheles). Or, as Edmund Burke centuries ago rightly remarked, all that is necessary for the triumph of evil is that good people do and say nothing. Concordia University, Irvine, California, ethicist James Bachman eloquently elaborates:

> History shows how dangerous it is to explore ethics and morality without any reference to God. As creations of God, we should not absolutize anything on earth. When God is removed from public discussion, ethics and morality are reduced to a power play between political parties, social movements, corporations and would-be dictators. Today, confidence in universal reasoning is waning, and there is general confusion in discussions of public policy. This is a crisis that will continue if a Christian voice is not included in discussions of public policies. The Christian voice, in the context of respecting others and the value of human life, is anchored in respect for God who created us all.[31]

Again the value of every human life is central to the Christian ethic. If Christians don't speak, if the church doesn't speak, who will?

In his incisive essay[32] preeminent Reformation theologian Robert Rosin indirectly indicts all who would use their historical or theological affection for Martin Luther as *de facto* acquittal or excuse from demonstration, action, and activism in the civil realm. Rosin points out how the *Gottesdienst*, adoration and service to God, is necessarily carried out in everyday Christian vocation. Human service flows from God's primary saving service to the whole person—Word and Sacrament celebrated liturgically, then enacted. As healthy trees bear good fruit—spontaneously and without prompting—followers of Christ are appointed to do ongoing acts of unconditional, undeserved love (John 15:16–17). The arena of Christian action is the world, created for and loved by God. Human affairs are God's affairs. For Luther, walls between the secular and the sacred collapse. Wars between the spheres do not derive from God. God is Lord of both civil and secular society. Good words and good works flow from redeemed hands and freed hearts—liberated to freely serve. Good works also flow freely between the kingdoms of the Gospel and the world. While these realms must always be properly distinguished, they are never fenced off from each other.

Yet good works done in the name of Jesus are always carried out under the cross. Tragically, this planet is peopled with many self-justifying residents who have not appropriated authentic justification by grace in Christ. Luther's "Christian era" counsel to the towns of Wittenberg and Leisnig has meaning for our postmodern life and times. Namely, that biblical theology, like Law and Gospel, must be applied existentially, specifically, and contextually[33]—to be Lutheran is to be an "occasional theologian." Abstract, speculative theology finds scant place in the tradition of Luther. Luther's mission focus demands concrete "consideration of the theological/spiritual aspect where the dignity and worth of the individual is seen most in being created and redeemed by God."[34] A primary mentor for Martin Luther King, Howard Thurman, expressed his disdain for abstract claims of Christian action: "To speak of the love for humanity is meaningless. There is no such thing as humanity. What we call humanity has a name, was born, lives on a street, gets hungry, needs all the particular things we need. As an abstract, it has no reality whatsoever."[35] Luther the reformer, like his namesake Martin Luther King,[36] would find value in a personalist perspective, by being active in the world for the sake of the least, the last, the lost, and the left behind. That love takes on concrete incarnation, most recognizable at the cross.

The paradox persists. God's love is nowhere greater, access to the heart of God is nowhere more available, nor is it anywhere more hidden than at the cross.

URBAN APPLICATION
OF THE THEOLOGY OF THE CROSS

In the summer of 1986 I worked in Philadelphia with what was the Lutheran Church in America's Center City Lutheran Parish, a coalition of more than 20 congregations in the hard-core inner-city of Philadelphia. I was 23 years old when assigned to do evangelistic ministry on these raw, rough, and raging streets of North Philadelphia. This was a declining yet vibrant, vital community located at 9th and Lehigh.

This location was a veritable concrete jungle, a cauldron of race conflict: poor blacks, poor Puerto Ricans. and a splattering of poor whites who hadn't yet escaped the neighborhood or couldn't yet afford to do so. Ethnically, I am blessed with a somewhat ambiguous appearance. As a lighter complexioned black person working in this neighborhood, I possessed distinct survival advantage. I could fit in well with any group. In a sense I incarnated myself multiply. Among the

African American brothers my salutation was, "Hey, what's up man?" Among Puerto Ricans, "Yo, que pasa?" White guys didn't know quite what I was, so they left me alone. But at 9th and Lehigh, whom the streets don't get, drugs get; whom drugs don't get, gangs get; whom gangs don't get, the police get; whom the police guns don't get, bigger guns get. The bottom line is few—especially males—get out alive. This was *kill-adelphia*, not *philadelphia*, where kids carry guns too big for their adolescent hands to hold. Like Robert Service's poem, this was a place of "strange valleys that greet strange deaths." Of course it's not just the inner city, but it's any city or town or community. We didn't take care of the core of the apple, now the whole fruit is rotten—witness the nine *suburban* school shootings in the late twentieth century.

In that community, that church located at 9th and Lehigh was like a city set on a hill. Its name was Holy Cross Lutheran Church. It was the community center. In the middle of the madness of the day, I'd sometimes hide in the sanctuary, sitting alone; in the evening, I'd hide in the nave—just "chill and be still"—oblivious to the whizzing by of traffic and the trafficking of drugs and sex and other soul-destroying deeds done on mean streets.

I said Holy Cross Lutheran Church *was* located at 9th and Lehigh. A fire destroyed the beautiful church building. I remember that spanning the arch high above the altar were these four Latin words, probably quoting Martin Luther. They are burned into my psyche forever: "*Ave crux spes unica*"—"Hail cross, our only hope." Even amid a decaying, death-dealing neighborhood, I discovered consolation in the God-man whose death stands as a sign of hope against all death. For the kind of death that eventually kills us physically, for the deaths of the flesh we must die daily in the spirit, for the killers that threaten and frighten, for urban horrors that make life a living hell, this symbol of the death of Jesus Christ faces all death squarely, overcomes death, and becomes a sign of hope—the cross means Christ's death absorbs all death and dying.

APPENDIX

Many Lutherans are not aware that Martin Luther and Martin Luther King have much in common, though separated by centuries, ethnicity, and geography. Here are some quick and striking connections.

1. Both Martins were reformers, not revolutionaries.

   Dr. Luther's ecclesial reform was a consequence, not a goal, of his pursuit of the Gospel. Likewise, Dr. King did not strive to overthrow the United States. Both called for a return to first principles. In Luther's case, it was a recovery of justification. King's appeal was for a recovery of the U.S. Constitution's original promise of fair and equal treatment of all people. There was nothing essentially novel in either movement.

2. Both Martins reached beyond their own people.

Neither man was motivated by a narrow agenda. Although African Americans benefited from the civil rights movement and German people from Luther's reform, neither man was limited by his culture. Their global, exportable, and enduring impact attest to this.

3. Both Martins demonstrated a living spirituality.

Both movements were activated by faith in Christ. Neither exhibited raw, secular power. Later black power advocates of racial consciousness movements attempted to wrest control of civil rights. Likewise, some empire politicos tried to co-opt the Reformation for their gain. Yet both men drew strength and vision from God's promise and presence in their lives, not from their effective politics.

LESSONS FOR TODAY'S CHURCH LEADERS

- Seek first to work within the God-ordained institutions, whether the government or the church.
- Build bridges with good traditions and visionary allies wherever possible.
- Do what's right, not just convenient or expedient, because morality matters more than power, and truth transcends culture.

NOTES

1. Booker T. Washington, *Up from Slavery* (New York: Oxford University Press, 1995).
2. William Edward Burghardt Du Bois, *The Souls of Black Folk* (New York: Fawcett, 1961). See especially chapter 3, "Of Mr. Booker T. Washington and Others," 42–54.
3. Samuel Proctor, epilogue to *The Preacher-Prophet in Mass Society*, by Jesse Jai McNeil Sr. (Nashville: Townsend, 1994), 113.
4. Elliot Cuff, "Black Preaching in the Church," in *African American Jubilee Edition* (New York: American Bible Society, 1997), 220.
5. LW 31:53.
6. Quotation from personal correspondence with the Rev. George D. Schaetzle, Cincinnati, Ohio.
7. C. Eric Lincoln and Lawrence H. Mamiya, *The Black Church in the African-American Experience* (Durham: Duke University Press, 1990), 123.

8. "Deep River," v. 1.

9. From "Nobody Knows the Trouble I've Seen."

10. From "Sometimes I Feel Like a Motherless Child."

11. "African Americans among the Most Religious People in the World," *Emerging Trends* 21.5 (May 1999): 1. Published by the Princeton Religion Research Center.

12. David T. Shannon, "An 'Ante-bellum' Sermon': A Resource for an African-American Hermeneutic," in *Stony the Road We Trod: An African American Biblical Interpretation*, ed. Cain Hope Felder (Minneapolis: Fortress, 1991), 122.

13. Albert J. Raboteau, *Slave Religion: The "Invisible Institution" in the Antebellum South* (New York: Oxford, 1978), 259.

14. "Were You There," various verses.

15. Marvin B. Tolson, "Dark Symphony," as recorded on compact disc by Marvin B. Tolson in *Our Souls Have Grown Deep Like Rivers: Black Poets Read Their Work* (Rhino Entertainment Company, 2000).

16. Stanley Crouch, *The All-American Skin Game, or The Decoy of Race* (New York: Pantheon, 1995), 43–44.

17. *This Far by Faith* (Minneapolis: Augsburg Fortress, 1999), 102.

18. Dr. Martin Luther King identified Dr. Benjamin Mays as his "spiritual mentor and my intellectual father."

19. Louis A. Brighton, *Revelation* (*Concordia Commentary*; St. Louis: Concordia, 1999): 127. Also in this volume, see Brighton's extended discussion of "The Restored Physical Creation," in which he describes the results of Christ's redemption and resurrection, 631–33.

20. Eric Schmitt, "Segregation Growing Among U.S. Children," *New York Times* (6 May 2001): from the Internet, www.nytimes.com.

21. *For the Sake of Christ's Commission: The Report of the Church Growth Study Committee* (St. Louis: LCMS, 2001), 13.

22. David H. Benke, *The Nehemiah Plan: New Jerusalem in East Brooklyn* (D.Min. project thesis, Union Theological Seminary, New York, 1983), 63.

23. Excerpted from Eva S. Moskowitz, *In Therapy We Trust: America's Obsession with Self-Fulfillment* (Baltimore: Johns Hopkins University Press, 2001) as "Self-Help as a Substitute for Activism," *The Chronicle of Higher Education*, Ex Libris, (6 April 2001): B16.

24. John J. Ansbro, *Martin Luther King Jr.: Nonviolent Strategies and Tactics for Social Change* (Lanham, Md.: Madison Books, 2000), 71–109.

25. John Nunes, *Voices from the City: Issues and Images of Urban Preaching* (St. Louis: Concordia, 1999), 84.

26. Geoffrey Wainwright, *Doxology: The Praise of God in Worship, Doctrine, and Life* (New York: Oxford University Press, 1980), 418.

27. Jose Yglesias, "Dr. King's March on Washington, Part 2," *New York Times Magazine* (31 March 1968): 270–71.

28. James M. Childs, *Joined at the Heart: What It Means to Be Lutheran in Social Ministry* (Minneapolis: Lutheran Services of America, 2000), 17.

29. Martin H. Franzmann, *New Courage for Daily Living* (St. Louis: Concordia, 1963), 60.

30. A. L. Barry, "Why Churches Speak Out," *Dallas Morning News* (1 July 2000).

31. James Bachman, "Speaking Out: Christian Voices in Secular Settings" *Concordia Today* (Winter 2000).

32. Robert Rosin, "Bringing Forth Fruit: Luther on Social Welfare," in *A Cup of Cold Water: A Look at Biblical Charity* (ed. Robert Rosin and Charles P. Arand; Concordia Seminary Monograph Series 3; St. Louis: Concordia Seminary, 1996), 117–64.

33. Charles Arand compellingly points out this characteristic of Luther's catechetical theology in *That I May Be His Own* (St. Louis: Concordia Academic Press, 2000), 106. He notes that Luther used "concrete and familiar everyday nouns" to describe the gracious provision of God. Further, Luther ordinarily described the Creator's work in "understandable and dynamic" terms. Finally, Luther told the story of God's saving work as personally applied; specifically, in Baptism God "puts a stamp on me."

34. Rosin, "Bringing Forth Fruit," 164.

35. *For the Inward Journey: The Writings of Howard Thurman* (San Diego: Harcourt Brace Jovanovich, 1984), 193.

36. See Appendix, page 230–31.

FOR FURTHER READING

Featherstone, Rudolph R. "The Theology of the Cross: The Perspective of an African in America." In *Theology and the Black Experience*. Edited by Albert Pero and Ambrose Moyo. Minneapolis: Augsburg, 1988.

Felder, Cain Hope, ed. *Stony the Road We Trod: African American Biblical Interpretation*. Minneapolis: Fortress, 1991.

Fulop, Timothy E., and Albert J. Raboteau, eds. *African American Religion: Interpretive Essays in History and Culture*. New York: Routledge, 1997.

Johnson, Jeff G. *Black Christians: The Untold Lutheran Story*. St. Louis: Concordia, 1991.

McGrath, Alister E. *Luther's Theology of the Cross: Martin Luther's Theological Breakthrough*. New York: Basil Blackwell, 1985.

Sernett, Milton C., ed. *African American Religious History: A Documentary Witness*. Durham: Duke University Press, 1999.

Spencer, Jon Michael. *Black Hymnody: A Hymnological History of the African-American Church*. Knoxville: University of Tennessee Press, 1992.

13

The Cross and the New Age

═══─═══

ROLAND C. EHLKE

The 1970s musical *Hair* told the public that the world was entering
a new era, "the dawning of the age of Aquarius."[1] According to
astrologers, for two thousand years our planet has been under Pisces,
the astrological sign of the fish. What many have seen as an era of violence and disillusionment, beginning with the death of Christ, is supposedly giving way to a time of joy and aspiration. The song predicts a
time for "the mind's true liberation." We are said to be in the beginning of the Age of Aquarius, better known as the New Age.

Our study will (1) look at the definitions and the roots of the New
Age movement; (2) examine some of its key ideas, see how they compare with Scripture, and what points of contact they afford; (3) take
note of distinctive New Age practices and their relation to Scripture;
and (4) provide a Law-Gospel witness to the cross that is faithful to
Scripture and speaks to the anxieties and cultural vacuums present
within the New Age movement. Because the New Age is less established and less familiar than longstanding world religions, such as
Islam, we will go into some detail on key components and leaders of
the New Age.

Before that, it is important to spell out what we mean by the theology of the cross, which lies at the heart of the Holy Scriptures and the
Christian faith. This theology is summed up in the word *grace*. Grace is
the undeserved love God has shown sinful humanity in Jesus Christ

235

(see Romans 3:22–24). When Jesus died on the cross, He paid for the sins of the whole world (1 John 2:2). Only Jesus could make such a sacrifice because He alone lived a sinless life. Because of human depravity, all attempts by sinful humanity to save itself are utterly futile (Romans 3:10–12). Indeed, the Bible clearly condemns such efforts. Our eternal salvation, then, is a free, unconditional gift from God (Ephesians 2:8–9). Living under the cross of Christ, believers need not look to outward circumstances of life or to their own good deeds. Rather, we live confidently—including during sufferings and in the face of death— knowing that God is with us now and that eternal life in heaven awaits us because of what Christ has already accomplished for us.

NEW AGE DEFINITIONS AND ROOTS

The forces that give impetus to the New Age movement (NAM) are many. At first blush NAM might appear to be a confusing kaleidoscope of influences and ideas. Yet as we look at the multicolored background, certain patterns emerge, and we are able to arrive at an understanding of the movement.

The strongest single influence on NAM is Hinduism,[2] with its teachings of pantheism and reincarnation. Buddhism, an offshoot of Hinduism, has influenced NAM with its emphasis on intuitive knowledge rather than logic and reason. Another source is the ancient Christian heresy of gnosticism, stressing the possession of insider, esoteric knowledge. Researcher Elliot Miller defines the New Age in this way:

> The New Age movement, properly defined, is an extremely large *metanetwork* ("network of networks") composed of people and groups who share common values and a common vision. These values are based on Eastern/occult mysticism and pantheistic monism (the worldview that all is One, and this One is God), and the vision is of a coming era of peace and enlightenment, the "Age of Aquarius."[3]

While this is an excellent general definition, some researchers see more elements beneath the NAM canopy. Often included in the New Age movement are American Indian ideas of the medicine man (the shaman), as popularized in the writings of Carlos Castañeda (*Journey to Ixtlan*, etc.), and other pagan religious elements, such as the worship of mother earth, Gaia.

At times, distinctions are made between New Age thought and other forms of paganism. In *Nature Religion Today: Paganism in the Modern World*, Richard Roberts argues that in some respects paganism is at odds with NAM, as well as with Christianity:

As a cultural practice, earth-centred, matriarchal Paganism embodies a relatively cohesive belief-system enacted through a core of common practices, of which the central and decisive feature is the ritual celebration of the annual life-cycle of birth, childhood, sexual maturity, fertility, old age and decay, death, and so on. In its matriarchal manifestation, however, the chthonic imperative shares with Christianity a drive toward the integral and the total. Unlike diversified New Age, in which any unifying ideological drives are undercut by pragmatic eclecticism enacted in a marketplace of spiritual hybridities, Paganism and Christianity are effectively incompatible. The former celebrates earthbound existence, not the least through sexuality; the latter involves constant vigilance with regard to the flesh (*sarx*) that wars against the spirit (*pneuma*).[4]

Even within a broad definition of NAM, we can readily discern common elements. Both paganism and the New Age's Hindu connections reject biblical revelation. Both are earthbound in their worship of the earth itself and in the assertion that everything is part of God, though Hinduism attempts to transcend this material world, which it considers illusion (*maya*). Moreover, as practiced in India, Hinduism shows the compatibility of pantheism with polytheism: On a popular level people worship some 300 million different gods while at a philosophical level all are seen as one.[5] In a sense, of course, Christianity is also earthbound because it is incarnational; in Jesus Christ, God takes on human flesh and blood.

Other New Age sources include nineteenth-century American spiritualists who claimed to communicate with the dead (for example, the famous "Rochester Rappings" of 1848, which gave rise to spiritualism).[6] The German hypnotist Franz Anton Mesmer (1734–1815), from whom we get the word *mesmerize*, and the healer Phineas P. Quimby, a mentor of Mary Baker Eddy, the founder of Christian Science, are also recognized as forerunners of the New Age.[7] The New England Transcendentalists, in particular Ralph Waldo Emerson (1803–1882), helped pave the way for the New Age. In his essay "Fate," Emerson wrote, "Let us build altars to the Blessed Unity that holds nature and souls in perfect solution . . . all is made of one piece."[8]

Given its links with Wicca, it is fitting to describe NAM with the metaphor of a witches' cauldron that includes a strong potion of the occult, with its delving into hidden, secret things through fortune-telling, magic, and mediums. Final ingredients incorporate a dose of secular psychology with its stress on self: self-love, self-esteem, self-image, self-actualization, self-fulfillment.[9]

Among other things, the New Age can be understood as a result of religious pluralism. Rather than trying to distinguish differences among the many religions and worldviews that now exist side by side in our "global village," more and more people simply see them all as various expressions of God and basic spiritual truth. This presents numerous logical problems (for example, reconciling contradictions such as pantheism and the concept of a transcendent God). It also runs counter to the biblical injunction to worship the one true God (see Exodus 20:3; Psalm 96:4–5; John 14:6–7).

Although NAM has been stirring in the Western world for more than a century, as the twentieth century progressed, the movement gained momentum. The poet William Butler Yeats, who was heavily into the occult, spoke of a turning of the gyres, cyclically ushering in a new age: "When the old primary becomes the new antithetical, the old realisation of an objective moral law is changed into a subconscious turbulent instinct. The world of rigid custom and law is broken up by 'the uncontrollable mystery upon the bestial floor.' "[10] The "world of rigid custom and law" refers to the Christian centuries, while "the uncontrollable mystery . . ." is a reference from Yeats's poem *The Magi*. In *The Second Coming* (1920), Yeats described the new revelation as the arrival of a "rough beast" whose "hour come round at last, Slouches towards Bethlehem to be born."[11]

Until the 1950s, the New Age remained a movement of an isolated few outsiders to the mainstream of Western civilization. The Beatniks—a la Jack Kerouac and Allen Ginsberg—turned their backs on society's stale materialism as they experimented with drugs, free sex, and Eastern religion. Then, in the 1960s came the Hippies, flower children with their communes, more drugs, meditation, and gurus from India.

The year 1971 has been referred to as NAM's "galvanization date," when it entered into the mainstream of American society. That year marked the first publication of the periodical *East-West Journal*. It also ushered in the first truly representative book, *Remember: Now Be Here, Now Here Be* by Baba Ram Dass, Jewish-born Richard Alpert. This former Harvard professor and co-worker of Timothy Leary of LSD fame recounted his journey from professor into the world of psychedelic drugs, then into becoming a yogi, that is, a practitioner of yoga. Ram Dass urged, "Don't just think about the future. Just be here now. Don't just think about the past. Just be here now."[12] Ram Dass's journey into Eastern mysticism is one that more and more people are following. Recent years have seen the New Age boil over into society at large, as a plethora of best-selling books attests.

Liberal Christian theology has been moving away from its biblical, Christ-centered foundation and thus opened itself to non-Christian influences. Friedrich Schleiermacher (1768–1834), generally considered the founder of modern Protestantism, shifted the basis of theology away from the Holy Scriptures to the inner consciousness of the individual heart, that is, to subjective feelings. Victor Raj points out how other influential theologians, such as Roman Catholic Teilhard de Chardin (1881–1955) and Protestant Paul Tillich (1886–1965), have followed that path. Raj notes:

> Tillich's theology is a classic model of modern-day universalism [the notion everyone will be saved] . . . His view of Christ readily takes on varied shapes, forms, and meanings . . . . But his conclusions are far removed from the biblical concept of God's unique revelation in Jesus Christ. In this sense Tillich's theology becomes a welcome contribution to the philosophy of the New Age.[13]

NEW AGE THOUGHT

Four basic concepts run through New Age thought. One is the idea of *pantheism*. Everything is God. This means that people are also divine. "Kneel to your own self. Honor and worship your own being. God dwells in you as you."[14] These words of Swami Muktananda sum up what the New Age is all about. Dr. Deepak Chopra, author of more than 25 books, reverts to classic Hindu pantheism when describing what he calls the highest stage of spirituality. He quotes the famous saying from the Vedanta: "I am That, You are That, and all this is That."[15] In contrast to the biblical concept of a transcendent God who is separate from His creation, everything is part of God.

This search for all in one is an expression of the human need for community. Ironically, though the Bible does not teach pantheism, it does teach an even more wonderful connection between God and His creation. That is the incarnation. Although this world is separated from God—both in its creation and, even more so, in its fallen, sinful condition—in love God has come into the world, become a part of it.

Sadly, when the New Age speaks of Jesus Christ (frequently as two separate personages), it misses this truth. Rather than the incarnate God-man of Scripture, the New Age Jesus is a guru, enlightened master, or avatar and Christ is a universal spirit or cosmic force that guides the spiritual evolution of humanity.[16] During His so-called "lost years," Jesus supposedly traveled to India where He studied under gurus before returning to Palestine. Christians need to be clear that the "God" and the "Jesus Christ" of the New Age are far removed from the Scriptures.

Such clarity is vital not simply for the sake of making an academic distinction. It is only in clearly seeing Christ—who is both our Creator and Brother—that true fellowship with God can be appreciated and enjoyed. In John's words, "[T]he Word [Jesus Christ] was God . . . Through Him all things were made . . . The Word became flesh and made His dwelling among us" (1:1, 3, 14). Through faith in Jesus, we "become children of God" (John 1:12).

Hand in hand with pantheism goes *reincarnation*. While secular humanism argues that individual human potential ends at death, according to the New Age humans last forever. We are divine and pass from one temporal body into another. Problems arise because at some level, perhaps unconsciously or in a previous life, we have willed them. Reincarnation rests on *karma,* the Hindu idea of justice. If our negative karma (bad deeds, thoughts, motives, etc.) outweighs the good, we are assigned a more miserable life the next time around or vice versa. The process has no room for mercy or forgiveness.

Shirley MacLaine, who has done as much as anyone to popularize New Age thought, tends to glorify the concept of reincarnation. In her book *The Camino: A Journey of the Spirit*, she describes her pilgrimage to Spain, where she recalled a former life she lived there in the days of the Christian-Muslim conflicts: "I was on a horse riding into the sunset . . . I had long curly black hair and skin the color of cappuccino coffee . . . Following far behind I saw soldiers covered in armor. The lead soldier carried a cross, which he held upright as he galloped west after me."[17] This romantic view of reincarnation is hardly that held by the masses in India who eke out an existence amid squalor, poverty, and disease. In his *Letters to a Disciple*, Mahatma Gandhi spoke not of the remembrance of lives past but of forgetting them as a blessing: "It is nature's kindness that we do not remember past births. Where is the good . . . of knowing in detail the numberless births we have gone through? Life would be a burden if we carried such a tremendous load of memories."[18]

While offering a sanitized view of reincarnation, MacLaine takes a harsh look at those not as well off as she is. Seeing a paralyzed man in a wheelchair on the pilgrimage, she can only comment, "I wondered what his karma was."[19] How different all this is from the simple proclamation of Scripture that we die only once and then face the judgment (Hebrews 9:27) and from Jesus' loving invitation to the downcast and burdened, "Come to Me, all you who are weary and burdened, and I will give you rest" (Matthew 11:28).

While reincarnation is at odds with biblical doctrine, once more there is a point of contact. Instead of karma and reincarnation, Scripture offers Christ's cross and resurrection. The Bible teaches that by His

death on the cross that Jesus has paid for our sins, and that by His resurrection from the dead, He has guaranteed us eternal life. In the words
of St. Paul: "He was delivered over to death for our sins and was raised
to life for our justification" (Romans 4:25).

A third New Age emphasis is on *consciousness*. According to New
Age thought, humanity's problem is not sin but lack of knowledge. We
need to be conscious of our divinity. MacLaine puts it this way: "The
knowingness of our divinity is the highest intelligence."[20] Which begs
the question: Why, if we are God, do people need to spend several
hundred dollars for a weekend seminar with New Age luminaries to
learn this? The answer usually is that some beings are more highly
evolved spiritually, farther along the path of reincarnation. Especially
in its emphasis on consciousness, New Age thought dovetails with the
theory of evolution. Supposedly, humanity in general has now evolved
to a point where it is ready for the new consciousness.

In holding out the promise of a special, higher consciousness,
the New Age rings of gnosticism. Ultimately, however, the hope of special consciousness leads to hopelessness. Chopra offers little consolation when he promises readers: "God lives in the unknown, and when
you can embrace it fully, you will be home free."[21] Again the line
between this and Christianity could not be drawn more sharply: "No
one has ever seen God, but God the One and Only, who is at the
Father's side, has made Him known" (John 1:18); in Christ, the hidden
God is made known. Although NAM sharply contrasts with scriptural
truth, again there is common ground for communication, understanding, and sharing. The special consciousness the New Age proffers is, in
fact, not just for a few but for all who come to know Christ. Indeed,
God "wants all men to be saved and to come to a knowledge of the
truth" (1 Timothy 2:4). Jesus personally identifies not merely with an
enlightened few, but especially with those who are most in need, "the
least of these" (Matthew 25:31–46).

The need for consciousness leads to a fourth New Age tenet: *transformation*. Somehow we need to break through from old ways of thinking into the awareness of our divinity. We need to be transformed; our
consciousness needs to be altered. At the heart of this transformation
is an emphasis on love. Chopra writes: "Only after years of cleansing
out the inner blockages of repression, doubt, negative emotions, and
old conditioning does a person realize that God's force is immensely
powerful. When this occurs, nothing can pull the mind away from
love. Love as a personal emotion is transmuted into a cosmic energy."[22]
When enough individuals are transformed, there will be global transformation. According to New Agers, this transformation began when in
the 1960s people started to see a paradigm shift, an "emerging spiritual

awareness," that today has reached widespread acceptance in NAM. This new sense of "cosmic consciousness" is epitomized in *The Celestine Prophecy* by James Redfield.

Because it is typical of many, Redfield's journey into the New Age is worth a thumbnail sketch. James Redfield was born in 1950 and grew up near Birmingham, Alabama. He was brought up in the Methodist church, but because the church could not adequately answer his questions concerning spiritual experience, he began to study Eastern philosophies. He majored in sociology at Auburn University and graduated with a master's degree in counseling. For more than 15 years, he was a therapist for abused adolescents. He was drawn into the human potential movement and to the work of Carl Jung. In 1989 Redfield quit his job as a therapist to write full time.

Within five years of its publication in 1993, *The Celestine Prophecy* had sold nearly eight million copies in more than 40 countries. It stayed on the *New York Times* best-seller list for more than 115 weeks, making Redfield the world's best-selling hardcover author in 1996. According to Redfield:

> . . . a new consciousness has been entering the human world, a new awareness that can only be called transcendent, spiritual. If you find yourself reading this book, then perhaps you already sense what is happening, already feel it inside.
>
> It begins with a heightened perception of the way our lives move forward. We notice those chance events that occur at just the right moment, and bring forth just the right individuals, to suddenly send our lives in a new and important direction. Perhaps more than any other people in any other time, we intuit higher meaning in these mysterious happenings.[23]

Following Jung's lead, such chance occurrences that seem to be more than chance are called "synchronicity," a phenomenon seen as supporting evidence for New Age beliefs. There are, of course, other ways to explain these occurrences. For Christians, God in His providence and saving activity uses "all things" for our good (Romans 8:28).

With New Age talk of transformation, we once again have the paradoxical separation from and connection with biblical Christianity. While Christians do not look for a utopian heaven on earth, they do live new lives. In Christ, we are a "new creation" (2 Corinthians 5:17). Paul says,

> Therefore, I urge you, brothers, in view of God's mercy, to offer your bodies as living sacrifices, holy and pleasing to God—this is your spiritual act of worship. Do not conform any longer to the pattern of this world, but be transformed by the renewing of

your mind. Then you will be able to test and approve what God's will is—His good, pleasing and perfect will. (Romans 12:1–2)

As for the New Age focus on love transforming the world, the Bible also says much about love. The Christian concept of *agape* love is unique. Independent of friendship (*philos*), passionate love (*eros*), or familial relations (*stergo*), this is the giving, self-sacrificing love of God in Christ (John 3:16). In witnessing to New Agers, Christians will want to reflect this unique and matchless love.

New Age Practices

There are many techniques available for the transformation that is supposedly taking place in the world today. It doesn't matter so much which one(s) people follow, as long as they somehow make the shift into the new consciousness. More than offering a change in consciousness, New Age practices also offer something concrete to take hold of and a means to establish a sense of belonging with others.

Techniques for altering consciousness include chanting, primal therapy, dream therapy, body disciplines, diet, yoga, drugs, acupuncture, channeling (contacting the dead through mediums), hypnosis, holistic healing, crystals, etc. An army of therapists, psychics, channelers, and gurus stands ready (for a price) to help the novice make the journey into an altered state of consciousness. Crystals, in particular, have become the symbol of the New Age. These quartz rocks have predictable vibratory qualities, which make them useful in science. New Agers believe that crystals can also channel wholesome vibrations into the human mind, body, and emotions.

Neale Donald Walsch's hugely popular *Conversations with God* series is an example of writing that is akin to channeling. In the opening pages of the first volume, Walsch describes how his writing took place:

> In the spring of 1992 . . . an extraordinary phenomenon occurred in my life. God began talking with you. Through me.
>
> Let me explain.
>
> I was very unhappy during that period, personally, professionally, and emotionally, and my life was feeling like a failure on all levels. As I'd been in the habit for years of writing my thoughts down in letters . . . I picked up my trusty yellow legal pad and began pouring out my feelings.
>
> This time, . . . I decided to write a letter to God.
>
> It was a spiteful, passionate letter, full of confusions, contortions, and condemnation. And a *pile* of angry questions . . .

> To my surprise, as I scribbled out the last of my bitter, unanswerable questions and prepared to toss my pen aside, my hand remained poised over the paper, as if held there by some invisible force. Abruptly, the pen began moving on its own. I had no idea what I was about to write . . . Out came . . .
>
> Do you really want an answer to all these questions, or are you just venting?[24]

Walsch's *Conversations* books recount his questions and comments to God and God's responses. Underlying the *Conversations* is the predication, "Feeling is the language of the soul" while words are "the least effective communicator."[25] Here we see the gap between this religion and biblical truth, in which the Word *is* God's revelation. Walsch's god—a. k. a. "That Which Is All Things"—chides those who would "accept the interpretation of others (even others who lived 2,000 years ago)" rather than listen to their own feelings.[26]

Not everyone involved in the New Age is involved with all the practices connected with the movement. Nor is everyone who uses them aware of their New Age connections. For example, many who read New Age literature or practice yoga may be unaware that these activities are intimately tied with the New Age and Hindu thought. According to one report, in gyms "where once was heard the throbbing beat of [aerobic music] . . . New Age woodwinds now reign." For some, it is a "spiritual elevation," and one instructor "was pleased to find her students readily took to the traditional [Hindu] 'Om' chant before and after class."[27] Numerous large companies involve their employees in training seminars that espouse New Age principles. Already in 1987, America's major corporations were putting "about $4 billion in corporate spending" into New Age self-improvement programs for employees.[28]

A number of New Age causes are ones that Christians would endorse, without accepting the mind-set behind them. The New Age concern with the environment and ecology, for instance, springs not from a Christian concern for being good stewards of God's creation. Rather, it comes from the notion that we are one with mother earth. In this schema, human beings are a part of nature as are whales; while it may be important to fight for whales as an endangered species, human abortion may be perfectly acceptable as a means of keeping a balance in nature. The biblical idea of people subduing the earth and ruling over the animals (Genesis 1:28) is foreign to the New Age. In this regard, Christians may have to recognize that ecology has not been a high priority for the church during much of its history.

New Ager Marilyn Ferguson correctly notes that NAM has infected medicine, education, business, the sciences, and even government with it implications.[29] Meanwhile, George Lucas's Star Wars movies have spread the New Age concept of "the Force," a power that exists in all nature and into which Force-sensitive individuals can tap. It is ironic that in our scientific age so many people are turning to fortune-telling, the occult, Eastern mysticism, nature worship, astrology, and other "new" age practices that are really nothing but a return to ancient paganism. In this, New Age practitioners are ahead of secular materialists. New Agers recognize that for all its accomplishments, modern technology cannot give ultimate meaning to life.

Moreover, while such practices often counter what the Bible teaches, they all reflect the need for a sacramental dimension in life, that is, a connection with the divine and with other people. Through the sacraments of Baptism and the Lord's Supper, Christians not only receive forgiveness, life, and salvation, they also enter into a community, in Alberto García's words, "the coming together and the mutual support of all God's people."[30] Concern for holistic health (treating the whole person), for example, is a common bond that can bring Christians and New Agers into contact.[31]

It is significant that both in its thought and its practices, NAM is what we might call a nature religion. That is, it posits a worldview that is closely linked to the natural world of creation and that, in Ferguson's words, "sees mankind embedded in nature."[32] It gives credence to the power and guidance of the heavenly bodies (astrology), earthly materials (such as crystals), and the forces of nature (pantheism). In some cases, the New Age has even returned to the ancient worship of various aspects of nature (Gaia). Religions of nature are distinct from religions of reason, which seek ultimate meaning in the conclusions of the human intellect (for example, secular humanism). They also stand apart from religions of revelation, which, to use Ludwig Wittgenstein's famous dictum, recognize that "the sense of the world must lie outside the world"[33] and turn to "revealed" scriptures for guidance (for example, Judaism, Islam, Baha'ism, Mormonism).

THE NEW AGE AND THE CROSS OF CHRIST

Some see a conspiracy behind the entire New Age movement. The fact is that NAM is hardly an organized movement. Some who share New Age ideals do not even like the label because it can carry negative, eccentric connotations. Far from being simply another organization or new cult, NAM encompasses people from many religions, cults, and organizations. NAM represents not so much any one organization as a way of thinking. It is the ushering in of a new consciousness, the awareness of our divinity.

In another way, the New Age *is* a conspiracy. The lure of godhead is Satan's age-old lure, going back to the Garden of Eden: "You will be like God, knowing good and evil" (Genesis 3:5). In its assertion that fallen humanity is divine, the New Age is the quintessence of what Luther called a theology of glory. As Luther put it in his Heildelberg Disputation: "A theologian of glory calls evil good and good evil. A theologian of the cross calls the thing what it actually is."[34] The New Age is a theology of glory, disseminating the notion that human beings are their own gods and saviors.

Nevertheless, as we have seen, there are points of contact with Christianity on every major New Age theme: pantheism (the need for community as met by the incarnation and all that implies), reincarnation (the need for transcendence as fulfilled in the resurrection), consciousness (the need for knowing as met by the saving knowledge of Christ), and transformation (the need for love as met in the love of God in Christ and reflected in the lives of Christians). New Age practices touch on the need for the sacramental (as met in the sacraments and Christian community). These points relate to the "felt needs" that people try to fill and that ultimately are filled only in Christ.

Examining the New Age as a religion of nature helps us see the movement from another angle and brings to the fore two points of contact that fit the uniquely Lutheran distinction between Law and Gospel—the natural knowledge of God and of the Law. Far from undermining the felt-need approach, a Law-Gospel presentation undergirds and empowers that witness. Sensitivity to individual and cultural circumstances involves the thoughtful application of Law and Gospel.

The psalmist David alludes to the natural knowledge of God: "The heavens declare the glory of God; the skies proclaim the work of His hands" (Psalm 19:1). The argument from design is still a strong tool in Christian witness. The intricacies and interactions of everything from the movement of the galaxies to the functioning of the human eye bear witness to the work of an omniscient and omnipotent Creator. Moreover, rather than evidencing an eternal existence, the material universe shows signs of running down, as the second law of thermodynamics testifies.

Although NAM teaches people to look inside themselves, it is striking that at the same time many New Agers look to astrology for guidance. This is a strong testimony to humanity's inability to find direction and purpose in life entirely from within itself. People need something outside themselves—as Augustine put it, the soul is restless till it rests in God. But if that something is not the true God, it is an idol.

The other point of communication is the individual conscience.

> Indeed when Gentiles, who do not have the Law, do by nature things required by the Law, they are a law for themselves, even though they do not have the Law, since they show that the requirements of the Law are written on their hearts, their consciences also bearing witness, and their thoughts now accusing, now even defending them. (Romans 2:14–15)

Although people might "defend" ungodly behavior, they need to suppress their own consciences to do so. While New Age adherents might argue that they are beyond good and evil, their consciences will tell them otherwise.

In *The Foolishness of God,* Siegbert Becker discusses the limited value of the natural knowledge of God and His Law:

> "Nothing in us follows [God's] will," says Luther, and so the natural knowledge of the law finally becomes "a damnable knowledge (*ein verdamlich erkentnis*) of our own eternal damnation." There will be all too much of that knowledge when a man is overcome by fear or when he finds himself in danger of death. So it always remains useless, vain knowledge, which cannot bring salvation, for by it a man knows and feels the wrath of God all too well, and it becomes a very difficult and bitter task for men to unlearn this knowledge and to forget it in the knowledge of Christ.[35]

Although Luther clearly saw natural knowledge as useless for salvation, he recognized its value in maintaining outward order in the world. New Agers may speak in terms of pantheism, yet they also speak of values, of good and evil, and of harmony. In Deepak Chopra's words, they are aware of the necessity for "more love and compassion."[36]

While Chopra may talk of transcending good and evil, he still assigns values. For example, as he watched the cremated ashes of his father floating away on the Ganges River, he felt both grief and celebration "for the great, joyous life" that had come to an end.[37] It is meaningless even to use such terms as love, compassion, great, and joyous unless, in fact, such values exist. Christians will differ with New Age devotees as to what constitutes a great or joyous life, but the very discussion is a concession to the truthfulness of the biblical worldview. There is right and wrong, sin and judgment because there is a personal Creator who has established such categories and to whom we must all answer one day.

Natural knowledge has value in Christian witness. Both creation and the conscience can be used as preachments of the Law. The power behind the universe is not some blind, impersonal force. Rather, it is

God. The universe attests to His infinite power and wisdom; the conscience attests to His justice.[38] Luther comments on Romans 2:12:

> This [natural] law is impressed upon all people, Jews and Gentiles, and to this law all people are bound. Therefore the Lord says in Matt. 7:12: "Whatever you wish that men would do to you, do so to them; for this is the Law and the Prophets." You see, the whole transmitted law is nothing but the natural law, which cannot be unknown to anyone and on account of which no one can be excused.[39]

Someone like Shirley MacLaine may have hardened her conscience to the point where she is proud of her many love affairs, even "chronicling" one in a book and movie.[40] As St. Paul put it, such people "live as enemies of the cross of Christ. Their destiny is destruction . . . and their glory is in their shame" (Philippians 3:18–19). Yet MacLaine, too, has had moments of "anxiety over an unknown future, both for herself and the planet."[41] If all is one, and if everything ultimately absorbs into that great oneness, then why the anxiety? MacLaine might argue it has to do with not being entirely free from old thinking patterns. Yet the awareness of some ultimate, overarching system of values attests much more powerfully to the natural knowledge of God and of His Law.

Without the Gospel such knowledge remains useless. In his treatment both of Psalm 19 and Romans 2, Luther immediately moves to Christ, who alone is the bringer of good news, the Gospel. Luther calls Psalm 19 "a prophetic and didactic psalm."[42] His words on verse 1 are significant:

> The emphasis is on the word "telling" [declare], to remind us that we should esteem the oral and external Word.

> The "glory of God" is the Gospel, for through the Gospel God is known.

> The "handiwork" of God is all the works wrought by the Gospel, like justification, salvation, and redemption from sin, from death, and from the kingdom of the devil.[43]

While Luther's directly Christocentric interpretation goes beyond what most modern interpreters might do with this passage, we see his eagerness to behold and proclaim Christ and the Gospel throughout Scripture. Without getting into a digression on hermeneutics, it suffices to say that Jesus Himself declared, "You diligently study the Scriptures because you think that by them you possess eternal life. These are the Scriptures that testify about Me" (John 5:39). The whole Bible points to Christ.

As for the Romans 2 statement that the requirements of the Law are written on people's hearts, Luther comments: "How do they show this? First, they show it to others by doing those things which are of the Law. Second, they show it to themselves now and to every man in the Judgment through this, that their conscience gives witness to themselves about themselves."[44] Luther proceeds to assert that this knowledge of the Law leads either to despair or self-righteousness and that "only from Christ" can we find the solution to this human dilemma.

The application of Law and Gospel to specific situations is, as Luther put it, the highest art. Lutheran Christians would do well to review on a regular basis C. F. W. Walther's classic *The Proper Distinction between Law and Gospel*.[45] As Luther and Walther explain, there is a time to present God's Law, showing people that they are sinners, and a time to present the Gospel, directing them to the Savior. Those who think they are without sin will need to hear the Law, while those whose consciences have been touched with an awareness of their sinfulness will need the comfort of the Gospel.

Recently, Deepak Chopra successfully sued a magazine for alleging he had an affair with a prostitute. He called his successful suit "an act of love" to raise the publication to "a higher state of awareness."[46] For Christians there is no greater act of love than to proclaim Law and Gospel. The New Age movement tries to brush off sin; it needs to hear the bold proclamation that there is a judgment to come. People caught in the deception of the New Age need to be brought to the higher state of awareness that though they cannot save themselves, Jesus died for them, as He did for the whole world.

Only the Gospel proclaims a loving God who has made Himself known in the incarnation. The man Jesus Christ is the eternal Son of God, who is both Creator and Redeemer. Faith in Him brings true union with God—not in pantheistic absorption into the mysteries of nirvana or moksha but in knowing we are His forgiven children. In Christ there is life after death—not in a dreary cycle of millions of reincarnations but in the mansions He has prepared for us in heaven. In His Word lies true consciousness—not of esoteric knowledge but an awareness of our sinfulness and redemption through the Savior. And in Him we find the only real transformation that comes through the love of God in Christ.

The New Age cannot and certainly will not bring the enlightenment and liberation it offers. Jesus Christ alone can do that. Witnessing with their lives and words, Christians will joyfully and sensitively share the love of Jesus. He who was crucified and rose again offers the best and only real assurance for this or any other age: "Surely I am with you always, to the very end of the age" (Matthew 28:20).

NOTES

1. James Rado and Gerome Ragni, librettists, *Hair,* produced by Michael Butler, Broadway, 1967.

2. See A. R. Victor Raj, *The Hindu Connection: Roots of the New Age* (St. Louis: Concordia, 1995).

3. Elliot Miller, *A Crash Course on the New Age Movement: Describing and Evaluating a Growing Social Force* (Grand Rapids: Baker, 1989), 183.

4. Richard Roberts, "The Chthonic Imperative: Gender, Religion and the Battle for the Earth," in *Nature Religion Today: Paganism in the Modern World* (ed. Joanne Pearson, Richard H. Roberts, and Geoffrey Samuel; Edinburgh: Edinburgh University Press, 1998), 71.

5. In its earliest forms, Hinduism was polytheistic. This was in the times contemporaneous with Abraham and Moses (1800–1400 B.C.), when the Middle East was also steeped in polytheism. The earliest Hindu scriptures, the *Vedas* (about 1500 B.C.) reflect this, while later writings, the *Upanishads* (800–600 B.C.), have a more philosophical bent and develop the concept of *Atma,* the "world soul."

6. See Slater Brown, *The Heyday of Spiritualism* (New York: Hawthorn Books, 1970).

7. See John P. Newport, "Tracing the Origins of New Age," chapter 2 in *The New Age Movement and the Biblical Worldview: Conflict and Dialogue* (Grand Rapids: Eerdmans, 1998), 19–39.

8. Ralph Waldo Emerson, *Ralph Waldo Emerson* (ed. Richard Poirier; New York: Oxford University Press, 1990), 365–66.

9. See, for example, Paul C. Vitz, *Psychology as Religion: The Cult of Self-Worship* (Grand Rapids: Eerdmans, 1977).

10. William Butler Yeats, *A Vision* (New York: Macmillan/Collier, 1966), 105.

11. William Butler Yeats, *Selected Poems and Three Plays of William Butler Yeats* (ed. M. L. Rosenthal; New York: Collier Books, 1986), 90.

12. Ram Dass, Baba (Richard Alpert), *Remember: Now Be Here, Now Here Be* (San Cristobal, N.M.: Lama Foundation, 1971), 90.

13. Raj, *Hindu Connection,* 163.

14. Quoted in Tom Minnery, "Unplugging the New Age," *Focus on the Family* 11:8 (August 1987): 2.

15. Deepak Chopra, *How to Know God: The Soul's Journey into the Mystery of Mysteries* (New York: Harmony Books, 2000), 178.

16. See Ron Rhodes, *The Counterfeit Christ of the New Age Movement* (Grand Rapids: Baker, 1990).

17. Shirley MacLaine, *The Camino: A Journey of the Spirit* (New York: Pocket Books, 2000), 44–45.

18. As quoted in Michael Arvey, *Reincarnation: Opposing Viewpoints* (Greater Mysteries: Opposing Viewpoints; San Diego: Greenhaven, 1989), 95.

19. MacLaine, *Camino,* 121.

20. As quoted in Minnery, "Unplugging the New Age," 2.

21. Chopra, *How to Know God,* 305.

22. Chopra, *How to Know God,* 146.

23. James Redfield, *The Celestine Prophecy: An Adventure* (New York: Warner Books, 1993), Author's note opposite p. 1.

24. Neale Donald Walsch, *Conversations with God: An Uncommon Dialogue* (New York: G. P. Putnam's Sons, 1996), 1.

25. Walsch, *Conversations with God,* 3.

26. Walsch, *Conversations with God,* 7.

27. *Newsweek (*3 February 1992).

28. *Newsweek* (4 May 1987).

29. Marilyn Ferguson, *The Aquarian Conspiracy* (Los Angeles: J. P. Tarcher, 1980).

30. Alberto L. García, "Signposts for Global Witness in Luther's Theology of the Cross," page 29 in this book.

31. See Miller, *Crash Course on the New Age,* 187.

32. Ferguson, *Aquarian Conspiracy,* 29.

33. Ludwig Wittgenstein, *Tractatus Logico-Philosophicus* (trans. D. Pears and B. McGuiness; London: Routledge & Kegan Paul, 1961), 145.

34. LW 31:40.

35. Siegbert Becker, *The Foolishness of God: The Place of Reason in the Theology of Martin Luther* (Milwaukee: Northwestern, 1982), 58–59.

36. Richard Scheinin, "Father's Death Sends Deepak Chopra Back to the Basics," *Milwaukee Journal Sentinel* (15 April 2001): E5.

37. Scheinin, "Father's Death Sends Chopra to the Basics," E1.

38. The initial point of contact with any non-Christian religion is some form of preachment of the Law because that is all any religion outside Christianity knows. With nature-bound religions, such as the New Age, we find that starting point in creation and the conscience. With religions of reason, such as atheism, that point of contact can be a discussion of the inadequacy of reason to come to terms with life's ultimate questions, such as the existence of God and the meaning of life (see 1 Corinthians 1:18–21). With religions of revelation, the point of contact is Scripture itself. Because other religions "of the book" recognize the Bible, they must be consistent with it and come to terms with its teachings (see Galatians 1:8–9).

39. LW 25:180.

40. Jean-Noel Bassior, "Shirley's Way," *Modern Maturity* (January-February 2001): 69.

41. Bassior, "Shirley's Way," 36.

42. LW 12:139.

43. LW 12:140.

44. LW 25:187.

45. C. F. W. Walther, *The Proper Distinction between Law and Gospel* (St. Louis: Concordia, 1986).

46. Gretchen Passantino, "New Age Guru Deepak Chopra Leaves Legal Troubles for Lucrative Book Tour," *Christian Research Journal* 22.4 (2000): 52.

FOR FURTHER READING

Standard Christian works on the New Age

Groothuis, Douglas R. *Unmasking the New Age.* Downers Grove: InterVarsity, 1986.

Miller, Elliot. *A Crash Course on the New Age Movement: Describing and Evaluating a Growing Social Force.* Grand Rapids: Baker, 1989.

Newport, John P. *The New Age Movement and the Biblical Worldview: Conflict and Dialogue.* Grand Rapids: Eerdmans, 1998.

Raj, A. R. Victor. *The Hindu Connection: Roots of the New Age.* St. Louis: Concordia, 1995.

Various Issues of the *Christian Research Journal.*

New Age (and neopagan) books by key people in the movement

Chopra, Deepak. *How to Know God: The Soul's Journey into the Mystery of Mysteries.* New York: Harmony Books, 2000.

MacLaine, Shirley. *The Camino: A Journey of the Spirit.* New York: Pocket Books, 2000.

Pearson, Joanne, Richard H. Roberts, and Geoffrey Samuel, eds. *Nature Religion Today: Paganism in the Modern World.* Edinburgh: Edinburgh University Press, 1998.

Redfield, James. *The Celestine Prophecy: An Adventure.* New York: Warner Books, 1993.

Walsch, Neale Donald. *Conversations with God: An Uncommon Dialogue.* New York: G. P. Putnam's Sons, 1996.

Contributors

DR. ESHETU ABATE is a translation consultant of the Bible Society of Ethiopia and lecturer at the Ethiopian Graduate School of Theology. He served until recently as dean of the Department of Theology at Mekane Yesus Seminary, Addis Ababa, Ethiopia. He is also a contributor to *Issues in African Christian Theology* (ed. Samuel Ngewa; Nairobi: East African Publishers, 1998). He obtained his doctorate of theology in systematic theology from Concordia Seminary, Saint Louis, Missouri.

PROFESSOR ROLAND EHLKE is an assistant professor of literature and theology at Concordia University Wisconsin. He is a consulting editor for Christian Research Institute, Irvine, California. He is also the author of *Christianity, Cults and World Religions* (Milwaukee: Northwestern, 1992) and several other books.

DR. RICHARD C. EYER is assistant professor of philosophy and director of the Concordia Bioethics Institute at Concordia University Wisconsin. He is also the author of *Pastoral Care under the Cross: God in the Midst of Suffering* (St. Louis: Concordia, 1994) and most recently of *Holy People, Holy Lives: Law and Gospel in Bioethics* (St. Louis: Concordia, 2000).

DR. C. GEORGE FRY is a retired bishop of the Lutheran Church in the USA. He has served as a university and seminary professor in the United States and as a guest professor in several parts of the world. He has written several books and numerous articles in the areas of historical theology, Islam, and the Middle East.

DR. ALBERTO L. GARCÍA is professor of theology and director of the Lay Ministry program at Concordia University Wisconsin. He has served as an assistant professor of systematic theology and director of the Hispanic Ministries program at Concordia Theological Seminary, Fort

Wayne, Indiana, and as an adjunct professor of religion and culture at Florida International University, Miami, Florida. He is also coeditor and contributor to *Christ and Culture in Dialogue: Constructive Themes and Practical Applications* (St. Louis: Concordia Academic Press, 1999).

DR. WON YONG JI is professor emeritus of systematic theology at Concordia Seminary, St. Louis, Missouri, and editor emeritus of *Missio Apostolica*, the journal of the Lutheran Society for Missiology. The article contributed for this book is a somewhat condensed and edited version of a paper presented at the Ninth International Congress for Luther Research, which met at the University of Heidelberg, Heidelberg, Germany, 17–23 August 1997. A similar edition of the essay was published in *Concordia Journal* 24.2 (April 1998): 130–37.

DR. ROBERT KOLB is missions professor of systematic theology and director of the Institute for Missions Studies at Concordia Seminary, Saint Louis, Missouri. He is also an editor of *Missio Apostolica*, the journal of the Lutheran Society for Missiology. He is a prolific author of articles and books in the areas of Luther, the Reformation, and missions.

DR. PAUL MUENCH is an associate professor of communications at Concordia University Austin. He has served as a missionary in Papua New Guinea and Russia and as executive director of Lutheran Bible Translators.

REV. JOHN NUNES is pastor of St. Paul Lutheran Church, Dallas, Texas. He is the author of *Voices from the City: Issues and Images of Urban Preaching* (St. Louis: Concordia, 1999).

DR. A. R. VICTOR RAJ is missions professor of exegetical theology and assistant director of the Institute for Missions Studies at Concordia Seminary, St. Louis, Missouri. He is also an editor of *Missio Apostolica*, the journal of the Lutheran Society for Missiology. He was raised Lutheran in Trivandrum, Kerala State, South India. His publications include *The Hindu Connection: Roots of the New Age* (St. Louis: Concordia, 1995).

DR. ROBERT J. SCUDIERI is director of North American missions for the LCMS. He is also the author of *One, Holy, Catholic and Missionary* (Fort Wayne, Ind.: Lutheran Society for Missiology, 1997).

DR. GENE EDWARD VEITH is professor of English and director of the Cranach Institute at Concordia University Wisconsin. He is a prolific author. His books *The Spirituality of the Cross: The Way of the First Evangelicals* (St. Louis: Concordia, 1999) and the award-winning *Postmodern Times* (Wheaton: Crossway, 2000) offer further insights into his essay and the themes of this essay collection as a whole.